Wishing you an abundant harvest!
Ina Wallace

D1215974

THE TIMBER PRESS GUIDE TO GUIDE TO VEGETABLE GARDENING

in the
•SOUTHEAST•

THE TIMBER PRESS GUIDE TO VEGETABLE GARDENING

in the
•SOUTHEAST•

IRA WALLACE

Timber Press

Portland · London

To my grandmother, Estella,
and my daughter, Raphael,
who both loved eating
fresh from the garden every day.

Copyright © 2013 by Ira Wallace.
All rights reserved.

Chapter opening illustrations by Kate Giambrone and Julianna Johnson
All other illustrations © Julia Sadler

Published in 2013 by Timber Press, Inc.

The Haseltine Building
133 S.W. Second Avenue, Suite 450
Portland, Oregon 97204-3527
timberpress.com

6a Lonsdale Road
London NW6 6RD
timberpress.co.uk

Printed in the United States of America
Book design by Kate Giambrone and Julianna Johnson

Second printing 2014

Library of Congress Cataloging-in-Publication Data

Wallace, Ira.
   The Timber Press guide to vegetable gardening in the Southeast/by
Ira Wallace.—1st ed.
       p. cm.
   Guide to vegetable gardening in the Southeast
   Includes index.
   ISBN 978-1-60469-371-3
   1. Vegetable gardening—Southern States. 2. Vegetables—Southern
States. I. Title. II. Title: Guide to vegetable gardening in the Southeast.
   SB321.5.S74W35 2014
   635.0975—dc23   2013013712

.TABLE OF.
CONTENTS

Preface

Vine-ripened tomatoes, succulent figs, crisp winter salads, corn on the cob, and sweet braised greens are just a few of the fresh-from-the-garden delights awaiting gardeners in the Southeast. Working with long, hot summers and mild, uneven winters, southern gardeners from Thomas Jefferson to Barbara Kingsolver have feasted abundantly in every season. Every year at the Heritage Harvest Festival at Monticello, a celebration of heirloom varieties, local food, and sustainable agriculture at Jefferson's mountaintop home, I have the privilege of meeting hundreds of eager gardeners. The bountiful harvest on display at the festival is an inspiration to new gardeners. With a little planning and knowing how to make the right choices for a south-eastern garden, even beginning gardeners can have that abundance throughout the year.

I often run workshops on year-round gardening and growing garlic and perennial onions at the Monticello and Mother Earth News fairs, and afterward, eager participants frequently ask if I have a book. Finally, this is my offering, sharing what I have learned about year-round food growing in over 40 years as an organic gardener and over 20 years as an advocate and producer of heirloom organic seeds at Southern Exposure Seed Exchange (SESE) in central Virginia. Our motto at SESE is "Saving the Past for the Future"; we strive to preserve the knowledge that lets farmers enjoy abundant harvests without chemical fertilizers and pesticides. Our farm is certified organic and I am committed to keeping our spot of earth healthy and productive. Throughout this book, I have shared the information you'll need to make your own garden equally rich.

My gardening roots trace back to my grandmother's backyard in Florida where I grew up. We had something growing every month, although all I remember growing in late summer were black-eyed peas, okra, and sweet potatoes. That was the slow time, but it didn't last long. As soon as the weather started cooling off a little we went all out with greens, squash, peppers, tomatoes, and beans. Winter brought on lettuce, celery, and even more greens. I don't think I grew broccoli and other more refined members of the cabbage family until after I went off to college. But, boy, did we have some fine cabbages, collards, turnips, and mustards. These memories make fall and winter gardening special for me. Fall harvests provide fresh organic food just when it is most expensive in the markets and less available from local farms. And growing a fall garden is actually easier than summer gardening, once you get the timing down. In the July and August chapters, I'll go through the basics of summer planting for an abundant fall and winter harvest. I share the techniques and timing that work for us to start seeds in the heat.

In these hectic, modern times, many of you might feel that it is hard to find the time you need to produce your own food. Well, let me tell you that I struggle with having enough time myself. It's one reason that I am always looking for new ways—like creating no-dig "lasagna beds"—to make gardening easier. Gardening is still a lot of fun for me. I always make time to try out something new in the garden each year. This is how I find new and exotic tastes like Thai Red roselle for jams and refreshing drinks or delicious new-to-me heirlooms like Shronce's Deep Black peanut. I have tried to share many of my favorite heirloom varieties for those of you who want to be able to save seeds as well as enjoy fine flavors. I have included basic seed-saving instructions for each of the vegetables in the Edibles A to Z section.

There are almost as many reasons for gardening as there are gardeners. But whatever the reasons, in the last five years we have seen the number of new gardeners buying our seeds increase by 10 to 20 percent every year and the attendance at the Heritage Harvest Festival at Monticello has quadrupled. The question of what is going into our food and where it comes from has led many of us toward local and organic food, and that excitement is only growing. And what food is more local than the food from your own backyard? Whether you are new to gardening or an old hand looking for tips, I hope this book will give you the tools and motivation you need to get gardening straight away.

Acknowledgments

I have been giving talks on gardening in the Southeast, writing articles, and contributing to the Southern Exposure Seed Exchange catalog for many years. But it took surviving a life-threatening operation for me to finally agree to write an actual book.

It was Timber Press, and especially Juree Sondker, who got me started. I so appreciate her encouragement and editing, plus that of Michael Dempsey, for keeping me on track and making this a much better book.

Thanks also to my gardening friends Pam Dawling, Cindy Conner, and Ken Bezilla, who shared their experience and their years of gardening records, and answered so many of my questions along the way.

I am especially grateful to Lisa Dermer, organizer par excellence, and Gordon Sproule, who both worked with me from the beginning, helping whenever I asked—editing and offering insightful suggestions and personal encouragement whenever I needed them.

Thank you to all my friends and fellow worker/owners at Southern Exposure Seed Exchange and Acorn Community Farm for supporting me in writing this book by taking on a lot of my usual work in our gardens and in the office.

GET STARTED

WELCOME
TO THE SOUTHEAST

The climate in the southeastern states is warm and wet, with long, hot summers, high humidity, and mild winters with many rapid changes in temperature. Happily, gardening is a year-round activity in our region. The southeastern states covered in this book spread from the beaches of the Delaware and Maryland's Delmarva Peninsula across the Appalachians to the edge of Oklahoma and all the states south of that line, including the acid soils of east Texas. Our definition of the Southeast largely mirrors the native range of the American holly. This area includes USDA climate zones 6, 7, 8, and 9, with small bits of zone 5 at higher elevations, plus a little zone 10 in middle Florida and southern Louisiana. We leave the special conditions in the tropical south where it never freezes and the hot, dry, alkaline soils of west Texas to another volume. Gardeners in southeastern Oklahoma and southern Ohio may also find this book a valuable resource.

The climate zones we refer to throughout this book are based on the map of ten hardiness zones created by the United States Department of Agriculture in 1960 and most recently updated in 2012. Each zone represents a 10°F difference in minimum winter temperature. The number of freezing days in the Southeast has declined by four to seven days per year for most of the region since the mid-1970s.

Defining Our Climate

There are many ways of dividing the Southeast area and looking at its weather patterns, geography, and soils. For simplicity, the monthly to-do lists in this book will refer to two areas: the Upper South and the Lower South. When looking for best planting dates and other specifics for your garden, it is always good to also consult local resources like your agricultural extension agent, master gardeners, and experienced neighbors.

Upper South growing-season profile

Like the entire Southeast, states in the Upper South experience long, hot summers, but evenings cool off, especially in the mountainous area. The temperature can top 100°F, but usually only for a day or two before relief. Winter lows don't usually drop below 0°F, but an unusually harsh arctic front can bring lows of −20°F. This area includes zones 6 and 7, and scattered areas of zone 5 at higher elevations in the states of Delaware, Maryland, Virginia, West Virginia, Kentucky, and Tennessee, as well as the mountains of North Carolina, South

Carolina, Alabama, Mississippi, northern Arkansas, and southern Missouri. Crops like rhubarb, asparagus, raspberries, highbush blueberries, and spring broccoli do better in this region than further south. In the lower areas of the Upper South, gardeners enjoy great success with long, hot-season crops like okra, watermelon, and figs, as well as crops from almost any other region of the country, given proper location and timing.

Lower South growing-season profile

This is the land of peaches, Vidalia onions, rabbiteye blueberries, and abundant winter gardens. The warming influence of the Gulf of Mexico and the Atlantic Ocean makes winters short and summers long, hot, and humid. The Lower South includes zones 8 and 9 in the states of South Carolina, Georgia, Alabama, Mississippi, and Louisiana, eastern North Carolina, northern Florida, and the acid soils of eastern Texas plus a small area of zone 10 in southern Louisiana and middle Florida. Abundant rainfall makes for the verdant growth we often associate with the old south. In most areas, warm-weather crops like tomatoes are planted in early summer and again in fall to avoid the heat of August. Fall and winter gardens may be more productive than summer plantings if irrigation is an issue.

In the Southeast, summer heat is often as important a concern for gardeners as winter lows. The AHS Plant Heat Zone Map is a great tool for factoring in the heat. It has twelve zones that indicate the average number of days each year that a given region experiences temperatures over 86°F. These "Heat Days" are when many plants begin suffering physiological damage from heat. The zones range from zone 1 (less than 1 heat day) to zone 12 (more than 210 heat days). Taken in tandem with the USDA hardiness zones, this map and ratings can

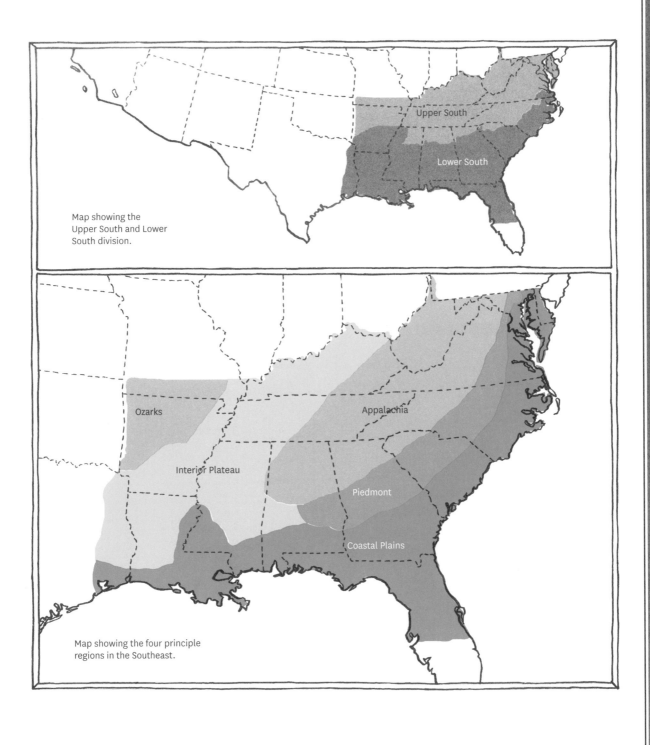

Map showing the Upper South and Lower South division.

Map showing the four principle regions in the Southeast.

really help gardeners plan ahead and get the most from their plantings. It's a particular help when choosing heat-tolerant vegetable varieties, berries, and fruit trees.

The southeastern gardener has many advantages in terms of climate. We have a long growing season, plenty of sunshine, rich soils, and ample rain. According to the national weather center data from 1981 to 2010, Mobile, Alabama, was the wettest city in the United States, with 67 inches of rain each year. It joined nine other major southeastern cities in having more rain than Seattle. On the other hand, gardeners in our region also face a number of climate challenges: high humidity, excessive rainfall, and droughts, sometimes all in the same year—all that while contending with the occasional hurricane or tornado.

Looking at first and last frost dates for a few major cities in the Southeast shows how much variation there is in this region. Gardeners should learn about their climate from local sources, like your cooperative extension agent, master gardeners, local garden centers, and neighbors with years of experience growing in your area.

For most of the country, the dates of the last spring frost and the first autumn frost indicate the beginning and end of the growing season. Gardeners in the far north are largely holed up for the winter. But in the Southeast, vegetable gardening can be a year-round adventure if you give some attention to scheduling. Indeed, throughout the South as much planning goes into dealing with the hot, humid summer weather as goes into extending the harvest through the winter.

Cool-season crops are easy to grow if planted in early spring or fall, and nearly impossible to grow in summer. In the lower and coastal South, warm-season crops also have an early and late-summer planting to avoid the hot, dry, "dog days of summer." All over the Southeast, gardeners need to remember the importance of summer planting for an abundant fall and winter harvest. Timing for starting transplants is important and often surprising for gardeners from other regions. For example, in Virginia, broccoli (a cool-season crop) should be started in late June to early July for fall transplanting, and in Louisiana, tomatoes (a warm-season crop) are started in early January for spring transplanting.

In our region's wettest areas, savvy gardeners make raised beds 8–12 inches high. These extra-tall beds warm up quickly and are ready for early spring planting when elsewhere the ground is still muddy. Prepare these beds in the fall and cover them with weed barrier fabric to have them ready for early spring planting.

AVERAGE FROST DATES FOR THE SOUTHEAST

CITY	FIRST FROST	LAST FROST	FROST-FREE DAYS
Nashville, TN	10/28	4/6	204
Amarillo, TX	10/20	4/18	185
Memphis, TN	11/13	3/22	235
Mobile, AL	11/29	2/28	273
Savannah, GA	11/25	3/1	268
Lexington, KY	10/25	4/15	192
New Orleans, LA	12/11	2/12	300
Fayetteville, NC	11/5	3/28	222
Parkersburg, WV	10/22	4/21	183
Norfolk, VA	11/23	3/20	247
Richmond, VA	10/30	4/6	206

Data courtesy of National Climatic Center

Looking at a map of the broad geographic areas in the Southeast can give us a wider perspective on the rivers, mountains, oceans, and other forces that shape our weather and help define our growing seasons.

Coastal Plains. This region is a vast, broad, flat coastal plain that stretches from the Delmarva Peninsula on the Atlantic coast, around the tip of Florida, and back along the Gulf Coast to Texas. Proximity to the Atlantic Ocean and the Gulf of Mexico make for short and mild winters as well as hot and humid summers, with plenty of rain all year. Average winter lows can vary from 17°F in southern Delaware to 25°F along the Mississippi Delta in Louisiana, where some years it doesn't freeze at all. Winter is perfect for growing greens and a variety of cool-season crops.

> **Growing season:** February to December (207–300 days)
> **Average winter low temperatures:** 17–25°F
> **Days above 86°F:** 45–180

The Piedmont. This area stretches westward inland from the coastal plains to the edge of the Appalachians and Blue Ridge Mountains, from Maryland south to Georgia. Summers are hot and humid and winters are cold, with lows from 20°F in the South to 7°F in the north. The Piedmont gets 44–48 inches of rain per year. Spring and fall are distinct and refreshing periods of delightful weather for gardeners. Because periods of drought are not uncommon in the Piedmont, it is best to plant early and late to take advantage of the cooler temperatures and abundant moisture in the spring and fall.

> **Growing season:** March to early November (180–243 days)

> **Average winter low temperatures:** 10–17°F
> **Days above 86°F:** 90–125

The Mountain South, including Appalachia and the Ozarks. In the southeastern shadow of the Blue Ridge, moist southerly winds rising over the mountains drop more than 80 inches of precipitation per year, making this region the wettest in the eastern states. Because of higher elevation, summer weather is cooler and less humid. Winter is colder than lower areas nearby, and surprise frosts are common in the late spring. Cooler summer temperatures make for excellent fall crops of broccoli and other brassica crops.

> **Growing season:** April to October (130–190 days)
> **Average winter low temperatures:** 0–10°F
> **Days above 86°F:** 14–90

The Interior Plateau. This area stretches from northeast Texas north to the edge of the Ozarks and east to the Appalachian foothills. The meeting of warm air from the Gulf of Mexico and cold arctic fronts makes for unpredictable weather in this area with annual rainfall varying from 22–52 inches. Summers are hot and humid. Timing is everything. You want most spring-planted crops to mature before the onslaught of hot weather (except okra, southern peas, and sweet potatoes, which thrive in warmer weather). Choose early maturing varieties and plant as early as possible to avoid the heat and possible droughts in late summer. Then plant a fall garden to extend the harvest season.

> **Growing season:** March to late October (180–240 days)
> **Average winter low temperatures:** −7–20°F
> **Days above 86°F:** 90–125

Weather

Climate and weather are distinguished from each other by time. *Climate* describes weather conditions over a long period of time. *Weather* is what's happening right now in terms of short-term variations tied to individual weather systems (fronts, hurricanes, air masses).

One of the strongest influences on weather in the Southeast is warm air moving north across the Gulf of Mexico and meeting frigid cold fronts heading south from Canada. Where the two meet, there are thunderstorms, heavy rains, or snow, and sometimes hail or tornadoes. In late summer and fall, tropical storms and hurricanes can move up the Atlantic coast or careen across the Gulf of Mexico bringing high winds and even more water to the region. This convergence zone is why the Southeast is home to many of the wettest cities in the United States.

According to the National Weather Service, another very important factor in forecasting seasonal weather in the Southeast is the El Niño/La Niña–Southern Oscillation (ENSO). It describes the variable surface temperature and atmospheric conditions far away in the Pacific Ocean near the equator. The strongest impacts are during the winter months. Usually, El Niño means a cool, wet spring and La Niña results in a warm, dry winter/spring. However, the northern sections of Alabama and Georgia are usually wetter with a La Niña winter. La Niña winters can sometimes lead to drought that summer, and El Niño may delay spring planting dates due to excess soil moisture.

Microclimates

While *climate* describes the weather over time in our region, microclimates are those small areas that are different than the larger general region. Microclimates bring us home to our yard and garden. They may be created by a number of things: buildings, extra-windy areas, topography, or large bodies of water. In urban areas, buildings can have a huge effect on the climate nearby and paved areas may act as heat sinks, keeping city gardens a few degrees warmer. Buildings and fences may act as wind barriers or create wind tunnels. If there's a large body of water nearby such as a lake or the ocean, this tends to moderate the air temperatures of nearby areas.

Living on top of a hill or deep in a valley plays a major role in microclimates. Warm air is lighter than cold air, so if a gardener lives in a valley they may have more frost problems than someone living higher up. In windy areas, the top of the hill can be several degrees colder than a spot along the slope. The gardens at Monticello are carved into the side of a south-facing slope to catch all that southern sun, while late frosts just roll on down the mountain. This makes it possible to grow figs that look more like they came from Savannah, Georgia, than Charlottesville, Virginia.

Other factors that can affect microclimates are rainfall, soil types, mulching practices, paved surfaces, fences, walls, raised beds, cold frames, balconies, and rooftops. A smart gardener will observe their microclimate and use it to their advantage, making modifications such as adding a brick wall or living windbreak of trees to trap heat or provide shade where needed.

Phenology

In these times of climate change and erratic, unpredictable weather, many scientists and gardeners are returning to the observation of nature as a guide to planting and predicting insect emergence. Phenology is the study of recurring plant and animal life cycles and their relationship to weather. Many historical figures, including Thomas Jefferson, recorded phenological observations that are being resurrected and used to understand how climate and weather have changed over the last century or more.

Plant and insect development is temperature dependent, not calendar dependent. After the winter dormancy period, temperatures rise and plants and insects develop. Growing degree days (GDDs) are a scientific measure of accumulated heat. Farmers and gardeners with a scientific inclination are using the GDD measurement of heat to predict which insects will be active at which point. Calculating GDD is a bit complicated for most gardeners because the base temperature varies with plant and insect species. Fortunately for us, recent research at the University of Ohio has confirmed the relationship between GDD and traditional phenological observations. The National Phenological Network allows you to add your observations to this work and draw from the information being gathered by fellow citizen scientists in your region.

So a gardener who records bloom times, insect occurrences, and bird migrations and uses the concept of phenology has another important tool for success at their disposal. For example, if you plant your peas when the forsythia blooms, you risk losing a few plants to late frost but you will be in the ballpark.

NATURAL GARDENING SIGNALS

PHENOLOGICAL SIGN	ASSOCIATION
dandelions begin to bloom	sow beets and carrots
daffodils begin to bloom	plant potatoes
forsythia begins to bloom	sow peas
redbuds begin to bloom	expect flea beetles
lilacs in full bloom	sow beans, squash, and cucumbers
oak leaves the size of "squirrel ears"	sow corn
foxgloves begin to bloom	bean beetle eggs hatch
fall dead nettle shoots emerge	sow spinach

Source: *Acorn and Twin Oaks Communities Garden Phenology Calendars and Records*

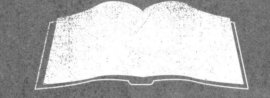

GARDENING
101

Until the 1950s, most families in the Southeast had a large vegetable garden. Today, most people live in cities or suburbs, and that means plots are smaller. But according to *Southern Living* magazine, we southerners still garden more than other Americans. You don't need a large space to begin a vegetable garden. Heck, if you use containers, you don't even need a yard. But you do need three critical elements to have your garden produce abundantly: sun, soil, and water.

Sun

••

Sunlight is the fuel for plant growth. If you want to grow a wide variety of vegetables including tomatoes, peppers, and others that produce fruit, you need at least six to eight hours of full sunlight each day between the spring and fall equinoxes. Ten hours is needed to bring out the full flavor of many large heirloom tomatoes. If there is any doubt, observe and measure how much sun you have. It's so discouraging to do all the work of starting a new garden only to find your spot is too shady for what you want to grow. Because of the high summer temperatures in the Southeast, morning light and afternoon shade are better if you have a choice when choosing the location for your garden.

With four to six hours of full sunlight a day you can grow good lettuce, arugula, cilantro, and other "greens" such as spinach, kale, collards, and cabbage. Both broccoli and cauliflower are actually modified flowers and need the same light as fruiting vegetables. Root crops need at least six full hours of sun to produce what you want. Except for parsley and mint, most common herbs also need a well-drained location with full sun.

If you only have enough hours of sunlight in fall and winter when the trees are bare, consider concentrating on cool-season crops. It may even be best to have your summer garden in a different location than your fall and winter garden. Adequate sunlight is one of the most critical elements in the success of your garden.

And while, yes, enough sunlight is crucial, too *much* sunlight and heat in late summer can be brutal! So in the deep South, some crops like sweet peppers, tomatoes, and chard benefit from shade late in the day in midsummer. We plant lettuce so that taller plants growing to the west and south provide shade. Planting tomatoes where dappled shade reaches them at about 4 p.m. seems to help with fruit set in August. Even in the upper South, many tomatoes, bell peppers, lima beans, and snap beans may stop producing fruit for a short time during the summer. When the temperature soars above 95°F, pollen is killed and the stigma (female receptacle for the pollen) dries up. This is only a temporary setback, so don't pull up the plants. They will probably fruit again when the temperatures drop. Duck the intense August heat by growing an early season and a late season of quicker-maturing varieties. You'll still have the real heat lovers like okra, southern peas, watermelons, Malabar spinach, and hot peppers to give you something to do during the hottest months. We'll cover more details of planning and locating your garden in the next chapter.

Soil

••

Healthy soil is more than just plain old dirt. It is a complex and living mixture of minerals, organic material (which was once alive, such as leaves and roots), humus (decayed organic matter), water, microorganisms, and other animals. Plant roots also need air to breathe and it is the structure of your soil that creates those breathing spaces, which are every bit as important as all that other stuff in the soil. Except for sunlight, and carbon dioxide, plants get everything they need from the soil. Build up healthy soil in your garden and that soil will give you great plants.

Gardens in the Southeast typically have either sandy or clay-rich soils. Both are subject to drought. Heavy clay soils can be as hard as concrete, often have lost their topsoil, and pose a formidable challenge to successful cultivation. This soil is often iron rich, leading to a distinctive red coloration and the common name, red clay. They are mostly quite acidic and require lime.

DIY SOIL TEXTURE TEST

A picture is worth a thousand words. This simple test will give you a quick picture of the relative amounts of clay, sand, and silt in your soil.

Here's what you'll need:

small trowel
wide-mouth jar with straight sides and a tight-fitting lid
soil sample
water
1 T powdered dishwasher detergent (optional)

STEPS

1 Remove sod and mulch from the garden area you are testing. Then use a trowel to dig a soil sample. I like to go down 6 inches to get to the area where roots grow. Sift the sample to remove rocks, roots, and other large organic matter. Then fill the jar halfway with soil.

2 Add tap water until the jar is ¾ full. (For a more accurate test, add 1 T powdered dishwasher detergent as a surfactant to keep the soil particles separated.)

3 Screw lid on securely and shake the jar for at least three minutes to thoroughly combine the soil, water, and detergent. Make sure there aren't any clods of soil stuck to the jar. Set the jar on a level surface in bright light for two days.

4 Check the sample periodically to watch the layers form. Coarse sand particles are the heaviest and settle out after a few minutes. Silt is next heaviest and will settle out after about an hour. Clay, the lightest particles in the mix, can take one to two days to settle and may remain suspended in the water. Organic material will float to the top.

Knowing the makeup of your soil helps you choose how to build rich, well-draining, moisture-retaining loamy soil teeming with microbial life. Most of the soil at our Southern Exposure farm is the heavy red clay so common in the Piedmont. We turn our red clay into brown gold by cover cropping with green manure crops such as rye, buckwheat, or clover, and working in lots of composted organic matter.

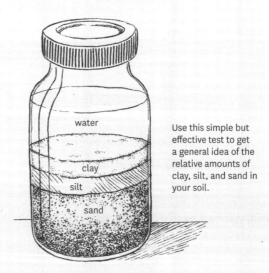

water

clay

silt

sand

Use this simple but effective test to get a general idea of the relative amounts of clay, silt, and sand in your soil.

Clay soil has a large percentage of fine particles leaving very little room for air spaces. It compacts easily, doesn't drain well, and sets like a brick in the summer heat. However, your average clay soil is very fertile and just needs to be loosened up a bit to allow tender roots to work their way down in there. Regularly adding organic matter (leaves, compost, and cover crops) will improve drainage, helps create airspaces, and makes a better home for beneficial soil microbes that actively help maintain soil fertility. The coarse, partially decomposed organic particles act like wedges, temporarily creating air spaces and the fully decomposed humus is sticky and acts like glue to clump the clayey soil together into larger aggregates, increasing pore space. Over time, this increases soil oxygen levels and improves soil drainage, which in turn increase the rooting depth so roots can reach more water and nutrients.

Sandy or rocky soils are low in organic matter and nutrients because water drains through them so quickly. Bare sandy soils are prone to erosion. When you improve these soils, organic material lodges between the grains of sand and acts like a sponge holding water and increasing nutrient availability.

Scattered throughout the Southeast, there are areas of rich, deep soils with lots of organic matter that are excellent for agriculture. The fertile Pamunkey loams near Jamestown in Virginia produced the food that sustained the early European settlers in the area. The Pamunkey and other Indian tribes were the first people to recognize the natural ability of this soil to produce abundant food. In recent years, these same soils have produced record yields of corn and wheat.

Healthy, balanced loamy soils like the Pamunkey are full of microorganisms, our little friends, that turn organic material into humus. The spongy humus holds water, minerals, and other nutrients in a liquid soup and makes them easily available to plants. Rich, natural soils take hundreds if not thousands of years to form and can be lost quickly to flood or poor management. If you should be blessed with such perfect soil, don't count on it lasting unless you work to maintain it with the regular addition of organic matter and other nutrients as needed. Good soil is a work in progress.

Compost

With our long growing season, high rainfall, and warm temperatures, gardeners in the Southeast need to work a little harder than those in the North to replenish the organic material removed with our abundant vegetable harvests. Think about all those baskets of greens, corn, beans, and tomatoes that your soil grows and then you haul away. An annual spreading of 1–2 inches of compost will provide all the nutrients most crops need for excellent growth and help improve soil structure. In the South, composting is the single best thing you can do for your soil. See the March chapter for more details on making healthy compost.

Water

Adequate moisture is essential for healthy plant growth and here in the Southeast we're blessed with ample moisture throughout much of the year. However, drought in the hottest months is also a predictable reality, so locate your garden near a reliable source of water. Plants need water to carry nutrients and keep their tissues hydrated. Even short dry periods can stunt plant growth, reducing yields dramatically. With landscape plants, you can select varieties that require less water, but choices for low-water vegetable plants are limited. Thankfully, there are simple ways you can increase water efficiency. Here are some tips:

Create windbreaks. Plant bamboo or build semi-permeable fences using shade cloth. This reduces evaporation from leaves and soil.

Apply mulch. Shredded leaves, pine needles, or other organic mulches keep the soil cool and help it retain moisture from rain and irrigation.

Improve your soil. Incorporating organic matter into your soil increases water-holding capacity and improves soil structure. Compost, animal manure, grass clippings, cover crops, and leaf mold are common ways to increase organic matter.

Plant in blocks. Planting in squares instead of rows creates a canopy of leaves that shades the ground and reduces evaporation.

Check plant needs before watering. Vegetable plants should be watered according to need, not on a schedule.

Water at the right time of day. Watering at night or early in the morning—thus avoiding the hottest part of the day—reduces water loss (and diseases as well).

Set up an efficient irrigation system. Switching from a sprinkler to a drip or soaker hose can reduce water usage by up to 50 percent.

In our fantasy garden, nature provides rains when needed, in the perfect amount. Alas, in reality, you'll often have to help nature along by watering by hand or with an irrigation system. How often you need to water depends on how often it rains, how long your soil retains moisture, how fast water evaporates in your garden, and sometimes even whether your plants are in a critical growth stage. Soil type is another important factor. Clay soils hold water very well (sometimes too well). Sandy soil, on the other hand, acts like a sieve, letting the water run right through. Happily, the amount of water stored in *any* soil can be improved with generous additions of organic matter and mulch.

When drought hits your garden, it's also hitting your whole region. For gardeners using municipal water, there are often restrictions on watering during the hottest months. Storing water for use during dry periods is not a new idea in our region. As recently as the early twentieth century, rainwater was the primary water source on many Texas ranches, with stone and steel cisterns still standing today on homesteads long converted to well water. A water-storage renaissance of sorts is happening in Texas, Georgia, Florida, and other drought-challenged states in the Southeast, as gardeners are waking up to the potential of water literally falling from the sky. Encouraged by the city of Austin's incentive program, homeowners in that city have installed more than 6000 rain barrels. Each can be filled by a brief cloudburst and save hundreds of gallons of water.

One of the beauties of rainwater harvesting systems is their flexibility. A system can be as simple as a whiskey barrel placed under a downspout for watering a small garden or as complex as an engineered, multi-tank, pumped, and pressurized cistern to supply both residential and irrigation needs.

Across the Southeast, Master Gardener groups and water districts offer classes on how to make your own rain barrel from a durable, food-grade, 55-gallon barrel, which can be filled from as little as a ¼-inch rain shower. Many local nurseries, hardware, and natural foods stores offer quality rain barrels ready to take home and install instantly. These units come with an opaque, sealed lid that blocks mosquitoes, prevents algae, and protects children and pets.

You can increase your harvest of rainwater by connecting multiple rain barrels fed by the same downspout or have a barrel under every convenient spout. Just fill your watering can or connect a gravity-fed hose to get a spray of nice soft rainwater.

Bigger and more complex systems use gravity to feed water from gutters to a larger cistern. Traditionally, cisterns were made of concrete and buried underground, but modern cisterns come in a variety of materials for use above ground as well. These large units hold hundreds of gallons of water and require care and adequate foundations for proper installation. You can find much of this equipment at online gardening sites. Many local businesses have sprung up to help with the engineering that assures your cistern and its piping system will safely and reliably deliver water when and where it's needed in your garden.

Most vegetable gardens need about an inch of water a week, ideally delivered in ½-inch gentle showers twice a week. There are a variety of ways to get water to your garden when rain keeps passing you by:

Watering cans. Every garden can use at least two sturdy watering cans (two are about as easy to carry as one). I like 1- or 2-gallon lightweight metal or plastic cans with a fine rose (the business end, where the water comes out) for gently watering in newly planted seeds or watering in new transplants and helping lettuce or other sensitive plants through a dry spell. Make a little circle of soil like a saucer around the plants before you sprinkle, so the water soaks into the root zone instead of running off.

Garden hoses. For the beginning gardener, time spent at the end of a hose is educational. You get familiar with your different plants and their different needs. But it's no fun dealing with pesky hoses that kink and just won't roll up easily. My advice is to buy the best-quality, most durable rubber hoses you can afford. And don't run over them with the lawn mower. Having shorter lengths of hose stationed strategically around the garden will save you a lot of lugging. Quick connectors and sprinkling heads make it easier to get water where you need it.

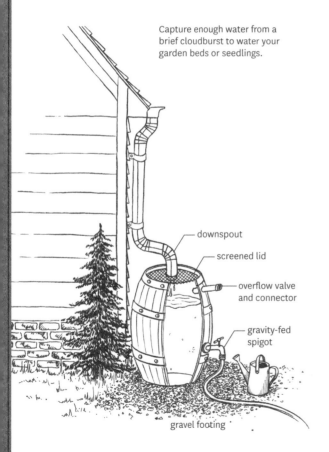

Capture enough water from a brief cloudburst to water your garden beds or seedlings.

downspout

screened lid

overflow valve and connector

gravity-fed spigot

gravel footing

Sprinklers. You can find various types of sprinklers in garden centers and catalogs. Sprinklers are easy to set up but distribute water unevenly and cause runoff, especially on slopes. They are best used before 10 a.m. because up to 50 percent of the water can be lost to evaporation during the hottest part of the day.

Drip irrigation. With frequent summer droughts and accompanying water restrictions, many gardeners in the Southeast have turned to drip irrigation. Soaker hoses are the simplest. These porous rubber hoses slowly ooze water into the soil where it encourages deep plant roots. Garden centers, hardware stores, and online merchants offer a variety of do-it-yourself drip systems with different prices and accessories. New services are springing up to help gardeners get a water-conserving drip system up and running for a modest fee. Whether you do it yourself or hire a garden service, don't forget to add a timer to your system.

Mulches for Your Garden

Mulch is one of the best things you can do for your garden. Placing a layer of organic material directly on the soil surface keeps the soil cool and moist, smothers weeds, feeds the soil as the material decays, and reduces soil splashing and soil-borne disease.

Mulching is almost always good for your garden, but of course there are exceptions. Hold off on the mulch if you want your early spring soil to warm up, or slugs and snails are a problem, or when drainage is poor. There are many different types of mulch to suit your various needs:

Grass. Fresh grass clippings are high in nitrogen and will feed your plants as the clippings decay. Peppers, tomatoes, and eggplant do well with grass clippings.

Newspaper. Throw out the slick sections of your local newspaper and use the rest for a great weed-suppressing mulch. Use shredded newspaper mulch on corn, tomatoes, and raspberries. Earthworms thrive under newspaper mulch.

Straw. Straw mulch is a good insulator for root vegetables left in the ground for harvest during the winter (especially the ones that overwinter well outdoors: carrots, parsnips, and salsify). It also has been shown to reduce soil-borne diseases like anthracnose, leaf spot, and early blight in tomatoes.

Other organic mulches. Use shredded leaves, pine straw, and sawdust as weed-suppressing mulches, or layer them with a higher-nitrogen-content material to compost in place and feed the crop.

Decorative mulches. Woodchips, bark, pecan shells, coffee grounds, and other slow-to-decompose materials add a nice touch for containers, fruit bushes, and perennial plantings. Non-organic material like stones or pebbles can be an attractive dressing, especially in pots.

Living mulches. In edible landscapes and herb gardens, controllable, low-growing plants such as creeping thyme, alpine strawberries, chamomile, and clover shade the ground to keep plant roots cooler and retain soil moisture.

Plastic mulches. Generally, I'm not a big fan of black plastic mulch; it is usually made from petrochemicals and it's hard to dispose of properly. These days, however, you can get biodegradable plastic made from cornstarch. It can be very handy for preventing weeds and maintaining soil moisture, especially for sprawling vining crops such as winter squash and melons.

Feeding Your Garden Soil

Soil is a sponge-like storehouse for nutrients, but many soils lack the proper balance of the nutrients needed to grow a healthy, productive garden. Luckily, we can rectify that. Let's start by looking at the major nutrients and what they do.

Of the 16 commonly known plant nutrients, nitrogen (N), phosphorus (P), and potassium (K) are called the *macronutrients* and are usually the only ones that gardeners will need to keep in mind. Nitrogen promotes leaf growth, which is great for leafy crops like spinach, lettuce, and cabbage, but don't overdo it on other plants or you'll have lots of leaves and not many fruits or flowers. Phosphorus helps grow strong root systems and supports photosynthesis, fruiting, and flowering. It doesn't travel well in the soil, so it needs to be available in the root zone to be effective. Potassium promotes the flow of nutrients throughout the plant, strengthens stems, improves fruiting, and enhances general health. It helps plants withstand drought, extreme temperatures, and other stresses.

Every fertilizer package lists three numbers representing the percentage of these three crucial elements, always in the same order. Organic fertilizers tend to have low numbers and inorganic fertilizers have higher numbers. So, for example, a box of organic fish meal labeled 8-13-4 contains 8 percent nitrogen, 13 percent phosphorus, and 4 percent potassium. A specialty, single-purpose fertilizer might have a strong imbalance, such as 22-2-2. This would be a nitrogen-rich inorganic mix for greening up the lawn in spring.

Plants are happy to use nutrients from either organic or inorganic fertilizers, but the impact on the soil is vastly different. Organic fertilizers slowly release nutrients giving a steady supply of food to your plants without disrupting the work of earthworms and other beneficial organisms. Repeated applications of inorganic fertilizers, especially without adding sufficient organic matter, lead to a buildup of salts that kill beneficial soil microbes and stop the formation of humus. The nutrients in chemical fertilizers are highly water soluble. This means that if they are not quickly absorbed by plants, they can easily become pollutants contaminating our waterways. In addition, many of the products are made with petrochemicals in ways that use large amounts of energy and further endanger the environment.

The following amendments are some of the most commonly available choices for home gardeners. Some amendments are rich in more than one element. For example, fish meal contains generous amounts of nitrogen, phosphorus, and potassium. This makes it a good all-around organic fertilizer for container gardens and new gardens with poor soil.

Blood meal (12-3-0) is a long-lasting, high-nitrogen fertilizer, made from dried slaughterhouse waste. Use it carefully when plants need a big shot of nitrogen.

Cottonseed meal (6-2.5-1.5) is a rich source of nitrogen, but many pesticides are applied to cotton crops and residues tend to remain in the seeds. Pesticide-free cottonseed meal is available in some areas.

Bone meal (2-22-0) is an excellent source of calcium as well as phosphorus for the typically acidic soils east of the Mississippi.

Fish meal (10-5-4) is a slow-release source of organic nitrogen, potassium, and phosphorus. It is also high in carbohydrates and proteins, which stimulate biological activity in the soil and improve tilth.

Feather meal (15-0-0) is fairly high in nitrogen but needs warmth and microbial action to release it.

Tobacco stems and stalks (2-1-7) are high in potassium and have a modest amount of nitrogen. They should not be used on tomatoes, peppers, eggplant, or other night-shades because of possible tobacco mosaic virus.

Wood ashes (0-2-6) are a good source of potassium, calcium, and phosphorus, but apply with care. Too many ashes can quickly raise the soil pH.

Rock phosphate (0-2-0) is a slow-release source of phosphorus; warm temperatures and biological activity in compost or soil speed up the process.

ORGANIC PLANT FOOD FOR N-P-K

NITROGEN	PERCENT	AMOUNT PER 100 SQ. FT.
blood meal	12.0	10 oz.
cottonseed meal	6.0	1.25 lb.
bone meal	2.0	2.5 lb.
fish meal	6.0	1.25 lb.
peanut meal	7.2	1.0 lb

PHOSPHORUS	PERCENT	AMOUNT PER 100 SQ. FT.
rock phosphate	30.0	0.75 lb.
bone meal	22.0	0.75 lb.
fish meal	3.0	1.75 lb
cottonseed meal	2.5	0.8 lb
peanut meal	1.5	3.5 lb

POTASSIUM	PERCENT	AMOUNT PER 100 SQ. FT.
wood ashes	8.0	14 oz.
tobacco stems	7.0	1½ lb.
granite dust	5.0	2 lb.
fish meal	4.0	2½ lb.
peanut meal	1.2	8 lb

Data from NCSU *Nutrient Content of Fertilizers and Organic Materials*

Getting the acidity right: Soil pH

An important factor in any conversation about plant nutrients is soil pH, the technical term for the acidity or alkalinity of the soil, with 0.0 being most acidic (sour) and 14.0 being most alkaline (sweet). If your soil's pH is way out of balance, no amount of fertilizer will help, because nutrients will remain locked up and unavailable to plant roots.

Soil pH influences soil bacteria, nutrient leaching, toxic elements, and soil structure. Bacteria that release nitrogen from organic matter and certain fertilizers are particularly affected by soil pH, because bacteria operate best in the pH range of 5.5 to 7.0. Vegetables vary, but most crops prefer a pH of 6.2 to 6.8. All of these numbers can be dizzying, but the take-home message is clear: your soil pH matters and there are easy steps you can take to keep it in a good range.

Adding dolomite lime or other ground agricultural lime raises the pH or "sweetens" acidic soil. Regular application is necessary in most gardens to replace the calcium and magnesium taken up by your crops and washed away by rain. Because it prevents runoff—meaning the nutrients stay in your soil—adding organic matter helps the soil maintain the correct pH. High organic soil matter also increases plants' ability to tolerate some acidity.

Most soils east of the Mississippi tend to be acidic

and benefit from periodic applications of lime, but it's still best to test your soil first to be sure. Many garden centers and online sources offer easy-to-use pH tests, but, unfortunately, independent consumer research has shown that these tests can provide inconsistent and even grossly inaccurate results. A soil test available through your extension service or several other labs listed in our resource section will tell you more accurately how much lime to apply. If you don't have recent test results, most gardeners in the Southeast can assume that their soil is slightly acidic and amend accordingly.

Prepare the ground

Your goal here is to make a comfy home for your little plants. You want to mix in any amendments needed, and loosen up the soil so your plants can grow easily and water can seep in. In a brand new garden, this can be a lot of work. Fortunately, it will be much easier for the next year.

For a small garden, I like double digging, a technique where you turn the soil using a shovel, to the depth of two shovel blades. If your soil is already quite loose, you may only need to turn the top layer. You can also use a broad fork to loosen the soil. For larger plots a rototiller can easily be rented, but it can seem quite heavy and unwieldy to the inexperienced user. If you have a large garden in the country, you may be able to hire a local farmer to till your soil with a plough or disk. Fortunately for new gardeners there are many services springing up all over the country to help with tasks like removing sod or initial tilling for a new garden space.

Use a garden rake (not a leaf rake) to break up clumps on the surface of your beds and make the beds smooth and level. You can also use a rake to mix amendments into the top few inches of soil.

It's All About the Plants

Every plant starts with a seed, and each seed is a living miracle containing everything necessary to make a new plant. It's just waiting for the right conditions to start growing. Our job as gardeners is to act as midwives by providing good soil, adequate sun, ample water, and ongoing attention to help each seed flourish. For most of us who didn't grow up on farms, our first seed-sprouting experiences were grade-school experiments, like growing bean babies in a paper cup. I still get excited watching my beans push up out of the soil and grow inches overnight.

To direct sow or transplant?

A packet of seeds is perhaps the best investment a gardener makes. For less than the cost of a large coffee or a mint julep you can have weeks of fresh greens, baskets of tomatoes, or bushels of fresh green beans. But saving money is not the only reason to start from seeds. Online seed companies and garden-center seed racks offer a larger selection of varieties to the adventurous gardener. Many vegetables and flowers are actually easier to grow from seed than as transplants. Dill, cilantro, and roots such as carrots produce abundantly with direct sowing (planting seeds straight into the ground) but do not take well to transplanting, as anyone who has ever purchased a $2 pot of cilantro that immediately went to seed can testify. Premixed collections allow the new gardener to try out a number of varieties with one packet, and the generous amounts of seeds in most packets make it easy to try succession plantings (that is, making several plantings over the course of the growing season to keep the fresh food coming).

Growing plants from seed can be easy and economical if you follow some simple guidelines: Don't rush the planting season. Use a planting calendar, available from your state or local extension agent or master gardener. Not all plants are suited for direct sowing. Spring cabbage, broccoli, and onions, as well as long- and warm-season crops like eggplant, peppers, and tomatoes, are best started indoors and then transplanted. Many gardeners purchase seedlings from a reputable local nursery or online source in their region. That way they get locally adapted varieties. Select small but sturdy, vibrant, green plants. Oversized starts suffer more transplant shock (disruption to growth while getting established in the garden). Reduce shock by waiting for the right time of day to transplant, handling seedlings gently, setting plants quickly into properly sized holes, and water, water, water.

Even some seeds that are best direct sown may rot before sprouting if left in cold, wet soil for too long. You never know what the weather's going to be. Planning for several smaller succession plantings allows you to try for the earliest harvest without risking losing your whole crop to a late frost or soil that isn't warm enough.

Some seeds, like peas, beans, and corn, should be sown directly into the soil outside. Watermelon, melons, cucumbers, and squash are also usually sown outside, because transplanting can easily damage their tender roots. But wait until the soil warms up before you start planting.

How to sow outdoors

Direct sowing is simple, but proper planning and preparation is very important. The Edibles A to Z section of this book gives directions on spacing and sowing depth for a variety of crops and will help you decide whether to sow in rows (furrows, or wide rows), in hills (stations, with large separation between plants), or to broadcast sow (thickly spreading seed over a large surface, with less attention to exact spacing).

Whichever method you choose, you'll need to sow extra seed to guarantee a good crop: you run a greater risk of losing young seedlings when sowing outdoors, because so much more is out of our control than when we sow in pots inside. If you're lucky, you'll have more seedlings than you need, and with greens, carrots, and beets, you can thin in stages and enjoy eating the young plants; for crops that transplant well, you can dig up extra plants to move to other parts of the garden or to give to friends (catch them before the roots are too well established).

Good soil preparation is critical. This is your chance to improve soil texture and fertility. Don't rush sowing and miss your chance to really give your plants a good start in life. First, properly amend your soil with compost and other nutrients and loosen the soil using your desired technique. Finally, before sowing, be certain you rake the soil to a fairly smooth surface. A few passes with a garden rake should do the trick. This will help prevent seeds from washing away, ensure that your plants are all on the same level, and make weeding with a hoe easier later on.

After you sow, cover the seeds with fine soil to the recommended depth (be careful here, as this can be very, very shallow for small seeds that benefit from some light). Finally, press down firmly so the seeds make good contact with the soil. This keeps the seeds moist by capillary action, which helps the water travel through the soil.

Here are the basic methods for direct sowing:

To sow in **furrows, or wide rows,** I run the corner of a hoe the length of the bed at the desired depth. Use a string (pulled tight between two stakes) as a guide to keep your furrows straight and spaced properly; then seed at the desired spacing. If the seeds are tiny, or the spacing is very close, you can save time by dribbling the seeds in at approximately the right spacing. On the other hand, for peas and beans I like to space more carefully so I won't have to bother with thinning.

Station sowing, or planting in hills, is the best technique for large plants like melons, squash, and cucumbers. Sow three or four seeds at each location where you ultimately want to have a plant. Dig compost and other amendments into the spot first. You could make hills, which are like tiny raised beds at each spot, but in the South, keeping adequate moisture is more important than warming up the soil. We generally station sow on the flat by working compost and any other amendments into an area and smoothing the soil level before planting. Once your seedlings have put on two or three true leaves, thin them to your desired final spacing by cutting off extra plants at the surface.

Broadcast sowing works well for salad mix and other cut-and-come-again greens, especially very small plants that don't need much space. Simply sprinkle the seeds evenly over the whole surface. This is often done with very small seeds, so you may find it's best to cover the area only very lightly with fine soil or compost, or simply to rake in the seeds so they rest just below the surface (which also helps ensure an even distribution).

Water your beds

Make sure to be diligent and keep your seeds moist until they germinate. I have a few tricks up my sleeve to do this without much fuss. For big seeds that we sow in

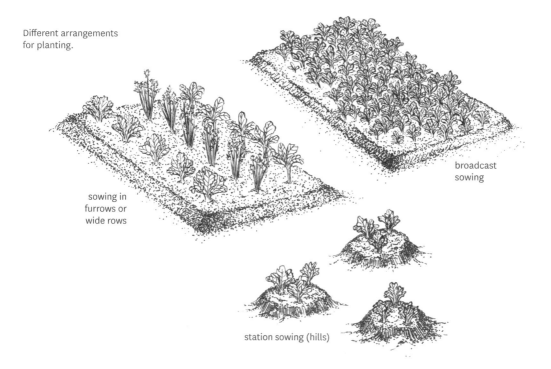

Different arrangements for planting.

sowing in furrows or wide rows

broadcast sowing

station sowing (hills)

furrows, like corn and beans, I first soak the furrow until the water runs over the sides (my British friend calls it "flooding the drill"). Your seeds will usually then have enough water until they come up. For smaller seeds such as brassicas, it's best to expect to water the beds every day until the plants come up (though maybe you will be lucky and it will rain!). I sometimes place a lightweight plank or board over the well-moistened furrow after I've covered it with soil. The board helps keep the soil very moist, so you can water less. Check under the board every day. You must remove it the moment you see the tiny seedling heads. (This doesn't work for seeds that need light to germinate, like lettuce and some herbs.)

Seed soaking and pre-sprouting

In the Southeast, we have a long enough growing season that we can wait for the soil to get warm before direct sowing summer crops. However, the window for direct sowing cool-season crops in both spring and fall is short. You want to get those seeds growing quickly even if the conditions outside aren't great for little baby plants. This is especially true if you're trying to start fall-season crops in midsummer when it's 95°F in the shade.

To pre-sprout peas in a jar, place the seeds in a quart mason jar and cover with room temperature water for four to eight hours. Drain the water and put the jar of seeds in a warm, dark place. Rinse daily until you see very small white rootlets emerge (four to seven days). Have the planting area ready before pre-sprouting so you can plant the pre-sprouted seed as soon as you see the root tips. Sow with the root end down.

For beets, chard, and sometimes corn, we soak the seeds overnight to give them a head start. Other smaller seeds, such as herbs and flowers, we sprout on a moist, rolled-up paper towel in a plastic bag, move to a flat for about four weeks, and put outside.

Sowing seeds for transplanting

In the spring, you sow seeds indoors because the weather or the soil is too cold outside. In the summer, you sow seeds indoors for quite the opposite reason: to protect them from heat. In addition, insect pressure is much worse in the summer months, and the high heat increases evaporation, making it more difficult to keep seedling beds evenly moist. Indoor sowing isn't the only option: outdoor nursery beds protected by shade cloth can improve your chances of success sowing outdoors.

You can grow spring seedlings in a south- or southeast-facing sunny window, but even with daily rotation your plants may still stretch toward the window. Growing under fluorescent lights can ensure that your seedlings get enough light and are sturdy, not leggy. See the January chapter for details. You can also start seeds in a cold frame (a small, simple structure that protects your plants from the cold, often made out of old window frames and haybales; see the February chapter for more information) or greenhouse if you have access to one.

We start most spring seedlings four to six weeks before the recommended transplanting date (tomatoes, sweet peppers, eggplants, broccoli, cabbage, kale, and collards). Onions, hot peppers, and celery need longer, about eight to ten weeks. Don't start your seeds indoors too soon; large seedlings suffer more damage when you move them outside.

Start your seeds in a good organic seed-starting mix from a local store or make your own. Purchased mixes are sterile, light, and hold moisture well. Use a large container to mix water into your soil mixture until it is moist, but not soggy. Fill nursery flats, small pots, or other containers nearly to the top with your mix. Make sure your containers have drainage holes.

Use your finger or a stick to make holes in the soil. The holes can be quite close together because you'll soon be moving your plants into larger containers. For large seeds, make holes about ½ inch deep. For smaller seeds, ⅛ to ¼ inch is plenty. Place one to three seeds in each spot (it's good to sow extra because not all your seeds will come up; pull out or snip off any extras once they sprout, or very gently move them to an empty spot). Cover the seeds with fine soil and press down gently. Water gently and sparingly, just enough to keep the soil moist but not soggy. It may be anywhere from a few days to a couple of weeks before you begin seeing your first seedlings break through the soil.

Potting up and hardening off

While your seedlings are growing in pots or flats, make sure they always have plenty of light, moisture, and space to grow. When they have two to four true leaves (the first one or two leaves to appear, the cotyledons, formed during germination, are not what you are looking for), it's time to move them into larger flats or pots (called potting up). Don't give them too much room too quickly. Seedlings grow best and are easier to care for if you choose *slightly* larger containers, not enormous ones.

This is a good time to make sure your plants get the nutrients they need. Do this by potting up into a fine, fertile compost/soil mix, either purchased or homemade. Moisten your potting soil first and fill the container nearly to the top. Use a narrow trowel or a Popsicle stick to make a deep hole, and while holding the soil aside, slide in the seedling. Gently press down the soil around

HOME REMEDIES FOR YOUR PLANTS

Every gardener runs into problems with insect pests, fungi, or other plant ills. When prevention doesn't work, the next step is safe, non-toxic solutions straight from the pantry. Whichever treatment you choose, it is best to spray in the early morning or the cool of evening. Do not spray when temperatures are above 80°F. Do a small test before you go all out.

Soap. Liquid soap (like Dr. Bronners), mixed with water, is a great aphid control. Mix 1 tablespoon per quart and use a spray bottle to spritz directly onto the bothersome bugs.

Sticky traps. My favorite sticky trap is to smear Tanglefoot (a sticky, non-drying paste made from natural gum resins, vegetable oil, and wax) or petroleum jelly onto the inside of a 5-gallon bucket. When flea beetles are attacking my eggplants, I just hold the bucket alongside the plant, and give the plant a good shake over the bucket, and many of the bugs will get stuck. Trap flea beetles this way once a day for a few days to give the plants a chance to outgrow the infestation.

Milk spray. Use for brown rot and other fungi that attack peaches and other stone fruit. New research from Australia and Brazil shows that spraying a 20 percent milk solution can also control powdery mildew on cucumbers and squash.

Hydrogen peroxide. Use as a dip for perennial onions and garlic before planting to prevent fungal diseases.

the base of the plant. It is best if the seedling roots are a bit spread out and generally point downward. Give each plant a bit more water and you're done!

A couple weeks before you expect to transplant outside, begin hardening off your plants so the seedlings gradually become accustomed to strong sunlight, cool nights, and less frequent watering. Start by moving your seedlings into direct sunlight for two to three hours each day, in a location sheltered from strong winds. Gradually increase daily exposure and reduce watering (but do not let the plants wilt) until your plants are ready for transplating.

Transplanting outdoors

To avoid stressing your tender spring seedlings, transplant them into your garden in the late afternoon on an overcast or drizzly day. Transplant shock is a big deal, so do everything you can to ease the transition. That means making sure your plants have all the water they need, especially if the weather is hot.

Use a garden trowel or shovel to dig a hole a few inches deeper and wider than the roots of the plant. I like to mix a shovel full of compost in with the soil I've removed. This ensures the plant is surrounded by fertility. If the soil is at all dry, fill the hole with water and let it drain first before planting.

Gently place the plant so the roots are spread out and directed downward. Refill the hole with your soil-compost mix. Press down firmly around the base of the stem.

Give the plants plenty of water just after transplanting; make sure to water the whole bed, not just the plants. Continue giving them lots of water until they're established and growing well. In the summer, I place mulch around the plants right after transplanting to help keep the soil moist and prevent weeds from coming up.

For spring plantings, I wait until the soil starts to warm before mulching.

Greener Growing

Gardeners are providing an important service to our environment just by growing their own local food. But there are lots of other choices we gardeners can make to ensure that we're growing in harmony with nature. Here are some tips for making your garden a more earth-friendly place:

Build your soil. Recycling all the organic waste from your yard and household to the soil doesn't just improve your tilth, it also reduces waste going into landfills and lessens your carbon footprint.

Watch your water use. Water bills tend to add up quickly in hot, dry summers, but you can reduce your water usage and still have a bountiful garden: choose varieties that need less water, keep your plants well mulched, and use a watering system that gets the water into the soil with minimal evaporation.

Prevent nutrient runoff. Don't over fertilize! Nutrient runoff from yards, gardens, and fields is a huge problem for waterways all over the Southeast. Keep your soil covered with mulch, dig your amendments into the soil, and use soil tests so you apply just what you need (this saves you money, time, and trouble, as well).

Use earth-friendly building materials. Choose untreated wood, recycled or repurposed materials, and be creative! There are lots of newfangled garden products available. Consider what you need before you purchase, and make sure it will last.

Encourage beneficial insects. Keep helpful bugs in your garden by providing nectar sources for as much of the year as you can. Mint-like herbs, umbels such as Queen Anne's lace and yarrow, and asters such as sunflowers, black-eyed Susans, and daisies, are the preferred flowers for many insects we want in our gardens. Oh, and never use broad-spectrum insecticides because they destroy all those beneficial bugs in the process.

Manage pests naturally. My favorite way to make the garden into a more balanced ecosystem is with chickens! Backyard chickens are all the rage, and for good reason. Rotate them through your garden and they'll add fertilizer right where you need it. Chickens eat weed seeds and insect larvae, and they even help remove weeds from the soil. Run them through before planting to reduce the work of preparing beds. Harvey Ussery's blog (TheModernHomestead.us) and book (*The Small-Scale Poultry Flock*) are chock full of good information on gardening with chickens.

Prevention is your first line of defense. Even organic pest deterrents and treatments have an impact on the environment. Your goal is to avoid needing any pest controls in your garden. Well-fed, well-watered, vigorously growing plants have fewer disease or pest problems. Choose insect- and disease-resistant plant varieties, and keep your plants happy with healthy soil, sunshine, and adequate moisture.

Plant the right varieties at the right time. Varieties well suited to our region are great for our environment. They're less troubled by pests and diseases and need fewer inputs and less water. At Southern Exposure, we've become true converts to the incredible heirlooms that ancient gardeners in our region selected and passed on to us: from pumpkins that originated with the Cherokees, to tomatoes originating from eighteenth-century southern plant breeders like Thomas Jefferson. Likewise, going with the natural rhythms of the seasons will get you better results with less work. For example, if you love potatoes, don't just plant them in the spring. Here in the South, you can plant a whole second crop starting in early summer that you'll be digging up around the first frost.

GARDEN
PLANNING

The first thing to consider when planning your garden is what you and your family like to eat. It doesn't do anybody any good to grow lovely looking vegetables that nobody wants. Next, check in with yourself: How much time and energy do you really have? After that, look at how much space you have. Does it have enough sun? It's important to make a plan that matches you and your situation. How will you use your resources? Every garden is limited. Even in the big gardens at Southern Exposure Seed Exchange, we have to make hard choices about what we'll grow. When I'm deciding what to grow, flavor is really important. Some things just taste better straight from the garden. Maybe you are into reducing your grocery bills. Fresh veggies can be expensive to buy, but cheap to grow. Or you might worry about the future and want a more sustainable lifestyle. These are all considerations when you plan your garden.

The Edibles A to Z section in this book will help you choose plants that thrive in our region. Some are traditional crops that have fallen out of favor but have a lot to recommend them. Why did the old-timers in this part of the world grow southern peas, okra, greasy beans, and sweet potatoes? Maybe it's because these are all disease-resistant, drought-tolerant, nutritious, and

delicious! I hope you'll be inspired to add some of these or other southern traditions in your garden.

For those new to gardening and with limited time, a small, well-cared-for garden will produce more food and more satisfaction than a sprawling, weedy garden that overwhelms you. Choose crops that thrive with minimal attention. I've made a chart to help you pick the easier crops to grow, but don't be afraid to mix in a few that need a little more care.

EASY-TO-GROW CROPS

WARM SEASON	COOL SEASON	IN NEED OF EXTRA SPACE
asparagus beans	beets	Swiss chard
bush beans (early and late plantings)	bunching onions	asparagus
	kale, broccoli, cabbage, kohl-rabi, rutabaga, turnips	cucumber
cherry tomatoes and paste tomatoes		grinding corn, popcorn
	lettuce	Jerusalem arti-chokes
ground cherries, husk cherries, and tomatillos	peas (snap and snow)	sunflowers
	radishes	sweet potatoes
hot peppers	shallots, garlic, and perennial onions	watermelon
lima beans		winter squash (*Moschata* types: butter-nut, tan cheese, seminole)
Malabar spin-ach and New Zealand spinach	southern greens and mustard greens (arugula, turnip greens, creasy greens)	
okra		
parsnips		
southern peas		
Swiss chard		

SLIGHTLY MORE CHALLENGING CROPS

WARM SEASON	COOL SEASON	IN NEED OF EXTRA SPACE
edamame	Asian greens	melons
eggplant	bulbing onions	sweet corn
peanuts	carrots	non-*Moschata* winter squash such as hub-bard, kuri, delicata
pole beans	leeks	
slicing tomatoes	peas (English/ shelling)	
summer squash (successions)	potatoes	
sweet peppers	spinach	

CHALLENGING CROPS

WARM SEASON	COOL SEASON	IN NEED OF EXTRA SPACE
celery and celeriac	Brussels sprouts	big pumpkins (*Maxima* type)
	fava beans	globe artichokes
	runner beans	

BUILDING YOUR SOIL WITH COVER CROPS

As you plan, you also should think about cover crops. They stabilize your soil as well as loosen it up. Plus, they add organic matter and nutrients right in place. Cover crops can be planned or spontaneous. Some you plan into your regular rotation. Others are "catch crops": fast crops when you happen to have a bit of open space before conditions are right for the next planting. Catch crops protect your soil and increase fertility. My preferred summer catch crop is buckwheat: the fast-growing plants crowd out the weeds and the early flowers nourish our bees. In the fall, I sow rye catch crops for the highest fertility boost, or oats (which are killed by frost) if I want the space available for easy early spring planting.

The grains I just mentioned add lots of biomass. You can also mix in a nitrogen-fixing cover crop. Rye and vetch are a fantastic, affordable combination. The vetch climbs right up the rye stalks. We grow rye and vetch over the winter where we'll transplant tomatoes in spring. We mow down the cover crop right in place and leave it as mulch (you can even do this with a scythe). Then we set out the tomato starts straight into the mulch without having to till the soil. The cover crop has loosened the soil for us, and the vetch has added plenty of nitrogen.

WARM-SEASON COVER CROPS

- buckwheat
- sorghum
- Sudan grass

NITROGEN FIXERS

- soybeans
- crowder peas

COOL-SEASON COVER CROPS

- wheat
- oats
- rye
- forage radishes
- leafy brassicas

NITROGEN FIXERS

- vetch
- Austrian winter peas
- clover

Locating Your Garden

First, look at where you will get the most sun. You can always amend your soil, install irrigation, level out grades, and makes lots of other changes, but you can't tell the sun where to shine. If you're planning in the winter, notice if you'll lose sunshine when the trees leaf out. Be aware of tall buildings and walls that shade your garden.

Once you've identified possible sites, try to locate your garden as near to your house and water sources as possible. I've had to haul water to my garden, and it's a whole lot of work. Think about access to your garden with a wheelbarrow or cart. You may be hauling a lot of produce out of there.

Choose soil with good tilth. A good mix of clay and sand is great, but you can always improve your soil. I really think that soil quality should be secondary to picking a site with good light and a convenient location.

When to Plant

In our climate, we can have something growing in the garden every day of the year. To get the most out of our gardens, we have to pay attention to timing: when to plant, but also when a planting is done. You might be able to get a few more vine-ripened tomatoes, but it's often better to pull all those old plants in time to sow your winter cover crop or spring spinach. (Plus you can ripen green tomatoes on the counter indoors.)

We have three distinct planting seasons. There's the spring cool season, the warm season, and the fall cool season. The spring cool-season plantings start as soon as the soil is workable. Warm-season planting begins in

CROPS BY SEASON

SPRING COOL SEASON	WARM SEASON	FALL COOL SEASON
Asian greens	celery and	Asian greens
beets	celeriac	beets
bulbing onions	corn	Brussels sprouts
bunching onions	cucurbits:	bunching onions
carrots	cucumbers,	carrots
fava beans	watermelon,	fava beans
kale, broccoli,	melons,	kale, broccoli,
cabbage,	winter squash,	cabbage,
kohlrabi,	summer squash	kohlrabi,
cauliflower,	Jerusalem	cauliflower,
rutabaga,	artichokes	rutabaga,
turnips	lettuce	turnips
leeks	Malabar and	leeks
lettuce	New Zealand	lettuce
peas	spinach	peas
potatoes	nightshades:	radishes
radishes	tomatoes,	shallots, garlic,
southern greens	eggplants, pep-	and perennial
& mustard	pers, ground	onions
greens (aru-	cherries, husk	southern greens
gula, turnip	cherries, and	& mustard
greens, creasy	tomatillos	greens (aru-
greens)	okra	gula, turnip
spinach	parsnips	greens, creasy
Swiss chard	peanuts	greens)
	potatoes	spinach
	runner beans	Swiss chard
	snap beans, lima	
	beans, aspar-	
	agus beans,	
	edamame	
	southern peas	
	sunflowers	
	sweet potatoes	

late spring when the soil is warm enough for heat-loving crops. The fall cool-season plantings actually begin in midsummer and continue at least through October. (Garlic and onions are even later.)

When planting perennials like berries and asparagus for the first time, they are generally best put in the ground in the spring and fall. See the Edibles A to Z section for details on each crop.

Succession Planting and Filling in Spaces

Some crops are simply ready when they're ready and that's that. To have a good supply over time, you have to stagger plantings to prolong the harvest. A benefit of doing several plantings is security in case of extreme weather. Here are other things to remember:

Frequent plantings of fast crops. We do frequent succession plantings for quick-growing crops that are best fresh from the garden. Think lettuce, radishes, peas, arugula, and bush beans. Frequent successions also let you take full advantage of the South's shorter planting seasons in spring and fall.

Multiple plantings of slower crops. Some slow-maturing crops we plant only once, because they provide continuous harvests from one planting, or a single harvest that keeps well in storage for months to come. However, some slow-maturing crops benefit from multiple plantings, especially crops that don't keep well in storage, taste best straight from the garden, or produce smaller harvests as the season progresses. It's not so sad seeing your old zucchini plants wither up when you've got fresh new ones coming on. Corn, cucumbers, carrots, winter and summer squash, pole beans, melons, broccoli, and cabbage all benefit from staggered plantings.

Intercropping and relay planting. Get more food from your garden space by planting a quick-maturing crop alongside a slow-maturing one (intercropping). You'll harvest the quick-maturing one in time to make space for the slower one to take over the rest of the bed. Relay planting is intercropping where you plant a new crop while the previous crop is still in the bed. We sow spring peas in between rows of overwintered spinach. When the peas are about a foot tall, we're done harvesting the last spinach leaves and we pull the plants.

Catch crops. When a space opens up that you're not expecting, take advantage of the situation! Mix in some compost and sow a quick-maturing crop of something or other. Or pop in a few plants from your seedling bed.

Make the most of each planting. Try planting shorter and longer season varieties of the same crop at the same time. The shorter season one will come on early and when it's done, the later one is getting ready to eat. We especially like doing this with sweet corn and broccoli. Or, you can choose a variety that doesn't mature all at once. Many heirlooms have this quality, because our gardening forebears wanted continuous harvests from one planting. You can also get more from one planting by choosing tall, continuously bearing, indeterminate types, rather than short, bush plants with more concentrated harvests.

Planting Systems

Gardeners have figured out a lot of different arrangements for putting plants in the ground. There are traditional rows, raised beds, broadcast seeding, hills, square foot gardens, containers, and so on. Don't feel you have to pick just one planting system. Mix and match. Go wild! On our farm at SESE, we have permanent raised beds in the herb garden, temporary raised beds (that change from year to year) for root crops and greens, and we garden on the flat for most everything else, some in rows, some in stations.

Raised beds

There are many advantages to raised beds, which is why they're so popular. The soil drains well and warms up faster in the spring. You fertilize just the bed and not the paths. You only walk on the paths, so there is no threat of compacting the beds. The extra inches of light, fluffy soil help plant roots get growing quickly.

You can frame your raised beds with lumber (salvaged is best) or other materials, such as bricks or stones. A framed border of some sort is attractive, prevents foot traffic, and defines your beds. (Unframed beds tend to creep larger with time, until you're tiptoeing down tiny aisles). But framing makes it harder to change your garden layout, and makes it harder to use tools like hoes to weed the edges of the beds.

How big should you make your beds? Well, how much space do you have, and how flexible and nimble are you? Commercial farm beds are usually 4 feet wide, with 12-inch aisles. This will give you the maximum space for plants. I find that 3-feet-wide beds with 18-inch aisles are much more comfortable.

To make a raised bed, begin by deeply tilling the soil. Then use a shovel to scrape off the top 2–4 inches of soil from the adjacent aisles and pile it on the bed.

We use raised beds for early spring planting and the winter garden, but we look to other planting systems when the soil is already warm, and especially when dry conditions are a concern.

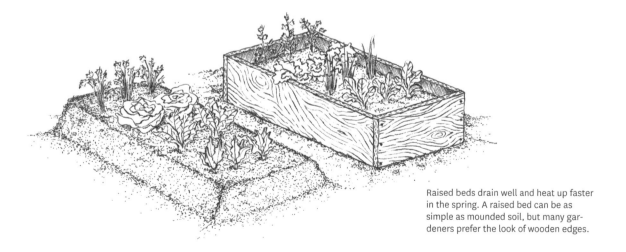

Raised beds drain well and heat up faster in the spring. A raised bed can be as simple as mounded soil, but many gardeners prefer the look of wooden edges.

Square foot gardening

If you have a very small garden, the square foot system is an effective way to maximize your space. Forget about rows—in this system you divide your raised beds into 1×1-foot squares and use the leaf area of each plant to determine how many will fit. The really close spacings get the most from small areas but require you to intensively improve your soil. This is a great choice for those with a tiny garden or poor soil, who don't mind buying a lot of compost and other amendments.

Gardening on the flat

Gardening on the flat is as simple as it sounds. In well-drained conditions it suits corn, vining crops like winter squash and melons, sweet potatoes, and other space hogs. Lay out your fixed paths and your garden beds. Enrich the planting areas but don't bother giving them the extra lift of raised beds. Keep everything on the same level. Your beds won't dry out as quickly as raised beds do in the summer. That's ideal for summer crops and hot-weather nursery sowings.

Container gardening

Don't have a yard to plant? Don't despair! People are doing incredible things with tiny spaces and container gardens. Containers let you take advantage of sunshine wherever you have it-—on your driveway, roof, patio, or in window boxes. Craig LeHoullier of Raleigh, North Carolina, who rediscovered the Cherokee Purple tomato, grows hundreds of tomato plants in containers lined up on his driveway!

Smaller containers are good for getting an early start with greens and herbs. For deep-rooted plants you'll need deep containers, 5 gallons or more. Get creative, especially with repurposed items, from 55-gallon metal drums cut in half, to whiskey barrels, to plastic buckets.

Whatever you choose, it needs to drain. Punch holes in the bottom and you're set. Use a tray underneath to protect the floor.

Keep in mind that straight soil doesn't work in pots. It cracks, drains poorly, and becomes compacted. High-quality organic potting soils or sifted compost are your best choices for containers. Keeping your container garden watered is crucial. Self-watering containers are great for people always on the go. Plans for making your own are available online, or you can purchase them premade from your local garden center.

Community gardens and other shared spaces

In the Southeast, we're just now seeing the big increase in community gardens that's been happening in other areas. People are excited about the local food movement and they want to be a part of it themselves. City dwellers as well as those in more rural places are getting together and turning vacant lots, church lawns, community centers, and other underused spaces into glorious gardens. These aren't usually official city projects. They can be informal arrangements between neighbors or landowners and the community or church-sponsored gardening projects for youth. Not only do these gardens give people access to land, they also allow for sharing of tools, information, and infrastructure. Find local gardening groups who'll help point you toward these projects. If there is not a community garden near you there are some great resources in print and online to help you start one.

Many community gardening projects are donating at least a portion of their produce to local food banks or other charitable organizations. One example is Plant a Row for the Hungry, a project of the Garden Writers Association. They can help you start your own local campaign if you're interested.

COMMUNITY GARDENING RESOURCES

With community gardens increasing in popularity in many areas, there is a lot of online information and support available. Try searching for "community garden support" on Google, and you'll see what I mean.

Here are some organizations that I've had contact with:

American Community Garden Association (communitygarden.org) supports the formation and expansion of state and regional community gardening networks, encourages research, and conducts educational programs.

Tricycle Gardens (tricyclegardens.org) has five community gardens in Richmond, Virginia, and runs a program of volunteers and workshops to support community gardens.

Yards to Gardens.org (y2g.org) lets gardeners in Northern Virginia connect and share garden space and tools.

Coalition of Austin Community Gardens (communitygardensaustin.org) fosters development and coordination of the many community gardens in Austin, TX.

Park Pride (parkpride.org) is a networking hub for the strong and growing community gardens network in Atlanta, GA.

Keeping Garden Records

Gardening is a never-ending learning experience, but it's surprising how hard it can be to remember what you've learned from one season to the next. Keeping a garden journal is one easy way to keep track of what is happening in your garden. A very simple system is to just keep track of what you planted and when on a wall calendar. But there's actually a lot more to record, and you'll be able to improve future garden plans by giving yourself space to get more details down about each crop. We follow the example of Thomas Jefferson and record everything: sowing and transplanting dates, varieties, first harvest, last harvest, how much was harvested, weather events, any pest or disease problems and what you did about them, and any stray thoughts for the future of your garden. Here at Southern Exposure on our certified organic farm, we keep extensive records. We prefer to use spreadsheets to plan and keep track of what actually happened in our gardens.

If spreadsheets aren't your cup of tea you can purchase a garden journal that helps with organization. Some gardeners find jotting down planting and harvest data on a wall calendar gives them all the information they need. For more detailed records, many tech-savvy gardeners use one of the new online garden-planning tools in the Resources section of this book. I have been enjoying getting reminders of when to plant in my inbox.

WHO'S IN THE FAMILY: GARDEN PLANT FAMILIES

- **Cucurbits:** cucumbers, melons, squash, watermelon
- **Nightshades:** tomatoes, eggplants, peppers, husk cherries, ground cherries, tomatillos, and potatoes
- **Brassicas:** cabbage, broccoli, cauliflower, kale, mustard greens, turnips, rutabagas, Asian greens, Brussels sprouts, radishes, kohlrabi, collards
- **Alliums:** onions, garlic, leeks, scallions, shallots
- **Legumes:** beans and peas of all kinds, peanuts, clover, vetch, Austrian winter peas
- **Composites:** sunflowers, lettuce, some leafy greens
- **Umbels:** carrots, parsnips, dill, fennel, celery, celeriac
- **Goosefoots:** spinach, beets, chard
- **Grasses:** corn, wheat, oats, rye

Creating Your Rotation

One of the simplest and best ways to prevent diseases and pests in your garden is to use a good crop rotation. Plants in the same family have similar nutritional needs and attract similar pests. A well-organized rotation helps to best utilize available nutrients and may reduce the chance of a soil-borne disease getting established or nasty bugs surviving over winter. The key here is to know your plant families and avoid planting related plants in the same area year after year. I recommend waiting three or four years between planting a crop from any given family in the same spot.

Getting to know plant families is not only good for planning crop rotation but also is an essential tool of the trade for being a good seed saver and being aware of things that might cross-pollinate and mix up your carefully tended seeds.

To get started planning your rotation, figure out your must-have crops for your garden and how much space each needs. Now divide them into families. Take out your garden map or draw a rough estimate. Divide the map into six to eight areas and try to fit everything, keeping the family groupings together and allowing at least one space for cover crops. This may take a bit of adjusting and in a small garden it won't always come out perfectly, but your goal is an allocation of space that lets you systematically rotate your crops around the garden so that no one family is in the same place more often than every three years. If you have enough space to allow for a longer rotation and more cover crops, all the better.

A six-bed rotation might start like this:

BED 1: all-season cover crop
BED 2: tomato, pepper, potato, eggplant
BED 3: onions, garlic, leeks, shallots, beets, chard
BED 4: peas, beans, southern peas, peanuts
BED 5: squash, corn, melons, pumpkins, cucumbers
BED 6: cabbage, lettuce, radish, broccoli, kale, turnip, Asian greens

For the second year, you could move your extended cover crop to Bed 6 and move everything else over one bed.

BED 1: tomato, pepper, potato, eggplant

BED 2: onions, garlic, leeks, shallots, beets, chard

BED 3: peas, beans, southern peas, peanuts

BED 4: squash, corn, melons, pumpkins, cucumbers

BED 5: cabbage, lettuce, radish, broccoli, kale, turnip, Asian greens

BED 6: all-season cover crop

For the third year, move your tomatoes and other nightshades to Bed 6 and again move everything else over one bed.

BED 1: onions, garlic, leeks, shallots, beets, chard

BED 2: peas, beans, southern peas, peanuts

BED 3: squash, corn, melons, pumpkins, cucumbers

BED 4: cabbage, lettuce, radish, broccoli, kale, turnip, Asian greens

BED 5: all-season cover crop

BED 6: tomato, pepper, potato, eggplant

A simple rotation makes things easy, but be sure to leave lots of room for flexibility in your plan. In the scheme above, if you wanted two beds of nightshades you have four beds to expand into that haven't grown anything in that family for two or more years.

QUICK TIPS FOR GOOD GARDEN PLANNING

Time your planting. Have your seeds and transplants ready when the timing and weather are right. Don't rush planting out tender seedlings when the soil is too cold or wet in the spring, but at the same time don't delay or the hot weather will come and you'll have to wait until fall.

Prepare the soil. Work the soil and prepare beds ahead of time so that you'll be ready when the seedlings and weather are ready. I try to prepare some beds for spring planting in the fall or during a "January thaw" when we have a week where highs are more than 60°F. This avoids the need to work soil that is too wet at planting time. A nice mulch will keep down winter weeds and can be pulled aside a few days before planting to warm the soil in winter or thoroughly watered to cool the soil for summer planting. "Feed the soil" to grow your plants.

Plant enough for losses. Losses due to insects, weather, and neighborhood critters, from deer to dogs, can be expected, so plant extra until you gain experience and know what to expect. Seed is inexpensive and gardening friends are so happy when all goes well and you have extra seedling "starts" to share. Do take good care of your seedlings, keeping them covered if it is too cold or shaded in the summer heat as well as regularly watered and weeded. You'll be rewarded with an abundant harvest.

GET PLANTING

PLANNING
FOR FRESH FOOD
ALL YEAR

Even in the sunniest parts of the Southeast, January brings some rainy days well suited to sitting in a warm, cozy chair, planning for the year ahead. The prep work you do now—garden maps, a planting schedule, testing seeds left over from last year and ordering any you'll need for this one, and setting up a spot to start your own plants from seed indoors—ensures a bountiful garden for the year to come. There's plenty to do outside as well, from pruning perennials to taking soil samples for testing, to preparing beds (if the soil dries out enough).

If you are new to growing your own food, the Get Started section of this book will help you learn about the climate and soils in our region, pick a good location for your garden, and get started growing healthy, fresh, delicious food for a twelve-month harvest. Let's start planning!

TO DO THIS MONTH

PLAN, PREPARE, AND MAINTAIN

- Organize catalogs and order seeds (making sure to first inventory your old seeds that might still be useable; see the "Vegetable Seed Viability" chart at the end of this chapter)
- Review last year's gardening successes and problems; consider what you would like to add to the garden and what you want to repeat from last year
- Get your soil tested, if you haven't done so recently
- Make a garden map and planting schedule
- Finish pruning fruit trees and bushes
- As the weather permits, prepare beds for early spring planting

SOW AND PLANT

- Start onions, hot peppers, globe artichokes, and rhubarb from seed inside in flats
- (In the Lower South) Start peas, onion sets, asparagus, and Irish potatoes outside, and plant bare root fruit trees, vines, and bushes

FRESH HARVEST

- arugula
- Asian greens
- Brussels sprouts
- cabbage
- carrots
- collards
- Egyptian onions
- kale
- leeks
- lettuce
- mustards
- spinach
- turnips

Check beets, carrots, garlic, onions, potatoes, squash, and sweet potatoes in storage for bruises, damaged rinds, or other signs of decay. If you have them, you should also check on your celeriac, kohlrabi, rutabaga, turnips, and winter radishes. (In the Lower South, many of these roots will still be in the ground.)

Garden Maps and Planting Schedules

There are many joys to vegetable gardening, but there are also a few predictable and avoidable frustrations. One of these is having everything ripen at once. Planning for a *continuous* harvest of fresh, tasty, homegrown produce is one of the major challenges for a beginning vegetable gardener.

In the previous chapters, we discussed locating your garden, succession planting, types of planting systems, and other things that will help you with your garden planning. Take some time to review those chapters and think about how much time you have, what you want to grow, how big you want your garden to be, where it will be located, and what type of planting system you prefer. A smaller, well-maintained garden is often more productive and a better situation for gaining experience than a larger garden that is a bit out of control. Once you make these decisions about the size, type, and location of your garden, it's time to make a map and create a planting schedule to keep your garden producing all year.

Measure your garden plot and plan the spacing of paths, rows, and beds. Note the location of any buildings, large trees, or shrubs that will shade your garden in the coming months. Include the north-south orientation on your map. Show sources of water and any areas with obvious drainage problems.

Graph paper is the traditional way to make an accurate, easy-to-use map of your garden. Using one square to show one foot of garden often works well for home gardeners. Make the map as large as you can with the size of paper you have so there is lots of room to write and revise. Make copies so you have maps for the different seasons you will be gardening, including succession planting and cover crops.

These days, many computer-savvy gardeners use spreadsheets or an online garden-planning tool for making their garden maps. All have many useful options for bed size and shapes, vegetable selectors, harvest log, and field notes. They even send you email reminders for planting dates. If you have a large yard or country property, Google Maps (maps.google.com) can show the exact placement of your house, outbuildings, large trees and shrubs, and north-south orientation.

You may want to make a new map for each season. By planting a spring crop, a summer crop, and a fall or over-wintered crop, a gardener can get three to four crops from the same space. The more you want to grow, the more attention you need to pay to close rotation of crops (this is where good maps will help). For example, plant spring lettuce, followed by summer green beans, followed by fall spinach; usually you will plant a cool-season crop, then a warm-season crop, and finish with another cool-season crop. Careful attention to days to maturity for each crop will tell you the best rotation period.

So now that you have a map, it's time to locate your plants and create a planting schedule. Here are some considerations.

Sun and shade. Greens can tolerate shadier areas but fruiting plants such as tomatoes and peppers need full sun at least six to eight hours a day.

Height. Trellising and caging can help you make better use of your space, increase air circulation, and reduce diseases. In general, grow taller plants like corn and trellised beans on the north side so they won't shade the shorter plants in your garden.

Rotation. Organize your planting choices for a smooth crop rotation and easier maintenance by keeping similar plants together. For example, group together all your nightshades (tomatoes, potatoes, peppers, and eggplants). A three-year rotation will help minimize plant diseases in your home garden.

Succession planting and relay planting can really improve yields in your garden. Use planting dates and the days-to-harvest information from your seed catalogs to plan succession plantings. See the previous section for more information on these techniques.

To determine your best planting dates, determine your climate zone but also be sure to talk to experienced neighbors, local master gardeners, and your cooperative extension agent. Don't forget your fall and winter garden. Allow space for later crops.

Starting seeds versus buying seedlings. There are advantages to both. Ask yourself if you have enough space, with enough sunlight, to grow your own seedlings. Can you control the temperature? Do you have the time and attention to tend your seedlings? Growing your own seedlings is easier for some crops than others. You can start some and buy others. Also remember that starting seeds isn't just a winter or early spring activity. In many areas, gardeners interested in growing organic or heirloom varieties will need to start their own plants from seeds rather than buy conventional transplants from the garden center.

Getting away. Make sure to plan ahead if you'll be going away for vacation.

Starting Plants Under Lights

With your map drawn and your planting charts completed, it's time to think about the indoor starts you're choosing to do. Timing is important. You want healthy, vigorous seedlings to transplant. Don't start too soon before the date you will set them outside.

There are a number of ways to start plants at home. A sunny window can work if you give regular attention to rotating plants to avoid phototropism (leaning toward the light) and leggy growth. Tall, skinny plants don't transplant well. You can also grow nice, sturdy seedlings in a cold frame or greenhouse if you have one, but I find that for many home gardeners, the most reliable way to have stout, green plants for early season plantings is to

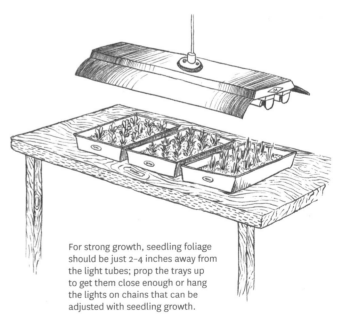

For strong growth, seedling foliage should be just 2–4 inches away from the light tubes; prop the trays up to get them close enough or hang the lights on chains that can be adjusted with seedling growth.

grow them under fluorescent lights. These lights give you better control of light and temperature.

Starting your own seeds is usually easy. In the Southeast, start most spring seedlings four to six weeks before the recommended setting-out date. Onions, hot peppers, and celery need longer, eight to ten weeks. Check with your local Master Gardeners or extension agent for best planting dates in your area.

Buy a good organic seed-starting mix from a nursery or natural products store. These mixes are sterile, light, and hold moisture well. In a 5-gallon bucket, add water to your soil mixture until it is moist without being soggy. Use nursery flats or other containers with drainage holes that are 2–3 inches deep and at least 3 inches wide. Fill them nearly to the top with your seed-starting mix. Use your finger to make small indentations in the soil about ¼ inch deep. Put one or two seeds in each spot. Cover with fine soil and tamp down to ensure the seed has contact with the soil. Gently water the seeds and keep the soil evenly moist, but not soggy.

Put the containers in a warm place with the fluorescent or grow light suspended 2–4 inches above. This may seem quite close, but I find it's better to have the plants very close than too far away. Check the plants regularly so you'll remember to raise the lights as they grow. Grow lights are broader-spectrum lights that cost about twice as much as regular fluorescents. They weren't around when I started gardening, and I think the fluorescents work just fine, but some people swear they grow stronger seedlings with grow lights. Hang the lights in a way that allows you to adjust their height as the plants grow. Keep the light on twelve to fourteen hours a day. A timer is helpful. When the plants have two to four true leaves, it is time to move them into bigger pots or deeper flats.

I like to move the plants into fine, fertile, well-screened compost to keep them growing steadily until it is time to transplant to the garden. Keep evenly moist and rotate the flats regularly. After four weeks, the plants can be moved to a cold frame or set outside for several hours each day to harden them off before planting in the garden. To avoid stressing our tender little friends, transplant in the afternoon of an overcast or drizzly day. Press down the soil firmly around each plant and, for most crops, add mulch to retain soil moisture and reduce weeds. Keep transplants well watered until established. See the previous section for more information on seed starting and transplanting.

SKILL SET

A SIMPLE HOME GERMINATION TEST

Germination testing at home is easy. Count out 10 seeds and spread them in a line, lengthwise along the middle of the top half of a thick paper towel (unbleached is best). Use a spray bottle of water to make the towel moist but not soggy. Fold the towel in half, roll it up, and loosely close it with a rubber band. Put the towel in a clean plastic bag and leave it in a warm 70–80°F location. Every few days, check to see how many seeds have germinated, adding moisture if necessary. Most crops will have fully germinated after a week. Some, such as peppers and herbs, may take two to four weeks. When that time is up count how many have sprouted. If it's less than 50 percent, plan on buying new seed. You can, of course, choose to plant your older seed anyway, but the seedlings may not be vigorous.

VEGETABLE SEED VIABILITY

When you buy a packet of seeds, the packet will usually say something like "Packed for 2013" (or whichever year the seeds were intended to be sold) or include a percentage that indicates the seed viability: the percentage of seeds that sprouted well in the test environment. However, seed viability isn't so simple, and it's not static: seeds lose viability over time, but some naturally last longer than others. When seeds are stored poorly, they lose viability much more quickly—and retail stores don't have the best conditions, as they are too warm and often too humid. A reputable seed company will have excellent storage conditions for packages, right up until they ship, so you might have better luck ordering direct than buying retail.

This table is for seeds that are stored well: in a cool, dark location with low humidity. Freezing seeds in a well-sealed container can extend viability for many more years (be sure to let the container come to room temperature before breaking the seal, otherwise condensation can form on the seeds and cause rot).

If you do use older seeds or poorly stored seeds, sow a fair amount extra and be prepared to fill in gaps. Seedling vigor, or how strong the tiny plants are when they come up, is different from viability, which is simply an indication of how many will come up. Vigorous seedlings withstand disease better by getting a faster start on life, which is a good reason to use fresh seed or store your seed well.

SEED LIFE

ONE YEAR	TWO TO FOUR YEARS	FOUR TO SIX YEARS
leeks	beans	brassicas
onions	beets	cucumbers
parsnips	carrots	radishes
	corn	spinach
	lettuce	squash
	muskmelons	tomato
	peas	watermelon
	peppers	

·FEBRUARY·

SOWING SEEDS
INDOORS

As winter fades away, gardeners throughout the Southeast are enthusiastically starting their spring vegetable gardens. Those in the Lower South will be planting in open ground, while those in the Upper South must plant more cautiously or under cover.

Throughout the region, February is marked by rapid and unpredictable weather changes, occasionally moving from 70°F highs to 25°F lows, with freezing rain and snow, almost overnight. To take advantage of the increasing warmth and be prepared for the unpredictable cold spells, the savvy food gardener makes liberal use of flats and transplanting. Like all good southeastern gardeners since Jefferson, we take advantage of warm days and dry ground to work the soil and prepare our beds, so they are ready and waiting

CONTINUED ON PAGE 58

TO DO THIS MONTH

PLAN, PREPARE, AND MAINTAIN

- Spread compost and till beds for carrots, spinach, beets, lettuce, onions, turnips, cabbage, kale, collards, broccoli, and potatoes when the soil is dry enough to be worked
- Finish weeding perennials; give them (including strawberries and grapes) some compost, if you haven't done so already in the fall
- Prune grapes and finish pruning blueberries, raspberries, and currants
- Buy seed potatoes mid-month in order to have time to green sprout (chit) in bright, indirect light for two to four weeks before planting
- Weed overwintered spinach, kale, collards, garlic, onions, and other greens

SOW AND PLANT

- Transplant perennial bushes, canes, and crowns if needed and apply generous mulch
- Sow in flats: cabbage, cauliflower, collards, senposai, kale, kohlrabi, peppers, broccoli, celery, celeriac, hot peppers, and spinach; sow fast-growing lettuce varieties every fourteen days
- Sow outside: pre-sprouted spinach seed, small amount of radishes and arugula; use row cover if extra protection is necessary; if mild, sow carrots, turnips, and fava beans; when forsythia blooms, sow peas and spinach under row cover
- Pot on (transplant into larger, deeper containers) cabbage, broccoli, lettuce, and kale; begin to harden off
- Transplant spinach (from flats), kale, and fall-sown onions
- (In the Lower South) Direct sow outside hardy roots, Asian greens, collards, and Swiss chard
- (In the Lower South) Transplant outside cabbage, broccoli, lettuce, onions, and Brussels sprouts
- (In the Lower South) Plant potatoes that have been green sprouted (chitted)

FRESH HARVEST

As spring warms up, new baby salad greens and radishes join the overwintered bounty.

- arugula
- Asian greens
- Brussels sprouts
- carrots
- collards
- Egyptian onions
- kale
- leeks
- lettuce
- mustard
- spinach
- turnips

Check beets, cabbage, carrots, celeriac, garlic, kohlrabi, onions, potatoes, rutabagas, sweet potatoes, turnips, and winter squash in storage

for our transplants. Spun polyester row covers, low tunnels, and hoop houses help us plant earlier and guarantee our crops get off to a strong start.

Great Garden Gear

Garden shows and plant symposiums abound in February and let us indulge in visions of the season to come. The larger garden shows come complete with "real" gardens and talks by garden experts on everything from container planting to the newest All-America Selection (AAS) winners. These shows are a great place to see firsthand many of the tools, planters, and garden gadgets advertised in catalogs and garden magazines. Take the opportunity to look and ask questions, but limit your purchases to fit your budget and garden size. Go to as many of the talks as you have time for. Both new and experienced gardeners can enjoy learning about novel approaches to traditional tasks. I remember first seeing Reemay at a garden show and wondering if that funny stuff would work. Reemay is a lightweight spun polyester row cover that lets through water and about 75 percent of light, while providing frost protection to 30°F or lower, depending on the thickness. Nowadays, a wide array of spun polyester and polypropylene row covers are mainstays of year-round organic food gardening.

After a visit to a big garden show, you may feel like gardening is an expensive business. Don't despair: it doesn't have to be. You only need a few good tools to get started.

Tips for stretching your garden budget

As an organic gardener, I always strive to "reduce, reuse, recycle" in my garden, and I really like to save money whenever I can. For those of you with similar goals, here are some interesting options.

Market bulletins. Many departments of agriculture publish old-fashioned market bulletins free online or just for the price of postage. These bulletins offer all sorts of strange and wonderful plants, bulbs, and seeds. The bulletins are also great places to find hay, manure, and other organic farm waste if you live in a rural area (print versions cost $10 to $15 a year).

Craigslist (craigslist.org). The go-to place online for free and inexpensive garden goodies for both city and country folk. Used tools, tomato cages, mulch, fencing, and plants are often advertised on Craigslist.

Freecycle (freecycle.org). A grassroots and entirely non-profit movement of people who are giving (and getting) stuff for free in their own towns. It's all about reuse and keeping good things out of landfills. Each local group is moderated by local volunteers.

Found, used, and repurposed materials. Junk art and homemade trellises can be a wonderful addition to your garden, from bamboo trellises and rubber tire planters, to stepping stones made out of pieces of a broken concrete sidewalk or driveway.

Seed swaps and community garden exchanges. Southern gardeners are neighborly and really like to share. Attending or, better yet, helping to organize a seed swap or community garden exchange is a great way to share your gardening excess, find new treasures in what might otherwise have become trash, and talk to neighbors about cooperating on bulk purchases such as compost. Such events are also a good place to begin organizing projects such as seasonal work parties and tool-sharing community coops.

Plant a Row for the Hungry. This is one of the many projects in our communities working to combat hunger and reduce wasted food. Find a group who needs your extra seeds, plants, and garden supplies, and that can use your extra garden produce at harvest time. Keep the sharing going around.

My Favorite Tools for the Garden

I like to save money, but cheap tools are no bargain. They break, dull quickly, rust, and have to be replaced, doubling the cost. My advice is to buy the best quality tools you can afford. Here are a few of the basic tools I like for my garden:

- A long-handled spade, fork, or shovel will be the first tool you need for digging a new garden. Stainless steel tools are long lasting, easy to clean, and don't rust—but they're expensive. Tools made from carbon steel are a cost-effective alternative to stainless steel tools because they are sturdy, durable, and easy to sharpen. Tools with ash shafts and steel-strapped or forged sockets handle pressure and stress well. Choose the handle length to best fit the person who will be using the tool. I like a short-handled fork or spade. Some small women even prefer an edging spade or one specially designed for a woman's proportions.

- A strong, metal garden rake is essential for smoothing beds and removing loose stones on top. An old-fashioned bamboo or metal fan–type rake is great for leaves and raking grass clippings. The new adjustable rakes are prone to break with heavy use, so they're not a good choice.

- I love hoes because a quick timely hoeing at the right time, when the weeds are still very small or just sprouting below the soil surface, can save hours of back-breaking hand weeding later on. I indulge myself with hoes of several different types and sizes, but to begin with one or two hoes will do nicely. You need a hoe to open the ground and cover seeds when planting and also to cultivate the soil to keep down weeds. You can start with one general-purpose tool like the swan neck hoe (half-moon hoe) for both tasks, but I prefer to also have a scuffle hoe just for weeding. It is a unique tool that easily slices through small and pre-emergent weeds just below the soil line. It's also called a stirrup

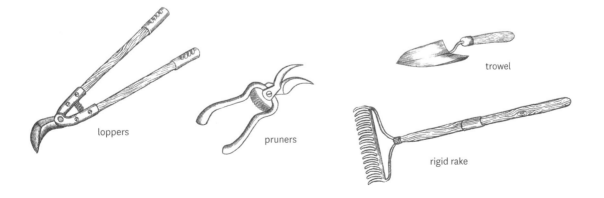

loppers

pruners

trowel

rigid rake

hoe. Winged weeders, diamond hoes, and other variations on double-sided hoes are all good choices. You'll find hoeing weeds much easier if you keep a sharpening stone in the garden shed and give your hoe a sharp edge each time you begin (and as often as every 15 minutes while hoeing).

- A good heavy-duty, metal hand trowel will serve for most transplanting and hand-weeding tasks. I use the new "iron fingernail" tool to make quick work of close hand weeding that I can't do with my scuffle hoe, and have even started using it for most transplanting now that I have a long-handle version.

- Sturdy hand pruners with replaceable parts will last a lifetime if properly cared for and kept out of the rain. I prefer bypass style pruners because they make a cleaner cut. Longer-handled pruners and loppers have better leverage for cutting large branches.

- Stakes and string are essential for marking rows in a larger garden and for locating plants more accurately in an intensively planted bed.

- For only a few dollars, a reliable soil thermometer will make deciding when to plant or transplant a much easier task.

Find a bucket, basket or bag to keep your tools together and organized. Add a few extras like twine, scissors or snips, plant labels and markers, and laminated copies of your garden map and planting schedule. Now just round up your garden hat, some sunscreen, garden gloves, comfy garden shoes (that are easy on, easy off), and you are ready to hit the garden running.

Choosing and Planting Bare Root Plants

Trees, strawberries, blueberries, cane fruits, and other perennials are sold as bare root plants for transplanting, but only during late winter and early spring. Bare root plants are dug while completely dormant and have the soil completely removed. They must be planted before they start to leaf out. In the Southeast, the bare root season is very short and it often passes by before gardeners realize the great savings and increased selection available compared to container plants. Healthy bare root trees and vines properly handled get established quickly and grow faster. February is the perfect month to find them online and at local garden centers.

- Look for varieties well suited to your location and climate. When buying online, choose reputable nurseries that cater to the Southeast. At local nurseries, look for plants that are truly dormant (no buds are open enough to show a leaf) with no damage to the roots, main stem, or branches.

- Look for strong, healthy stems and twigs that are firm and plump right out to the tip. Look for uniform branching and a good overall shape.

- Plant your transplant as soon as possible after you get it home. If you can't plant it right away, then heel it in in a shady place. That is, you temporarily place the plant in a shallow hole with the roots on an angle and loosely cover with sawdust or light soil, making sure the roots are completely covered and kept moist, but not soggy, until you can plant.

- Before planting, trim any broken, dead, or damaged parts and soak the roots for one to two hours before planting (only 15 to 20 minutes for strawberries and asparagus).

- While your plant is soaking, dig a hole twice as wide as the root ball and deep enough to keep the plant at the same level it was growing. Grafted trees have an obvious bulge that should be at least an inch above the ground. Make a small mound in the center of the hole to help you spread out the roots. Get a friend to help you place the plant so it's straight and at the right level, and then refill the hole with soil, patting it down to remove air pockets.

- Make a ring of soil about a foot in diameter around the trunk to form a shallow pan for water—be sure not to mound soil up around the trunk. Water well

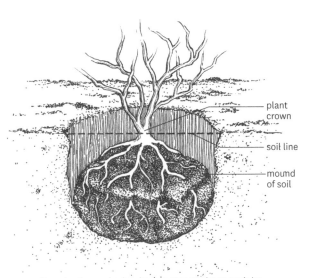

plant
crown

soil line

mound
of soil

For selection and price, bare root transplants can't be beat. Place bare root plants with the crown at soil level and the graft above. Spread the roots out over a ball of soil to guarantee your perennials a good start.

and mulch with compost, wood chips, or hay. Stake if necessary to keep plants straight while their roots are getting established.

Season Extension

Simple techniques like cold frames, low tunnels, and row covers let gardeners achieve remarkable results. It's amazing what a difference a little protection can make.

Even in the sunny Southeast, we have to give our garden extra protection to get the most from our long growing season. Variable February weather, from 70°F highs to 25°F lows, means you have to be prepared for the worst to take advantage of the warmth. Fortunately, the periods of low temperatures are brief. Floating row covers, cold frames, low tunnels, and small hoop houses are all low-cost tools that protect plants from rapid temperature changes, high winds, or frozen precipitation.

The simplest and easiest to use are floating row covers. These are lightweight spun or woven polyester or polypropylene fabrics that allow rain and sunlight to pass through while keeping out insects, reducing wind chill effects, and upping the temperature under the cover by up to 10°F. Row cover comes in different thicknesses. The lighter weight covers can be draped directly over crops, even the youngest seedlings, and held down by stones, soil, or ground staples. Heavier weights of row cover provide more frost protection and can result in even earlier harvests when used on extra-early tomatoes and cool-season crops (but you won't get extra benefit during the warm season, when plants don't need the extra heat). The heavier-weight covers require support and cost more. A medium-weight cover can be supported by hoops made from 9-gauge wire or plastic pipe bent and anchored on 2-foot pieces of rebar half pounded into the edge of the planting bed. For squash and other plants that need insect pollinators, row cover needs to be removed or opened daily after flowering begins. A bonus is that with careful use and storage, row cover can be reused many times for season extension and insect pest control.

Cold frames are simple structures for capturing the sun's heat and protecting plants from wind chill. They are easy to make from everyday materials and range from elegant well-insulated permanent features in the garden to temporary structures for extending the harvest of cool-season veggies and starting seedlings in the spring. We place straw bales around already prepared garden beds and cover the beds with used windows or lightweight, wooden, plastic-covered frames. Corrugated polycarbonate makes a lightweight, durable, and insulating cover for any type of cold frame. A nice thing about using straw bales is that when summer rolls around you have mulch handy. Lightweight portable frames are available for sale from several sources. Or you can put together a low-tech wooden box and cover it with an old storm window for a lid. If the sidepieces are thin wood, you might want to hammer in 2-foot stakes every few feet. Since it can be easily cut with a small saw, 1×2-inch lumber is ideal.

Crops growing inside cold frames need little or no watering or other attention over the winter months. But keep a close eye on plants growing in cold frames during the fall, and especially during the spring. They need even moisture and you'll have to vent the cold frame on warm days to prevent overheating.

BUILDING A LOW TUNNEL

Plastic-hoop low tunnels warm the soil for early spring planting and protect frost-sensitive plants in spring and fall. A hoop tunnel provides the same benefits as a cold frame by insulating the plants inside and keeping frosts at bay. These tunnels are easy to make and once you get the hang of it, you can make them in different sizes for different beds and different crops.

HERE'S WHAT YOU'LL NEED (for a 3 × 10-foot tunnel)

5 6-foot lengths of ¾-inch plastic pipe

10 18- to 24-inch pieces of steel rebar for stakes

1 piece of 3- to 6-millimeter-thick plastic sheeting or polyester row cover, approximately 5×12 feet (UV-resistant greenhouse plastic lasts longer than regular clear plastic)

12 garden clamps or clips, or larger binder clips (garden clips are available online or from some garden centers)

approximately 20 feet of scrap lumber or bamboo (for weighing down the sides)

large rocks, bricks, or lumber pieces to weigh down the sides

steel or rubber mallet

STEPS

1 Start by adding soil amendments and preparing your bed for planting before constructing your low tunnel over the bed. You can also construct a tunnel over an already growing bed.

2 Hammer a rebar stake in at each corner and every 2½ feet along the 10-foot sides. Leave 10–12 inches of each stake above the ground.

3 Starting at one corner, push a piece of pipe over the rebar stake, bend it into an arch, and work it down over the stake on the opposite side. Repeat for each pair of stakes.

4 After all the hoops are in place, stretch the plastic or row cover material over the hoops.

5 Bunch the covering together at one end, tie it with rope or baling twine, and stake it to the ground at one end. Pull the covering fairly tightly over the frame and bunch and stake the other end.

6 Secure the covering to the hoops with the garden clamps or clips. Make sure the covering completely covers the bed and plants.

7 Wrap the sides of the covering around lengths of scrap lumber or bamboo to hold them down. Use rocks or bricks as necessary to protect from the wind.

8 If you staple the edges to lengths of wood, it's easier to ventilate the low tunnel by rolling up the sides on warm days.

It is best to construct your tunnel on a warm day because the plastic contracts when it is cold. Some gardeners in the Southeast also like to make low tunnels with clear, slitted plastic row cover placed over wire hoops to form small tunnels, creating a self-ventilating greenhouse environment to promote the extra-early growth of heat-loving plants.

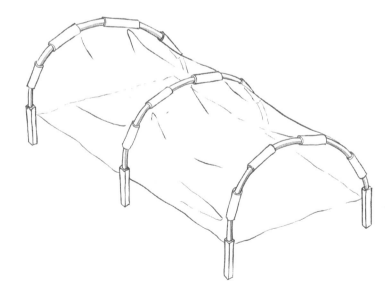

Rounded lengths of flexible plastic pipe held in place by rebar stakes span the garden bed. They provide support to a protective cover, giving your plants a snug environment protected from cold and wind, or cover with shade cloth to protect from scorching summer sunshine.

·MARCH·

DIRT

MOVING THE
GARDEN OUTDOORS

All over the South, folks are taking to their potting benches and "potting on" (transplanting their best little seedlings into larger pots from the sprouting flats). In most areas, we're talking about cool-season crops. In the Lower South, gardeners are already potting on hot-weather seedlings to get that first crop finished before it is too hot and dry. Wherever you are, this is the time to get a head start on what's next. The lengthening days, spring rains, and warming temperatures make for fast growth. So finish up your spring cleaning. Let's get planting for the season ahead.

TO DO THIS MONTH

PLAN, PREPARE, AND MAINTAIN

- Chit your seed potatoes in flats for two weeks with bright indirect light; then cut and heal them for three days before planting
- Side dress garlic and onions with compost tea, or foliar feed—they are about to really start to grow
- Order more seed potatoes for late planting and refrigerate them until June
- Prepare your beds: add compost; till before the weeds get started; cover with mulch or landscape fabric if you won't be planting anything soon—you'll be glad you did once the spring really gets going
- Weed perennials and fertilize; generously mulch them now and you won't have to weed so much later; early in the month plant new blueberries, raspberries, and strawberries.

SOW AND PLANT

- Plant potatoes when the weather becomes suitable (when daffodils are at full bloom or soil temperature is 60°F)
- Direct sow: radishes, turnips, carrots, beets, fava beans, kohlrabi, and leeks—and, of course, spinach (pre-sprout it for up to a week); when the Forsythia blooms, sow peas (cover them if necessary to protect from hard frost); under cover sow more lettuce, scallions, and heat-tolerant broccoli
- In flats, sow main crop tomatoes, insectary flowers; pot on peppers and eggplant; protect cabbage and broccoli from cold stress
- Transplant outside: senposai, early cabbage, collards, kale, kohlrabi, broccoli, and fall-sown storage onions singly; spring-sown onion seedlings in clumps of three to five
- Cover prepared beds with black or clear plastic to pre-warm the soil for extra early tomatoes, peppers and eggplant plantings
- Cover crops: sow oats in raised beds that you won't need for at least six weeks
- Divide and transplant rhubarb
- (In the Lower South) Finish plantings of cool-season crops early in March
- (In the Lower South) Later in the month start planting warm-season crops like cucumbers, beans and tomatoes outside but wait for the ground to get warmer for corn and peppers; be prepared to water and cover plants even after the last frost date

FRESH HARVEST

- arugula
- asparagus
- Asian greens
- beets
- cabbage
- carrots
- cilantro
- collards
- fresh herbs
- kale
- leaf celery
- lettuce
- mustard greens
- radishes
- spinach

Check beets, carrots, garlic, kohlrabi, onions, potatoes, rutabagas, sweet potatoes, turnips, and winter squash in storage

Adding Perennials to Your Edible Garden

Fruiting woody plants, cane berries such as raspberries and blackberries, and edible vines add a certain beauty and structure to a garden throughout the year. For a lovely, living open-work fence all year, prune your fruit trees into espaliers (flattened, branched, and usually fairly short shapes, for easy harvesting and maintenance). I find pear trees are easier than apple and other fruits to train into these elegant structures. Kiwis, grapes, and other trellised vines add interest in winter long after fruit is eaten and leaves have fallen.

Even in our sunny region, many gardeners with limited space are reluctant to allow space for fruit trees in their edible gardens for fear of shading the vegetable garden. New research at the University of Georgia trials from 2007 to 2011 is encouraging. Experiments with various degrees of shade found that with 30 percent shade, photosynthesis and general health of peppers increased and yields of useable peppers doubled. Yes, you can have your pears and peppers, too.

Our experience here at the Southern Exposure trial gardens also supports this conclusion. We find that peppers and tomatoes, as well as leafy greens, benefit from the partial shade created by dwarf, semi-dwarf, and espaliered trees as well as trellised grapes in late spring and summer.

Speaking of perennials, remember that early spring is a great time to practice your plant propagation skills. Start new plants from cuttings, divide and transplant overgrown rhubarb, thyme, oregano, tarragon, and other perennials in your garden. You can also start most of these from seeds, as well as many others like sorrel, rosemary, and chives.

PERENNIAL EDIBLES FOR THE SOUTHEAST

In every area of the Southeast, a variety of edible plants continue growing throughout the year. Although the plant may die back or even disappear above ground during the coldest or hottest months, the roots remain and the same plant springs back with vigorous growth. These are our perennial edibles. Many perennial edibles are most productive early in the season (a desirable quality, as this is a time when fresh harvests can be scarce) and often their yields increase over the years.

We use a variety of different techniques to keep our perennial edibles refreshed and bountiful, including appropriate pruning and a generous supply of nutrients. Here are a few perennial edibles to consider adding to your bounty:

Asparagus. Flavorful spring asparagus spears are definitely worth the time it takes to get the plants established. Fresh asparagus is high in glutamates, the chemicals that make the "umami" flavor that makes mushrooms and steak taste delicious, but the levels diminish within a few hours of harvest. The tall, highly ornamental ferns provide shade just when the sun is strongest, perfect for giving your lettuce and leafy greens summer relief.

Jerusalem artichokes. These Native American sunflower relatives make crisp, sweet roots and are so easy to grow that they're practically invasive. For best results, divide annually.

Raspberries and blackberries. These luscious berries are closely related, but their growth habits are very different. Blackberries thrive throughout the Southeast, but raspberries are better suited to cooler

continued next page

PERENNIAL EDIBLES CONTINUED

mountain areas and the Upper South. New blackberry varieties don't spread like their wild cousins and there are even thornless types available.

Strawberries. These are the first spring fruit for many gardeners. Pick the right strawberry varieties for your area and find a system to keep your beds refreshed, and you'll be rewarded with an extended harvest.

Grapes. For ecologically minded gardeners in the Southeast, the best choice is always muscadine grapes, our native grape. There's nothing sweeter than popping one out of its skin, straight into your mouth. You need a strong trellis, but these prolific vines won't disappoint.

Goumi berries. These sour berries are a great source of vitamins A and E, and have the highest lycopene content of any food. The big bushes are covered with bright red berries in the spring. There will be plenty for both you and your feathered friends. They're a great alternative to currants, which can introduce pine blister rust to our forests.

Blueberries. Rabbiteye and southern highbush blueberries are much bigger and more productive in the South than their northern relatives. You may need to cover them to keep out the birds.

Serviceberries. Besides the berries, which make wonderful jam, the bushes are attractive all year round with pretty flowers, colorful fall foliage, and interesting bark and form. Again, you will be competing with the birds.

Perennial herbs. Rosemary, thyme, sage, tarragon, and lavender are all Mediterranean herbs that like our warm weather but need good drainage. Chives, lemon balm, and mint all appreciate a moister site.

Perennial Propagation

For those who want a lot of perennials quickly and cheaply, there are several options. I prefer starting from seed, but it does require a little extra patience. Starting from seed isn't appropriate for every perennial crop, since many will not come "true" from seed: these are varieties that only retain their character when grown from cuttings or divisions: methods that actually clone the parent plant's genetics.

Even when growing from seed is an option, gardeners preferring to quickly establish their own perennials will want to make divisions or cuttings. The simplest option is to make divisions from a friend's established bed, which gives you a big head start. Making cuttings can also be quicker than starting from seed, but it's a bit more of an art. The cuttings will need lots of coddling while they're growing roots. What you choose to do depends on what you're growing and also on your temperament.

Making your own cuttings and divisions

Rather than buy expensive herbs from a nursery, you can do your own plant propagation at home. For herbs that don't grow true from seed, cuttings or divisions are your only options outside the nursery. Old-timers here in Virginia have a saying about divisions and cuttings: "First they weep, then they creep, then they leap!"

Separating root clumps, or making divisions, is an effective, quick, and simple method for creating new plants. It's also an essential part of maintaining some perennials, because it gives the roots needed breathing room to stay productive. Think of it like underground pruning—you'll need to have an established plant or a gardener friend who already has one. This is the method of choice for strawberries, raspberries, rhubarb, and many herbs. The best time to make divisions is just when the plants begin to grow in the spring, although many perennials can also be easily divided in the fall.

The easiest way to divide is when the plants have suckers or runners that you can dig up and transplant elsewhere. Strawberries and raspberries are good examples of this. But for plants that grow in clumps, it's actually not that much more difficult. You'll dig up the whole root ball and pull it apart or cut it into clumps with a shovel to make several plants. This is the preferred method for rhubarb and chives. Simply return a smaller plant to the original location. Herbs that take over a large area, like mint, can be dug up and moved elsewhere in patches.

Making cuttings is the method of choice for propagating your own kiwis, grapes, and blueberries. It's also an option for some of the bushier herbs, like rosemary and sage. It simply involves snipping off a section of a vine or branch and getting it to form roots and be its own plant.

There are two types of cuttings: early spring softwood cuttings and fall/winter hardwood cuttings. Hardwood cuttings are taken after the leaves have fallen, while softwood cuttings are best done in early spring. Cuttings are a convenient method for growing plants from your winter prunings of grape and kiwi vines.

To make a hardwood cutting, cut a branch or vine into sections that have at least two buds. Plant each section in a pot or outdoors, with the growing tip up, so that at least one bud is underground, and at least one

WHERE TO BUY PERENNIALS

It's wise to take care when choosing where you will buy your perennial edibles, especially if you are new to gardening in our region. Making your purchases from a reliable source knowledgeable of our climate can hugely improve your growing experience: choose the right varieties, and you'll have less trouble with pests and plant diseases, and your perennials will be adapted to our daylight and temperature patterns.

- A trusted local, independent nursery or garden center will have knowledgeable staff who can often assist you with making decisions, and they'll know your local growing conditions. This is a great way to pick up large plants in pots, without having to pay for shipping. Just make sure you have the right vehicle to bring them home!

- Pick a mail-order company that's growing plants locally and selecting varieties for organic growing conditions. One type of peach might grow great in Georgia only when it's sprayed with lots of chemicals, so you should take the time to know the varieties that do well without all the poisons. Small, regional companies that cater to organic gardeners are your best choice. Pay attention to the guarantee and look for lots of high-quality growing and varietal information on the website or in the catalog.
- Local plant societies, botanical gardens, and arboretums also often have annual plant sales. They may have more limited edibles, so get to the sale early to have lots of choices. I love discovering exciting new culinary herbs at these events, and it's a great opportunity to talk with the knowledgeable staff and volunteers.

is above ground. The underground bud will grow roots, but it can take some time for this to happen—sometimes it takes months! Softwood cuttings are made in the early spring from tender new growth, with a bit of older growth. Plant the 4- to 6-inch branch into loose soil and cross your fingers. You can improve their chances of rooting by covering the plant with a glass jar or plastic bag. Willow branch tea also promotes rooting, or you can purchase a rooting promoter from a nursery.

Perennials to start from seed

Starting perennials from seed is another inexpensive choice that lets you get a lot of plants established quickly, but it's only a good choice for some plants and it requires extra attention and patience.

The perennials you can grow from seed include rhubarb, asparagus, alpine strawberries, and many herbs, like thyme, sage, rosemary, winter savory, chives, garlic chives, and horehound. Many perennial herb seeds are quite small and take a very long time to sprout. Don't give up—keep the soil evenly moist—and never damp—while they're sprouting. I often cover the flat or pots with a plastic bag to keep the moisture in. Herb seedlings may be variable, so do some selection as you pot on. Or buy plants from a known cultivar.

Planting out your perennials

Planting a perennial is a big commitment. Even with strawberries, they may be there for at least three years. I spend some time carefully thinking about where to place my perennials first, before I plant them.

The edges of the garden and ends of beds are generally good choices. It's a big bother having to work around a patch of berries in the middle of the garden.

And, sometimes, bad things happen when someone doesn't know that your dormant crop is there, waiting below the ground: what looks like empty soil may be harboring your treasured perennials. Too many times we have had overeager garden help accidentally dig up a well-established perennial bed, thinking they were preparing fresh soil for planting, or weed out our treasured perennials just as they begin to sprout. Label your perennial beds well to avoid these unfortunate incidents.

It's also important to think about how the light will change in the coming years. Are there small trees nearby that will soon shade out your perennial beds? Or will your perennials soon be shading important garden space? I try to keep my tall perennials, like trellised grapes and cane berries, on the north side of my vegetables and herbs.

Think about the whole lifecycle of your perennials and try to group perennials together to their benefit. For instance, asparagus lets light through all winter and spring, but those dense ferns create a lot of shade during the summer. Rhubarb struggles in our harsh summer sunshine. We plant a bed of rhubarb between grapes and asparagus, so the rhubarb gets plenty of light in the spring, but is well shaded during the summer.

By the same token, I try to plant my leafy herbs to the east of vegetable beds, so they can benefit from a little afternoon shade during the summer.

Many perennials also make ideal landscape plants. Blueberries, bush cherries, and serviceberries don't just make tasty fruits, they're also gorgeous ornamentals. They come in lots of different shapes and sizes, so do a little research first and you're sure to find the plant that fits your space.

SKILL SET

LET'S MAKE COMPOST

Making your own compost is one of the best things you can do for your garden, and it's easy! Pick a dry, shady spot near a source of water and near your garden. All you need to make healthy compost is just three color-coded ingredients, plus some water now and then.

- **browns** (for carbon) such as leaves, pine needles, straw, or shredded paper
- **greens** (for nitrogen) such as kitchen scraps, grass clippings, and animal manures
- **blacks** (for beneficial organisms) such as soil, already finished compost, or worm castings; these speed up the composting process

At garden centers and online, you can find a wide assortment of manufactured compost bins as well as plans for making your own. These systems can make composting easier if you're limited by disabilities or pesky neighborhood association rules.

Start your pile with a 3- or 4-inch layer of coarse material like old hay or straw or chopped corn stalks to help with aeration and drainage. Next add some kitchen and garden waste such as leaves, coffee grounds,

crushed eggshells, etc. Then add a layer of nitrogen-rich material like chicken manure or fresh grass clipping. I like to add a layer of blacks like soil, finished compost, or worm castings after every other layer to add beneficial organisms that can speed up the process. This may not always be necessary because of the soil added on plant roots but I like to keep the pile "cooking" and get the compost finished quickly.

Water the pile after each layer and every few days to keep everything evenly moist but never soggy. The pile should have a slight indentation in the center to make sure water doesn't run off. Your finished pile should be at least 3×3 feet to gener-

ate enough heat for the 160°F needed to kill weed seeds during composting. If your pile doesn't feel warm to the touch within a few days, add more nitrogen-rich materials or water to get it going.

Lack of air can also slow down your composting. If the pile smells like ammonia, try adding more coarse material and turning the pile more often. Make sure that the materials on the outside are mixed into the center while turning. Good finished compost looks and smells like good humus-rich garden soil. The pile should decrease significantly in size and decompose. In two to four months your compost should be rich, crumbly "brown gold" and ready to use.

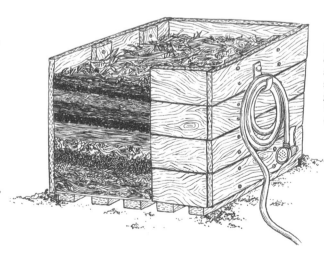

Moistened layers of green, brown, and black grass, soil, and coffee grounds quickly break down into compost.

· APRIL ·

PRETTY ENOUGH
FOR THE
FRONT YARD

Kitchen gardens were once tucked away out of sight, but no more. Many fruit and vegetable plants, flowers, and herbs are beautiful enough for the front yard. And front yard or back, they don't need mowing and invite beneficial insects into the garden, reducing pests and increasing yields. The warmth, frequent rains, and increasing day length of spring are great for your plants and the pests that love to feed on them. Take action now to gain control and maintain a healthy organic garden full of luscious produce.

TO DO THIS MONTH

PLAN, PREPARE, AND MAINTAIN

- Monitor and care for your indoor seedlings
- Install stakes or trellising for peas and pole beans
- Weed and thin greens and root vegetables
- Hill up potatoes by mounding soil over the plants from both sides, leaving only the top uncovered (potatoes grow off the stem above the seed piece, so a longer stem under the soil means more potatoes)
- Weed perennials as needed; mow paths; cover strawberries if frost threatens (pick flowers off any new spring plantings); thin fall raspberries to six canes per row foot
- Mulch to control weeds and preserve moisture
- Set up drip irrigation

SOW AND PLANT

- Harden off tomatoes, peppers, eggplants, celery, and celeriac beginning one to two weeks before scheduled transplanting; cover your cold frames when evening falls or bring the plants indoors for cold nights
- Pot on lettuce and any remaining tomatoes, peppers, and eggplant into larger pots
- Set sweet potatoes in flats for making slips by barely covering with potting mix or compost
- Sow early cantaloupes and watermelons in soil blocks or plug flats; sow some replacement tomatoes in case you need them; and sow more insectary flowers to keep the blooms coming
- Direct sow radishes, turnips, carrots, beets, parsnips, salsify, and early summer varieties of lettuce; when the lilac is in full bloom sow snap beans, cucumber, sunflowers, edamame, and sesame; when iris blooms fade (soil 65°F) sow peanuts, limas, and sweet corn; then one or two weeks later (soil 70°F) sow southern peas, squash, and watermelon; wait until the soil is really warm (75°F) to sow okra, cantaloupes, and sweet potatoes
- Sow cover crops in beds that will be open five or more weeks
- Set out transplants of cabbage and broccoli under row cover, insectary flowers, celery and celeriac; after your average last frost, set out tomatoes, peppers, and eggplant (always be prepared to protect from frost)

FRESH HARVEST

- arugula
- Asian greens
- asparagus
- broccoli
- cabbage
- carrots
- cauliflower
- beans
- beets
- collards
- fresh herbs
- garlic greens
- garlic scallions
- herbs
- kale
- kohlrabi
- peas
- lettuce
- mustards
- onions
- peas
- radishes
- (early) raspberries
- rhubarb
- strawberries
- spinach

Check beets, garlic, onions, potatoes, sweet potatoes, winter squash in storage

Inviting Beneficial Insects into the Garden

An edible flowering border alive and buzzing with beneficial insects is breathtaking. Supporting a healthy population of "good" insects is as important for an organic gardener as building healthy soil. Sweet, juicy melons, crisp, cooling cucumbers, and abundant fruit harvests all require insect pollinators.

Here's how to make your garden more inviting to insect helpers. First, stop spraying pesticides, even organic ones. Next, create year-round shelter and food for our native insects. Try to have flowers in bloom for as much of the year as possible, especially in early spring. Leave some leaf and plant litter on the ground over winter, as well as some bare ground for burrowing native bees. Finally, choose insect-friendly flowers. Lucky for us, many edible herbs and flowers are fantastic choices for tempting beneficial insects into the garden.

But which bugs are good bugs?

Everybody appreciates bees and other pollinators that bring us juicy apples and plump watermelons, but pollination isn't the only role that insects play. There are many beneficial insect predators that eat the eggs, larvae, or adult forms of common pests. The Southeast has hundreds of species of beneficial predatory insects, from hoverflies to parasitic wasps. Many serve a double role as pollinators during part of their lifecycle. Some of the good bugs to encourage in your garden are:

- lady beetles (or ladybugs) and lacewings eat aphids, mealy bugs, and spider mites

- big-eyed bugs, which are easily confused with squash bugs, eat insect eggs and larvae

- shiny ground beetles in a variety of colors eat slugs, cutworms, and many other soft-bodied pests;

- most wasps are either parasitic or predators playing a vital role in limiting the populations of thousands of bean beetles, caterpillars, and other insect species

- garden spiders consume huge numbers of insects pests

Choosing flowers and herbs that benefit the garden

Choose "user-friendly" flowers with easy-to-access pollen and nectar. There are three particularly good types: umbels are the flat-topped flower clusters of dill, fennel, cilantro, and parsley. Loose spikes of small flowers are common to many fragrant kitchen herbs, such as thyme, mint, and lavender. Daisy-type flowers are really tight clusters of miniscule flowers. They include chamomile, marigolds, chicory, dandelions, sunflowers, cornflowers, alyssum, and calendula.

Native plants support many more insect herbivores than non-natives, so select native plants like *Echinacea*, mountain mint, or redbud whenever possible.

Many plants that support beneficial insects are edible, attractive, and provide interest in multiple seasons. Anise-hyssop, rosemary, bee balm, lavender, and bronze fennel attract loads of insects and are easy to fit in most gardens. Buckwheat is an easy-to-grow, insect-friendly summer cover crop.

Insects need to eat all season, so try to arrange for successive waves of plants with different heights and flower types. Early spring can be a hard time for insects. Choose some plants that flower in early spring, like cilantro and arugula, and let some early chickweed or overwintered mustard flowers linger in your garden.

Edible Herbs and Flowers

In addition to providing food and habitat for our insect allies, herbs and flowers can add flavor and fragrance to all sorts of dishes and are a must-have for the kitchen garden. Herbs can be grown mixed in with your vegetables or edging your perennial border, but for cooking it is really most convenient to have a culinary herb patch close to the kitchen so you can run out and pick or snip fresh herbs for the evening meal.

How to grow

Most edible herbs and flowers are easy to grow. Plant where there's six or more hours of sun a day, and in soil with enough organic matter. (Most soils in the Southeast need generous amounts of compost or other organic material.) Herbs like rosemary, thyme, oregano, and sage prefer a well-drained location with good air circulation and possibly a bit of shade in the afternoon. Mint, lemon balm, violas, and lemongrass can tolerate more shade and prefer more moisture. I like to plant them under a roof drip line and spread an organic mulch to conserve moisture.

Arrange your herbs and flowers with an eye to how the area will look throughout the year, mixing evergreen plants and annuals while paying attention to the height and texture of each plant. Plant aggressive growers like mint in a sunken pot so they don't take over the bed. Colored basils and edible flowers can brighten your design. Grow what your family likes to eat. Place the plants you'll use regularly close to the path. Herbs are great in all kinds of containers if grown in appropriate potting soil, with holes for good drainage.

Most herbs and edible flowers grow easily from seed but many gardeners purchase perennials or get starts from friends in order to get the fragrance and taste they prefer. Whether you plant them in with the regular vegetables, create an edible insectary, or grow them in containers, herbs and edible flowers add a lot to a garden.

These are some of my favorite culinary herbs, edible flowers, and insectary plants:

Anise hyssop (perennial; seeds or divisions). The mint-like plants have a bushy growth pattern, so spreading isn't a problem (although they will self-sow in the spring.) Bees love them! The edible leaves and long flower spires make lovely licorice-flavored tea.

Basil (annual; seeds). The classic Italian herb for pesto, vinegar, and dressings, basil is now available in an astounding array of colors, shapes, and sizes. Holy basil (or tulsi) has a lovely, complex flavor and is grown outside sanctuaries in India. Lemon basils, purple basils, and tiny-leaved bush basils lend diversity to the table.

Bee balm (perennial; seeds or divisions). The fragrant flower spires attract bees, butterflies, and hummingbirds. The light, fruity taste makes a refreshing summer tea. Used by Native Americans as Oswego tea.

Borage (annual; seeds [self-sows]). One of the only truly blue foods, the edible flowers taste like sweet cucumbers. The early blooms are very attractive to bees and help fill the spring flower gap. Use the flowers in salads, teas, sandwiches, or to garnish a Pimm's Cup in New Orleans.

Calendula (annual; seeds). The attractive daisy-like flowers make glorious borders, and the bright orange petals give color to soups, custards, and rice. Try adding them to cookies or vinegars, or mix into salads for extra flare.

Catnip (perennial; seeds or divisions). A source of over-whelming excitement for your feline friends, you can also use the leaves to make a soothing tea.

Chamomile (annual; seeds [self-sows]). Use just the flowers (not the stems) for a calming tea. The small, fragrant plants tend to self-sow, tempting bees into your garden. Dry the plants for potpourri or use the tiny, yellow flowers as garnish in the spring.

Chives, garlic chives (perennial; seeds or divisions). Both chives and garlic chives are easy-to-grow perennials. Excellent as a garnish, tossed into salads, and as a fresh addition to dips. The flowers of both are edible and pollinator friendly.

Cilantro (coriander) (annual; seeds [self-sows]). Bring the smell of Mexico to your garden. Cilantro can be a love-it or hate-it thing, but Americans are being won over. The leaves bring pizzazz to salsa, and the seeds can be ground for coriander to spice curries and falafel. Let some plants grow tall and form flowers to keep your pollinators happy.

Daylily (perennial; divisions). Add these spectacular, large, edible flowers to salads, batter and fry them, stuff them with herbed cheese and bake them, or decorate a wedding cake! They're most often orange, but also available in red or yellow.

Dill (annual; seeds). The classic pickle spice. Add the leaves, flower heads, and seeds directly to your jars for a pretty garnish. Also an excellent addition to savory breads, herbed butter, vinegars, soups, fish, and salads.

Echinacea (perennial; seed or divisions). Often called purple coneflower. One of those daisy-family plants that are so inviting to insects. Ornamental plus many medicinal uses.

Fennel (hardy perennial; seeds). Tall, aromatic, drought-tolerant, anise-flavored plant used in teas, cooking, baking, and absinthe. Self-sows freely.

Lavender (perennial; seeds, divisions, cuttings). Use the unopened buds in cooking, such as the traditional Herbes de Provence. Use the fragrant flowers in potpourris, herb pillows, and crafts.

Lemon balm (perennial; seeds or divisions). Mint family plant that's a favorite of bees (it's genus name, Melissa, is Greek for "honey bee"). Use it in teas and lots of savory dishes.

Marigold (annual; seeds). Use the petals from lemon gem or tangerine gem. Other varieties are bitter. Often grown as a companion plant.

Marjoram (tender perennial or annual; seeds, divisions, or cuttings). Aromatic Mediterranean herb. Flavoring for meats, salads, omelets, vinegars, jellies, and teas.

Oregano (perennial; seeds or divisions). Closely related to marjoram. Needs good drainage. Flavors many savory foods, especially spaghetti and pizza.

Peppermint, spearmint (perennial; seeds, plants, or divisions). Somewhat invasive. Can be used as a ground cover. Tolerates partial shade. Use in teas, sauces.

Roselle (tender perennial or annual; seeds or cuttings). Hibiscus family. Tall, decorative plants. The red calyxes make "zingy" teas, jams.

Rosemary (woody perennial; seeds or plants). Drought tolerant. Flavoring for bread, vinegar, and many other foods, especially meats, vinegar, jam, bread, butters, vegetables, stuffing, and meat dishes.

Roses (petals and hips) (perennial; plants, cuttings, or divisions). Rose hips are famously rich in vitamin C (tea, jelly). Make rosewater or use in salads and many other foods.

Sage (perennial; seeds or cuttings). Ornamental, medicinal, and culinary herb from the Mediterranean in use for thousands of years. Seasoning for meat, vegetables, eggs, and especially stuffing.

Thyme (perennial; seeds, divisions, or cuttings). Easy-to-grow, aromatic herb available in many varieties. Essential for bouquet garni. Also use for teas (with lemon balm, for example) and flavoring poultry, fish, stews, soups, tomatoes, cheese, and eggs.

Viola (johnny jump up) (perennial; seeds, self-sows). Small, colorful early spring flower that looks like a mini pansy. Use to garnish meals and desserts.

SKILL SET

DRIP IRRIGATION AND WATER MANAGEMENT

As we plant out warm-season crops in earnest, it is important to make sure they will have all the water they need to thrive in the hot and sometimes dry months ahead. First, review your garden plans with an eye to efficient watering. Are plants with similar watering needs grouped together? Spreading a generous layer of organic mulch will suppress weeds (eliminating competition for water), conserve moisture, and moderate soil temperatures.

Most vegetable plants need at least an inch of water per week, which thankfully often falls from the sky. When you do have to irrigate, apply enough water to wet the soil deeply (at least 6 inches). Frequent, shallow watering leads to shallow-rooted plants that are less healthy and more prone to drought stress.

Drip irrigation is the most efficient way to get water to the root zone. It also saves you money on metered city water. Drip irrigation is so much better than other watering systems that it is often exempted from watering restrictions in drought-struck areas. Adding a timer to your system will not only save you time and water but will relieve you of worrying about watering while you're on vacation.

There is no one right drip system for your garden. A number of options work in most situations. Before you go shopping, gather some information.

- Determine whether you will be using city water, a well, a pond, or a cistern.
- Get out your measuring tape, or your garden map if it is drawn to scale, and do a rough estimate of the distance from your water source to your garden. Record how many row feet of each vegetable you will be growing, and the distance between plants.
- List and measure the spacing for any edible perennials, fruit trees, and small fruits you want on your irrigation system.

Take the information you have gathered to your local independent garden center where there is knowledgeable staff to help you pick out the right system. For the more confident or experienced gardeners there are many online retailers selling drip irrigation kits and supplies. Before you purchase any system, make sure that all of the individual components are available to purchase separately for future repairs or expansion. Any drip irrigation kit should include specific information on design, installation, and maintenance. Follow it carefully and don't be afraid to ask questions or get a different system if necessary. Prices of drip systems vary greatly according to the area size and the type of emitters and tubing being used. A very small patio container garden kit might be under $50. Materials for a vegetable garden might cost from $200 for a few beds to $600 for a large 5000-square-foot garden. My advice on buying drip irrigation is to educate yourself, start small, and keep it simple. You can expand your system as you gain experience and as your garden expands.

If all those pipes still seem more than you can handle, most areas have installation businesses. Or you can use soaker hoses. They are the easiest way to start with drip irrigation. Water just oozes out of the porous 25- or 50-foot hoses. They have removable end caps so multiple pieces can be joined together and laid out along rows or snaked around individual larger plants, fruit trees, or berry bushes. Cover the soaker hoses with organic mulch and you are ready to go.

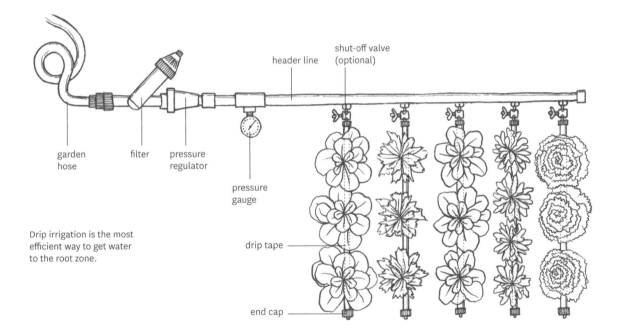

Drip irrigation is the most efficient way to get water to the root zone.

HARNESSING THE JUNGLE

As the days get longer and the weather really starts to warm up, tomatoes, summer vining crops, and weeds start to grow at an amazing rate and threaten to take over every inch of space in a small garden. If you have visions of lush, ripe melons, crisp cucumbers, baskets of juicy, vine-ripened tomatoes, and plump green beans, now is the time to finish the trellises and cages in your garden plans and perhaps add a few extras. "Growing up" is a great way to get more vegetables from your garden while making it a more attractive and comfortable area. Smart gardeners take action early to control rampant weeds, preserving available nutrients and precious water for your crops. In the meantime prepare to weed!

TO DO THIS MONTH

PLAN, PREPARE, AND MAINTAIN

- Plan fall and winter crops; make notes of planting, harvest, weather, weeds, insects and other conditions in your garden
- Scuffle hoe and hand weed all plantings weekly
- Hand pick potato beetles and asparagus beetles
- Stake, string weave, or cage tomatoes and peppers (only one row around peppers, using short stakes)
- Garlic: harvest garlic scapes, remove mulch from garlic, and weed; move mulch to weeded broccoli; check maturity of potato onions and garlic and start to harvest if ready
- Weed onions until three weeks before expected harvest date; weed each corn planting twice, undersowing at 30 days with soy or oats cover crop; be careful, corn roots are shallow
- Perennials: put up blueberry netting before fruit ripen; weed and water blueberries
- In early May, continue cutting sweet potato slips until you have enough

SOW AND PLANT

- Sow beans, carrots, and corn plus more radishes, peanuts, edamame, limas, cowpeas, and asparagus beans
- Sow winter squash, melons, cucumbers (picklers and slicers), summer squash, and zucchini; cover them with row cover to protect against cucumber beetles; keep them well covered until flowering starts
- Transplant (when hardened off) remaining tomatoes, peppers (mulch first to save weeding time), and eggplant (cover immediately with spun polyester fabric), and melons and watermelons at a maximum of four weeks old; do the same for okra, hot peppers, and sweet potatoes (mulch them later, when the soil has warmed to 70°F)
- Sow sorghum sudan, soy, buckwheat, or millet as summer cover crops

FRESH HARVEST

- arugula
- artichokes
- Asian greens
- asparagus
- beans
- beets
- beet greens
- broccoli
- cabbage
- carrots
- cauliflower
- chard
- cherries
- collards
- corn
- garlic scapes
- fava
- fresh herbs
- kale
- kohlrabi
- lettuce
- peas
- potatoes
- radishes
- raspberries
- rhubarb
- scallions
- spinach
- strawberries
- summer squash
- tomatoes
- turnips
- zucchini

Finish harvesting overwintered collards, kale, and kohlrabi beds by the end of the month if they are not already cleaned up

Dealing with Weeds

Gardens full of weeds produce fewer vegetables because the weeds compete for the available soil nutrients, water, air, and sunlight. Weeds also can provide a home for insect pests and plant diseases. So I recommend prevention as the first strategy. Leave no surface bare. Mulch, grow cover crops (if open for five weeks or more), and plant crops so the leaves of one plant will barely touch the next plant, covering the whole garden bed when mature and effectively shading out weeds.

A scuffle hoe is one of the most useful tools for fighting the war against weeds. Scuffle (stirrup) hoes come in many sizes all with a flat bottom that cuts weeds off just below the soil surface and breaks up the top ¼ inch of soil without bringing more weed seeds to the surface. When used properly, it is rather accurate, very selective, always effective, and inexpensive. Because it can be done while standing up straight, I even find scuffle hoeing enjoyable work. However, you won't be able to control all weeds with the hoe alone. Weeds at the base of the plant need to be pulled by hand. It is best to do this early because pulling large weeds can damage the root systems of vegetable plants. You can decrease the amount of hoeing necessary by generously applying organic mulches as a part of your weed-control program. Mulches help to retain soil moisture and reduce weed growth.

Organic mulches are by far the most common and preferred type. Bark, wood chips, compost, ground corncobs, chopped cornstalks, grass clippings, leaves, manure, newspapers, peanut shells, peat moss, pine needles, sawdust, straw, and wood shavings are common organic mulches. These mulches not only reduce weeding but also conserve soil moisture, add organic material, and reduce the soil temperature by 8–10°F during the summer. If organic mulches are applied to cold garden soils, the soils will warm up more slowly and plant maturity will be delayed. On the other hand, organic mulches can reduce soil crusting. After the soil warms in spring, an organic mulch can be applied to a depth of 2–4 inches around well-established plants. Be sure that there is adequate moisture in the soil before applying the mulch. Mulches such as sawdust, wood shavings, and corncobs can use up some of the soil nitrogen as they decompose. To compensate, you can mix compost or high-nitrogen organic fertilizer with each bushel of sawdust, wood shavings, or corncobs before applying them over the soil.

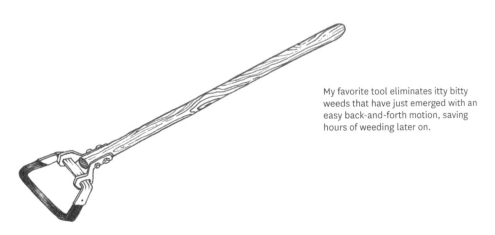

My favorite tool eliminates itty bitty weeds that have just emerged with an easy back-and-forth motion, saving hours of weeding later on.

Black plastic mulch is highly effective for early fruiting crops, such as melons, cucumbers, squash, and tomatoes. Its greatest value is its ability to increase soil temperature very early in the growing season when the soil is cool. But because of the need to dispose of plastic mulch at the end of the season I choose organic mulches whenever possible.

Vegetable crops that germinate quickly and grow fast in the garden can suppress weeds by shading. The North Carolina State Extension Service has done research on the ability of crops to suppress weeds by shading as the crop develops.

Smother crops is a term used for crops that are planted thickly to reduce weeds in the next crop. The straw residue from smother crops (like rye, ryegrass, etc.) can reduce early season germination of weeds such as common lambsquarters, common purslane, and redroot pigweed by 75 percent or more. According to research from North Carolina State University, smother crops are also effective in suppression of many winter annual weeds such as henbit and chickweed. Many of these same weeds are edible and can be harvested when young for salads or cooking greens.

What to Do About Bugs

Warm and wet weather not only encourages weed growth but also increases insect populations. Most bugs are not harmful and many of them are helpful. They are pollinators, and predators of pests. They speed up the decay of organic matter into compost and bring beauty and amusement into our lives and the lives of our children. Only a few damage your plants.

Here are some basics of organic pest management that you can adapt to your garden:

Prevention is the first line of defense. Build healthy soil, maintain even moisture, rotate crops, and choose appropriate varieties.

Know the pests most likely to cause problems in your garden. Learn to identify them, what their feeding preferences are, and the details of their life cycle. Often you can learn the pests for a whole plant family from dealing with just one example and know what to expect for any crop in that family. The brassica family (cabbage, broccoli, kale, turnips, mustards), for instance, counts caterpillars (including the cabbage worm and cabbage looper), aphids, harlequin bugs, and flea beetles among its pests. The nightshade family (potatoes, tomatoes, eggplants, peppers) has to deal with Colorado potato beetles, aphids, flea beetles, wire worms, and root grubs, among others.

ABILITY OF CROPS TO SUPPRESS WEEDS

GOOD	POOR
beans	broccoli and cabbage
corn, sweet	carrot
cucumbers	garlic
melons	greens
potatoes	lettuce
pumpkins	onions
southern peas	peas, garden (English)
squash	pepper
sweet potatoes	radishes
tomatoes	

Monitor your plants for insects. If you can detect an infestation early on, whatever you do for control will be more effective while populations are low. Use a head-lamp at night to scout for cutworms and also predators like spiders and soldier beetles.

Use simple, safe methods for manual control like row cover and hand picking. Your goal is to reduce pest population and increase predator population for a natural balance. Row cover comes in various thicknesses. The thinnest ones provide insect protection with little heat gain. Newer insect net products are less subject to tearing. If you didn't rotate your crop from last year, row cover may create a pest paradise. Some plants like peppers need wire support for row cover to prevent damage to leaves. Remember to remove row covers from squash, cucumbers, and other plants that need pollinators.

Hand picking can be very effective early in the season when pests are just getting started. Many insects can be knocked or jarred onto sticky sheets or into buckets. Predators are often more active and may escape being trapped.

Learn to recognize beneficial bugs like syphid flies, carabid beetles, big eyed bugs, lady beetles, etc., that prey on pests, and give them a helping hand with nectar sources and habitat.

Think twice before using insecticides—even organic ones. You may create more problems than you solve. If you must use them, be as specific as possible, such as using Bt (a group of insecticides make from *Bacillus thuringiensis*, which are naturally occurring soil bacteria) to help control cabbage worms.

Soap sprays (sometimes called "insecticidal soap") can help with aphids and other soft-bodied insects.

If in spite of your best efforts a crop is repeatedly damaged, remember that not everything you try to grow will do well everywhere or in all seasons. Experiment and learn about new controls every season.

Tomato Trenching: Giving Tomatoes a Head Start

Unlike other plants, heat-loving tomato seedlings should be planted in "trenches": set in the ground almost horizontally, so that only the top-most leaves remain above ground. This creates a very strong root base, giving additional strength and support to the plant. New roots form in the warm surface soil, which helps get the plants going strong in the spring. As the soil heats up, the roots will reach down deeper.

Here's how to trench tomatoes: Begin by snipping off any leaves below the topmost set. For each plant,

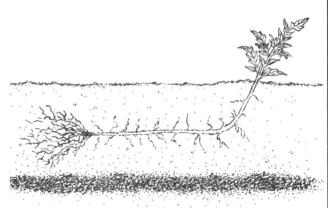

The trench method encourages tomato plants to make large root networks. Remove the lower leaves and lay the stem in a slanted trench.

dig a narrow trench, of the right size to fit the seedling. You'll place the plant at a slight downward angle, so that the stem is almost sideways and the top leaves and few inches of stem are above the soil. Point the existing root ball slightly downward and gently press down soil around the plant to snug it into place. New roots will grow downward from each old leaf node along the stem. Don't worry if the above-ground tops flop over to the side at first, they'll be reaching for the sky within a day or two.

Staking

As warm weather brings rampant growth to garden plants, gardeners with limited space can bring order to beds and make sure heat-loving tomatoes, beans, and melons get plenty of sun with the right trellising. Arches, arbors, and pergolas can provide focal points in the garden as well as keep fruiting plants off the ground with good airflow and plenty of sunshine. Staked, caged, or trellised plants can also provide shaded spots for nursing your fall plantings through the long, hot, dry spells in July and August.

Garden teepees are easily made from three to six bamboo, metal, or wooden poles held together with jute, wire, or electrical ties, and they provide support for all kinds of vining beans, pole limas, and even passion fruit. A large teepee even provides an excellent resting place for a young child helping in the garden—make sure to leave an opening for a doorway. Native people in the Southeast used living supports like corn stalks or giant sunflower stalks as poles for beans. Along the coast of the Carolinas and other places in the South it is traditional to grow vining crowder peas with corn or even popcorn for support.

I like to use cattle panels as a trellis support because they are rigid, easy to set up, and last forever. Small-fruited crops need no support for the fruits, but larger fruited veggies such as most winter squash, muskmelons, and watermelons require something to support the heavy fruit. Sections of hosiery, mesh citrus sacks, or anything strong that drains can be used to form a sling to support the fruit.

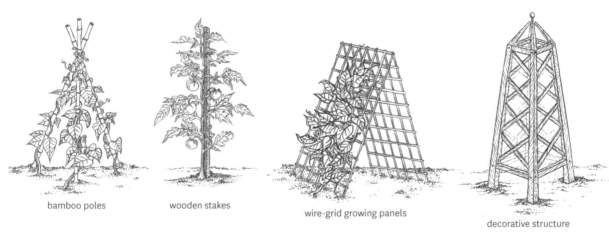

bamboo poles   wooden stakes   wire-grid growing panels   decorative structure

Simple or ornate, supportive staking or trellising brings order to the garden. Providing support also improves plant health.

SKILL SET

FLORIDA STRING WEAVING

Tomatoes are a garden favorite in the Southeast and with our abundant sun most gardeners who have enough space want to grow extra for canning or making salsa. String weaving is my pick for trellising paste (and other determinant) tomatoes.

HERE'S WHAT YOU'LL NEED

4 6-foot stakes (wood, rebar, or t-posts) per six plants
120 feet jute or other twine for a 12-foot bed
scissors

STEPS

1 Plant your tomatoes in a straight row 2 feet apart.

2 Drive a stake between every plant or two.

3 Weekly, starting when the plants are 12 inches, weave twine between the tomato stem and stakes. Start by tying the twine to the first stake and loop it tightly around the stakes along the row. When you reach the last stake, make a double loop and continue back on the other side of the row. When you get back to the first stake tie off with a strong knot and cut the twine.

4 Continue to run another line weekly (about every 4–8 inches) until the plants stop growing.

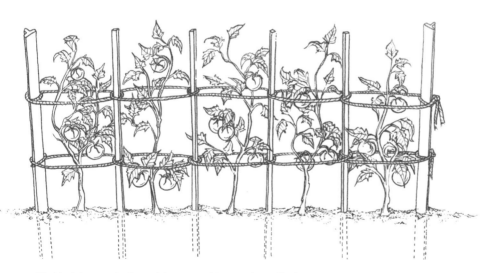

Florida string weaving is a quick, easy, and inexpensive method for supporting a range of tall crops.

·JUNE·

SUCCESSION
PLANTING

June takes us from the lovely, mild days of spring into the hot, humid days of the summer. The calendar may say that summer starts with the equinox on the 21st or 22nd of June, but gardeners in the Southeast know better and will laugh while offering you a nice, juicy, vine-ripened tomato. In this time of abundance, when the last of the spring lettuces are coming to table with the first of the summer cucumbers and tomatoes, it is easy to think about sitting back with a nice, cool glass of mint tea and enjoying the harvest. But if we want to keep this bounty coming all summer and into the fall, it is time to make the summer succession plantings, and plan the fall garden to assure produce through to winter.

TO DO THIS MONTH

PLAN, PREPARE, AND MAINTAIN

- Work on pest control: look for Mexican bean beetles on cloudy days early in June; order Pedio wasps when you first see beetle larvae; don't forget to order lacewings, praying mantises, and other predators too, if needed (for them to be effective, you'll still need a healthy habitat for them to survive; see previous chapter); hand pick Colorado potato beetles again, if necessary, every two weeks
- Harvest all your fruiting plants like tomatoes, summer squash, and beans frequently for premium quality and maximum continued production; harvest potato onions, onions, new potatoes, and garlic, and replant some of your smallest cloves immediately for garlic scallions
- Stop harvesting broccoli when it gets bitter; pull it all up and plant a cover crop, or southern peas
- Weed, weed, and weed again to preserve moisture and nutrients for your rapidly growing crops
- Mulch tomatoes, peppers, eggplant, okra, cucumbers, and asparagus
- Water! If you're not getting enough rain, make sure your vegetable plants get an inch or more of water each week (an inexpensive rain gauge saves time and anxiety)
- (In late June or July in the Upper South) If you haven't done so already, chit seed potatoes for two weeks in trays with bright but indirect light, before planting; hill rows by mounding soil over the seed pieces, cover with mulch, and water well immediately after planting
- Cut down buckwheat cover crop before it flowers, and mow sorghum sudan when it reaches 3–4 feet to encourage deep rooting.
- For perennials, weed asparagus in the last week of harvest (perhaps give more compost, and definitely mulch again); weed, compost, and mulch matted row strawberries to stimulate growth of runners (you can leave the runners in place to thin or transplant as needed in September); mow or mulch paths in grapes and raspberries

SOW AND PLANT

- Plant egg-size pieces of potato in late June or July in the Upper South; hill rows by mounding soil over the seed pieces; cover with mulch and water well immediately after planting
- Sow heat-resistant lettuces, taking special measures to keep the sowings cool (see below)
- Sow broccoli, Brussels sprouts, cabbage, and cauliflower for fall, making two or three sowings—a week apart as insurance—starting late in the month in the Upper South; plant them in a shaded greenhouse, cold frame, or specially prepared and covered outdoor seedling bed
- Sow southern (crowder) peas, cucumber, and zucchini
- Continue to plant successions of summer vegetables: beans, cucumbers, corn, edamame, summer squash, melons, limas, and winter squash; feed the soil with ample amounts of compost and organic fertilizer between plantings
- Sow winter squash and thin to 24 inches as soon as the plants have three true leaves
- Transplant sweet potato slips; finish planting watermelons (transplants or sprouted seeds)
- Remember your cover crops: good choices for sowing empty beds in June are buckwheat, millet, soy, cowpeas, and sorghum sudan

FRESH HARVEST

- artichokes
- Asian greens
- beans
- beets
- blueberries
- broccoli
- cabbage
- carrots
- celery
- chard
- cherries
- cucumbers
- eggplants
- garlic
- lettuce
- onions
- melons
- potatoes
- peas
- peppers (green)
- plums
- potato onions
- raspberries
- scallions
- southern peas
- summer squash
- tomatoes
- turnips
- zucchini

Put the Heat on Planting

If you haven't already planted okra, lima beans, sweet potatoes, and southern peas (black-eyed peas or crowder peas), now is the time. These drought-tolerant, heat-loving plants will keep growing through the "dog days of summer" and reward you with a bounty of real southern eating. If you haven't grown okra before, be patient with its slow germination. To accelerate the process, I often nick the hard coat of each seed with a file and/or soak the seed for a day before planting. Once the plants are up and growing they keep bearing and blooming with little attention. And they're decorative—consider an okra hedge, if you have room. The timing and habit of sweet potatoes and okra make them good garden companions. Try planting them next to each other so the vines of sweet potatoes can grow in below the okra.

If you don't have room for sweet potatoes in the main vegetable garden, they make a lovely ground cover in other open areas of the yard. Plus you'll get an amazing edible reward in the fall. For such a nutritious, easy-storing vegetable, it's worth looking for a space that will work.

Succession planting for fresh eating all summer

Making multiple plantings of the same crop is one of the central strategies for getting the most out of your space. You won't just have more food; you'll also be leaving less area open for weeds, saving yourself time, work, and money. That said, succession planting does take some planning and usually some trial and error. Some techniques might be considered advanced but the basics are easy.

First, there are vegetables we want to have garden fresh as much of the year as possible. Some are frost sensitive, so their outdoor growth is bookended by the last spring frost and the first fall frost. Green beans, southern peas, and corn have shorter harvest periods, so make weekly plantings or plant varieties with different maturities every three to four weeks until eight weeks before frost.

Other frost-sensitive crops like cucumbers, okra, summer squash, and melons have a longer window of harvest so we only make two to four plantings.

Many of our succession crops prefer cool weather but tolerate some heat. These include lettuces, radishes, mustards, carrots, and beets. In the Lower South, you might not plant them at all from June to mid-August. In the Upper South, you might make regular successions all season. The hotter the weather, the smaller the plantings and the more attention they will need to thrive.

Cool-weather crops like cabbage, broccoli, Brussels sprouts, Chinese cabbage, and cauliflower are the main stays of both the spring and fall garden. Succession plant in the early and mid-spring, stop planting in the hottest weather, and resume planting later. In the next chapter, we'll talk more about the difficulties of starting cool-season vegetables in the middle of summer.

Intercropping

If you have a small garden and some attention to detail, here's a gardening technique for you. Intercropping (sometimes called relay planting) will let you fit more successions into a small garden. Basically, using the same space, you grow two different vegetables with different growth patterns and nutrient needs. A common combination is planting tomatoes and lettuce together. The tomatoes are planted 2–4 feet apart, leaving plenty of room for the quick crop of lettuce to mature before the tomatoes need a lot space. Another example is growing smaller plants such as radishes at the base of taller plants such as beans or broccoli.

In the early spring, we plant four rows of a quick-maturing spinach in a 4-foot-wide bed with a row of dwarf snap peas in between. We pull out what's left of the spinach about the time we start harvesting the peas.

During the middle of the hot summer, shade-tolerant species such as lettuce, spinach, and parsley may be planted in the shadow of taller crops.

The more intensively you succession plant or inter-plant, the more important it is to pay attention to details such as watering, feeding your soil, and rotating your crops. You will then be rewarded by a dense, beautiful, productive garden! Keeping good records from year to year is also a big help.

Here are some tricks for keeping the garden full throughout many succession plantings in our long southeastern season:

Keep pulling up those old plants that are past their prime. Replant with new crops. In addition to your spring lettuce beds (which are probably ancient history by now) this might mean filling the space that opened up where a squash plant succumbed to vine borers or your cilantro bolts to seed. Have some seedlings ready to transplant into sudden gaps. This trick can more than double the yield in a small garden.

Add compost and any other nutrients needed before replanting. Remember that with later plantings it becomes a race with the clock, so it is more important than ever to help plants grow steadily. Fertilize and turn over the soil thoroughly before sowing successions of

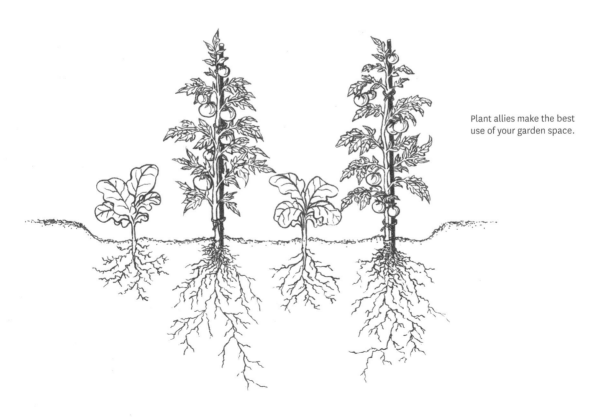

Plant allies make the best use of your garden space.

your new beans, beets, carrots, lettuce, and New Zealand or Malabar spinach.

Keep seeds moist until they germinate. It's obvious why this is so important but it's hard to do in June. Sow seed up to twice as deep as you did in spring. I sometimes cover the row with a board like the old-timers did, or use old window screen held up by rocks or bricks to maintain moisture and prevent crusting. Check your plantings daily and remove the board as soon as the seeds sprout. Water again if needed.

Screen young plants from too much sun. Use shade cloth, old snow fencing, turned-over light-colored pots, or the natural shade of tall plants like pole beans, corn, or trellised tomatoes.

Plant the right crops for later successions. Mid- to late summer is the time of the most diseases and pests, so choose resistant varieties that will mature in the time remaining before cold weather, or varieties that will continue to thrive in the cooling days of fall.

Starting the Fall Garden

In the Upper South, start your fall cabbage, broccoli, cauliflower, and collards in seedling beds, cold frames, or a shaded greenhouse for transplanting later. New gardeners often wonder exactly when is the right time to start different crops. Look at the seed packet to find the "days to maturity" number. Add 14 days to that number, count backward from the average frost date in your area, and that is your planting date for cool-weather crops. For successions of frost-tender crops like beans or summer squash, add 21 days instead of 14 to allow time for harvesting before frost. The next chapter includes a simple guide to planning your fall garden.

HEAT-TOLERANT LETTUCES AND GREENS

The following varieties germinate and grow well even in summer heat if you give them a little extra shade and water. These varieties have also survived the winter, under row cover, on our Virginia farm.

LETTUCES

- Jericho. 60 days. This large Israeli variety is the most heat-tolerant romaine around.
- Buttercrunch. 55 days. (1963 AAS winner) Small, fast-maturing, dark green bibb lettuce.
- Anuenue. 50 days. You might not be able to pronounce it, but this Hawaiian beauty is wonderfully crisp, glossy, heat tolerant, and bolt resistant.
- Sierra. 54 days. Glossy, crisp green leaves with reddish veins; holds well in heat.

- Thai oakleaf. 39 days. Selected in Thailand to produce well in high heat.
- Salad bowl. 40 days. (1952 AAS winner) Lovely long, frilly leaves in a rosette.

OTHER GREENS

- Swiss chards and leaf beets. 50+ days. All make excellent greens. The Bull's Blood is prized for baby salad mixes.
- Red Malabar spinach. 70 days. Colorful summer substitute for spinach. Requires trellising.
- Mayo Indian amaranth. 40 days for leaves to use as a spinach substitute or 90 days for grain.
- Goldberger purslane. 50 days. Upright plants with golden stems and large, smooth, mild, succulent, golden-green leaves. Cut-and-come-again for salad.

SKILL SET

LETTUCE ALL YEAR ROUND

Here is how you can grow and enjoy baby greens, Caesar salads, BLTs, and more throughout the year. Lettuce is a cool-season crop which does best at 50–70°F but survives from 32–85°F. Plus it appreciates partial shade during our hot summers. So in the Southeast, you can have garden-fresh lettuce pretty much all the time if you pay attention to variety selection, location, seasonal covering, watering, and planting timing.

First, here are some lettuce seed basics. The seeds sprout readily at 70–75°F, but they need light to germinate, so plant seeds no more than ¼ inch deep (some say just dust the seeds with fine soil, but in any case, be sure to keep them moist). Hot temperatures reduce germination, so store seeds in a tightly closed jar in the refrigerator between plantings. Now, decide how much lettuce you want each week. Remember you can harvest young lettuce by "mowing" (cut-and-come-again for mesclun or salad mix) and you can also harvest mature lettuce as whole plants.

Sow your first spring seeds about six weeks before your last frost, and sow again every ten to twelve days throughout the spring. Sow indoors in flats, in cold frames, or directly in the garden in covered seedling beds.

As the weather warms up, sow small amounts every seven days through the summer (in hot weather, keep shaded). Mixing different lettuce varieties each planting not only gives you beautifully colored and textured salads but also spreads out the risk of loss due to bolting or disease. When starting seeds in hot weather (the earlier discussion on succession planting is just the ticket for lettuce), put your seeded flat in a plastic bag to conserve moisture and put the flat in the fridge, an air-conditioned room, or a root cellar for about two days. If you're sowing outdoors in hot weather, plant in the late afternoon and water with crushed ice (really!). You can also pre-cool the outdoor soil by watering and covering it with a board or wet burlap for a few days before planting.

Keep transplanting seedlings from your nursery plantings into the garden, so that you have garden-fresh lettuces coming along in all sizes. Lettuce transplants easily so you can take advantage of bits of empty garden space for sowing or transplanting. Transplants tolerate bugs, diseases, drought, and other problems better than very young seedlings do. (But, still, keep them watered. It's the least you can do.)

In the early fall, even if it still feels like summer, start more frequent plantings. Sow small quantities of cold-tolerant varieties every three to six days in protected (cool, shaded) seedling beds. As day length decreases, a one-day difference in planting time can mean a one-week difference in harvest time. Most of the growth will happen in the warmer, longer days of September and October, but with luck and attention you will be harvesting lettuce from these early fall plantings through much of the winter.

For best quality and yield from these fall plantings, use floating row cover all fall. It protects your baby lettuces from nasty bugs early on, and from drying winds and lower temperatures later on.

Then come the depths of winter, when plant growth slows to a crawl. At that point, what you went into the winter with is what you will have to harvest from. You'll appreciate all those succession plantings when your winter garden starts to be a large outdoor refrigerator full of fresh salads ready for the picking. If you have started enough plants of cold-hardy lettuces, then row cover or a cold frame will usually keep your table supplied with salads until the spring sowings bring you a fresh crop of tender young greens.

·JULY·

THE DOG DAYS
OF SUMMER

It's not just an expression: "the dog days of summer" coincide with the rising of the Dog Star Sirius on 3 July to 11 August (according to *The Old Farmer's Almanac*). These are the hottest, sultriest, and driest days of the garden year.

In the Upper South, hot-weather crops are in full production and you are busy keeping them hydrated and weeded (and we all know that's tough). In the Lower South, the early summer plantings are petering out with only okra, sweet potatoes, and southern peas thriving in the heat.

Gardeners all over face the daunting task of starting their fall crops while the weather is still hot, dry, and otherwise miserable. But time is of the essence to get your fall and winter plants going, whether it's a second crop of tomatoes in Louisiana or fall broccoli in Virginia. The race is

CONTINUED ON PAGE 99

TO DO THIS MONTH

PLAN, PREPARE, AND MAINTAIN

- Shade your greenhouse with 30 percent shade cloth for increased production of high-quality peppers and tomatoes during July and August
- Hill up peanuts when the plants reach 12 inches; mulch them before they begin to peg (dropping runners to form peanuts)
- Harvest spring potatoes two weeks after tops have died; cure and store
- Spread compost, turn in spring cover crops, and prepare first beds for fall transplants
- Harvest any remaining spring carrots and store indoors for best flavor; sow a cover crop or fall greens in the carrot beds
- Clear out the trash from your spring peas, if you haven't already; plant cucumbers to use the pea trellis
- Harvest or cut down all the celery to encourage a second fall harvest
- Plan and order winter cover crop seeds
- Perennials: Finish renovating strawberries; water blueberries; take up and store bird netting once the harvest is over; weed, mulch, and water all perennials—they will thank you later

SOW AND PLANT

- Sow cabbage, broccoli, and other brassicas for the fall, as needed; plant your young seedlings under cover shelters; use row covers, or window screens on cold frames, or shaded, carefully tended seedling beds
- Sow heat-resistant lettuces in small amounts, every six or seven days (refrigerate seeds for two days before planting; sow in a flat indoors or plant outdoors in the evening and use frequent watering and shade-cloth or burlap or boards to keep soil temp below 80°F until seeds germinate)
- Cover crops: In your empty beds, sow buckwheat, soybeans, or sorghum sudan
- (In the Upper South) Sow last brassicas late in July for the fall
- (In the Upper South) Last chance to sow more cucumbers, zucchini, corn, beans, rutabagas
- (In the Upper South) Transplant out broccoli, cabbage, and cauliflower when the plants have three to four true leaves (three to four weeks old); protect from flea beetles with floating row cover; shade the transplants for the first few days; keep watered
- (In the Upper South) Plant chitted white potatoes for fall; hill, water well, and mulch

FRESH HARVEST

- asparagus beans
- beans
- beets
- blueberries
- cantaloupes
- carrots
- celeriac
- celery
- chard
- corn
- cowpeas
- cucumbers
- edamame
- eggplant
- figs
- hot peppers
- lettuce
- Malabar spinach
- New Zealand spinach
- okra
- onions
- peppers
- plums
- raspberries
- scallions
- summer squash
- tomatoes
- watermelons
- zucchini

Check potatoes, garlic, and onions in storage

on: will your garden amount to something before the first frost? And, more importantly, will it continue to produce after the frost, perhaps even all winter?

Many of the techniques for summer succession planting (see previous chapter) still work in July. We're sowing and transplanting brassicas (cabbage, broccoli, Brussels sprouts, etc.), and also lots of greens and roots. These cool-season crops will produce abundantly in the fall and winter if they get off to a good start now. Remember to keep the soil evenly moist, shade your tender young seedlings, use floating row cover to keep the bugs off, and keep everything weeded and mulched.

Dates for Fall Planting

Fall planting is really succession planting with a hard deadline: the fast-approaching first frost. Below are sample planting dates for whatever is your first average fall frost date. In this schedule, the earliest planting would be for Brussels sprouts; the latest would be radishes, with everything else in between.

The Southeast is a big region with a wide range of frost dates. The earliest frost dates are for the higher elevations in the mountains of West Virginia and Kentucky. There you're almost gardening in the north. The latest dates are for Florida and coastal Louisiana, where a frost is a fleeting event.

Actually, much of the Lower South is just as much a three-season climate as the north is, but reversed. In the Deep South, winter gardening is the norm and keeping the garden going through the hottest parts of summer is the challenge.

WHEN TO PLANT FOR FALL HARVEST

FIRST FROST	PLANTING DATES
8/30	6/1–7/15
9/10	5/15–8/1
9/20	6/1–8/15
9/30	6/1–9/1
10/10	6/10–8/20
10/20	7/5–9/20
10/30	7/5–9/30
11/10	7/15–10/10
11/20	7/25–10/20
11/30	8/5–10/30
12/10	8/15–11/10
12/20	8/25–11/20

If you are in doubt, check with your county extension office. Often the folks there have a table detailing what can be planted locally each month. By following these suggestions you can enjoy fresh produce on your table all winter.

HOW LATE TO PLANT? MATURITY DATES AND FROST TOLERANCE

CROP	DAYS TO MATURITY	COLD HARDINESS
Garlic	day-length and temperature triggered	overwinters
Onions	day-length and temperature triggered	overwinters
Brussels sprouts	90–100	down to 20°F
rutabaga	90–95	down to 16°F
peas	70–80	high 20s°F
cauliflower	60–80	light frost
cilantro	60–70	light frost
green onions	60–70	high 20s°F
broccoli	50–90	light frost
Cabbage	50–90	down to 20°F
Beets	50–60	survives high 20s°F
kohlrabi	50–60	light frost
Turnips	50–60	light frost
Kale	40–65	down to 20°F
radish, winter	50–60	down to 20°F
collards	40–60	down to 20°F
Swiss chard	40–60	light frost
Spinach	35–45	overwinters
radish, spring	35–45	light frost
mustard greens	30–40	light frost

Use this table to determine the right time to plant fall crops. Look up "days to maturity" and add 14 days to that number to allow for less daylight in the fall. Count backward from the average frost date in your area to determine your planting date. For fall successions of frost-tender crops like beans or summer squash, add 21 days instead of 14, to allow time for harvesting before frost.

TOOLS AND TECHNIQUES . . .

July has the highest evaporation rates of any month. According to the National Weather Service, you can lose up to a half inch of soil moisture per day in a typical July.

MOISTURE MANAGEMENT

You have to make sure your plants have enough water when they need it. First, conserve the moisture you've got. Here are some tips:

- Weed early and often. Weeds take moisture that your plants need. My favorite weeding tool is a scuffle hoe (see May chapter). It easily cuts off small weeds at ground level without breaking your back or disturbing the soil underneath.
- Harvest regularly and thoroughly (including damaged fruit), preferably in the morning. You'll get better-quality produce and give the plants more energy to deal with the heat and with ripening more fruit later. And by doing your work in the morning, you'll be done before the hottest stretch of the day.
- When planting, pre-soak seeds overnight to speed germination and sow them in well-moistened soil. Plant the seeds up to twice as deep as you would in the spring (in midsummer the soil is much warmer and the top layer dries out quickly.) A light sprinkling of straw or dry lawn clippings helps prevent the soil crusting that hinders seedling emergence.
- One trick for planting in hot, dry weather is known as "flooding the drill": Simply make a furrow and flood it to the top with water. Let the water drain into the soil, and then sow your seeds into the damp ground. Cover the seeds with some compost or potting soil and tamp it all down so the seed has good soil contact. Then cover the row with a board. The board helps keep the soil moist, but check your planting frequently, at least once a day. Promptly remove the board when the seedlings appear.

. . . TO BEAT THE HEAT

WATERING WISELY

What should you water first? Here's what I prioritize:

1 Newly planted seeds, transplants, and container plants.

2 Plants that will lose flavor or quality permanently from water stress (too much or too little water at the wrong time). For example, drought turns lettuce bitter and tomatoes will crack if they're too dry and then suddenly get a lot of water.

3 Prized perennials, such as blueberries, artichokes, asparagus, and figs after they've set fruit.

4 Herb and insectary beds.

SMART WATERING TIPS

- Drip irrigation is your most efficient option, whether with soaker hoses or a full drip system, but most gardeners still use sprinklers now and then.
- Clay soil needs deep soaking (rain or irrigation) once a week because water soaks in slowly and runs off uselessly if you water too much too fast.
- Sandy soils drain quickly so a thorough watering twice a week works best.
- Sprinkler irrigation loses up to half the water to the air due to evaporation. Minimize loss by watering in the early morning or overnight, if possible.
- For individual plants, make a portable drip station. Punch very small holes an inch from the bottom of a big plastic container. Fill with water and set next to the plant. The water in the bottom inch will keep the container from falling over or blowing away.
- Don't waste water. Replace leaking washers. Repair broken or leaky hoses promptly. Buy the best hoses you can afford.

SHADE YOUR PLANTS

In midsummer, too much sun is a problem. Here are some suggestions for providing a little protection:

- A well-placed section of lattice or snow fencing on the south or west side of tomatoes or a corn planting keeps the root zone cool and reduces evaporation even if the plants are too tall to be completely shaded.
- Recycled window screens or inverted, light-colored flower pots can help small transplants survive their first few days.
- Shade cloth works great when held several inches above plants by wire or PVC plastic hoops. The hoops don't have to be tall.
- Lightweight bed sheets and sheer curtains can be repurposed as shade cloth.
- Plant in a shady area of the garden or on the north or east side of tall plantings such as corn, pole beans, or caged tomatoes. Late summer greens are particularly suitable for planting in the shade of tall crops that are on their way out. Take out the dying taller plants as your greens are established and the weather moderates.
- A single-sided tent structure like the one shown on the next page gives you easy access to your plants, or gives taller plants room to grow. Place the shade cloth wall on the south side, or add an additional wall on the west side, for the best protection.
- The low-hooped structure shown on the next page can be made using the same techniques as we used in building a low tunnel (see February). The binder clips or paper clamps hold the cloth in place. Each hoop can be two or three wires, with one on the outside of the cloth: this will allow you to pull up the sides for better ventilation, and the wires will hold the cloth in place.

Finally, you know how much cooler you feel after an afternoon shower on a hot July day? Following that example,

TOOLS AND TECHNIQUES TO BEAT THE HEAT CONTINUED

give your heat-stressed plants a quick, late-afternoon shower. This won't wet the soil much, so it's not a substitute for whatever irrigation you use. And, as always, remember to take care of yourself as well as your plants when it's super-hot outside. Work in the mornings or early evenings. Drink plenty of water or cold tea and stay inside (or go swimming) during mid-day.

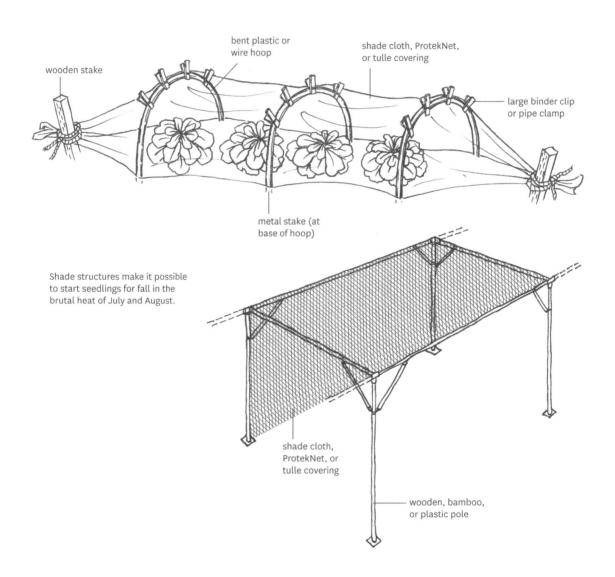

wooden stake

bent plastic or wire hoop

shade cloth, ProtekNet, or tulle covering

large binder clip or pipe clamp

metal stake (at base of hoop)

Shade structures make it possible to start seedlings for fall in the brutal heat of July and August.

shade cloth, ProtekNet, or tulle covering

wooden, bamboo, or plastic pole

· AUGUST ·

HEAT AND HARVEST

Being outside in the garden in August's heat and humidity can be tough, but this is also a month of abundant harvests and gleeful experimentation in the kitchen. The best time to enjoy your garden is the cooler hours of early morning. Gather the harvest and think of everything you can make with the abundance. Who can resist a tomato salad with nine different varieties of heirloom tomatoes, fresh garlic, and sprigs of seven different basils?

We still have many warm days ahead, especially if you're gardening in the Lower South. The key to keeping your plants happy and healthy is still rich, well-amended soil and even soil moisture. Irrigate deeply once a week and keep roots cool with a deep layer of organic mulch. We can take some comfort in knowing the worst is

CONTINUED ON PAGE 106

TO DO THIS MONTH

PLAN, PREPARE, AND MAINTAIN

- Roughly map out next year's garden so best choices for winter cover crops can be planted; pay special attention to planning early spring crops and order any additional seed needed
- Make notes in your garden journal about the weather, crop successes, and failures
- Learn about groups needing donations or other ways to share your excess produce
- Water sweet potatoes and other plants thoroughly and deeply for best production
- Water older strawberry plants for next year's crop, keep them weeded, and give them compost
- Prepare new strawberry beds for fall planting—compost, till, raise, mulch

- Sort early potatoes, carrots, garlic, and other produce in storage
- Keep up with weeding and harvesting to maximize yields and produce quality
- Cut back spring-planted chard to encourage new growth
- Thin carrots and rutabagas early (10 days after emergence)
- Weed earlier transplanted broccoli and other brassicas; undersow with clover for a cover crop through next spring

SOW AND PLANT

- Sow winter and summer radishes, kohlrabi, turnips, rutabagas, Swiss chard, collards, kale (cover with row cover against flea beetles), herbs, carrots, beets for fall and winter storage
- Transplant remaining cabbage, broccoli, cauliflower, collards, and broccoli seedlings for fall
- Direct sow spinach after the dead nettle has germinated, or sprout in fridge for one week before planting out—wait until September if it's really hot

- Sow cover crops buckwheat, soy, clovers and oats (or, possibly, winter barley)
- (In the Lower South) Transplant quick-ripening (under 80 days) tomatoes for fall harvest
- Continue weekly sowings of lettuce; switch to cold-tolerant varieties at the end of the month
- (In the Upper South) Early August is your last chance for cucumbers, squash, corn, beans

FRESH HARVEST

- Asian greens
- asparagus beans
- beans
- blueberries
- cantaloupes
- carrots
- celeriac
- celery
- chard
- corn
- cowpeas
- cucumbers
- edamame
- eggplant
- figs
- grapes
- herbs
- hot peppers
- leeks
- Malabar spinach
- New Zealand spinach
- okra
- peppers
- raspberries
- scallions
- summer squash
- sweet peppers
- tomatoes
- watermelons
- winter squash
- zucchini

behind us (July is usually the hottest month in the Southeast) and we enjoy small breaks in the heat and cooler nighttime temperatures, and anticipate the pleasantly mild autumn days ahead.

It may feel hot, but we have as much light as we did back in April, and we're losing it fast. Plants need lots of light to grow quickly, and quick early growth is essential to getting seedlings off to a strong start. Start fall and winter crops now, even if winter feels a long way off, to take advantage of the sunshine before we lose it.

The Juggling Act: Make the Most of Late Summer

Throughout our region, we are busy with harvesting, removing spent or declining plants, and preparing beds for the fall garden. Intercropping is one of my favorite ways to make this seasonal puzzle work. All of this juggling lets your plants take advantage of the favorable conditions for rapid growth in late summer and you'll keep harvesting your summer crops as long as possible. We plant a lot of broccoli, cabbage, and other brassicas that will be in the ground well into cold weather but not last through spring. We used to keep the ground covered with mulch, but in recent years we have taken to undersowing all of our fall brassicas with a clover cover crop. About a month after transplanting, we weed the area well with a scuffle hoe and broadcast the clover seed over the bed, either timing this just before a rain or running your sprinkler to settle in the seeds. On a small planting, you can use the bottom of your regular hoe or rake to tamp down the soil.

Planting lettuce and other greens at the edges of tomato and pepper beds is another combination we like because the taller plants provide shade and will be gone with the first frost. After the frost you can cut off and remove the tomato plants at ground level, then spread out extra lettuce and greens seedlings to use more of the bed space. Sprinkle on a layer of compost covered by mulch and your bed of fall salad is complete.

In small gardens, you can start small stations of greens anywhere an individual plant has been removed, or where there is space after an earlier planting is harvested.

Tall crops provide shade where it's needed in high summer, then die back in time to let in fall sunlight. Lettuce, chard, and spinach benefit from corn's late summer shade and make good use of the space.

Managing the Harvest

When we are planning our dream garden in winter, the harvesting part doesn't seem like work. Somehow getting those baskets of tomatoes, buckets of beans, and bundles of herbs will happen. It is so much more fun than weeding and watering that we sometimes forget to plan for how we'll get it all done.

In our Southern Exposure trial gardens, we harvest every day, but even in a small garden you need to plan to harvest at least two or three times a week. Otherwise you'll end up with zucchini the size of baseball bats! Harvest often and thoroughly to keep your plants productive and get the highest quality fruits and veggies. Pole beans, crowder peas, summer squash, okra, and tomatoes all produce better with regular harvesting. Keep your crops well picked if you want to keep picking. This maxim is also true for basil, parsley, most annual flowers, and other green herbs.

Your vegetables keep on producing while you are on vacation or even out of town for just two or three days. So ask a family member or neighbor to harvest and enjoy the produce while you are away. Offer to return the favor for them.

When to harvest

Harvest lettuce and leafy greens early in the morning before the day heats up, for the sweetest flavor and highest nutrition. Overnight, your plants have been working to hydrate the growing leaves and pump available nutrients out of the soil. So harvest early and move indoors as soon as possible. If you can't get out in the morning, wait until the early evening when it has started to cool again. If you must harvest greens in the heat of the day, soak

DIFFERENT STORAGE FOR DIFFERENT CROPS

- Peas are sweetest when eaten within a couple hours of harvest.

- Root crops like beets, turnips, and carrots can be left in the ground and mulched in well-drained soil for harvest as needed. However, this is only true in late fall when growth stops; spring and summer crops need to be pulled before they get large and lower quality. If the soil is heavy clay or has other drainage or pest issues, store these root crops in the refrigerator or in a cool basement with high humidity or in buckets of sawdust or sand.

- Most of us don't have a root cellar, but many have a cool area in the house. These crops may be stored in fridge, but use the crisper or increase the humidity: beans, broccoli, cabbages, Brussels sprouts, peppers, cucumbers, summer squash, and zucchini should be refrigerated for best storage.

- Potatoes must be kept in the dark in a cool room or basement to store properly.

- Store tomatoes, melons, and eggplants at cool, room-temperature conditions for best quality and eat as soon after harvesting as possible.

- Garlic and onions can be harvested any time it is dry and stored at room temperature. I'll talk more about curing and storing these culinary essentials in the October chapter.

- Cure winter squash and pumpkins at warmer temperatures; sweet potatoes can be stored at room temperature after curing.

them in cool water for half an hour before draining and preparing to serve.

The reverse rule goes for tomatoes, peppers, melons, eggplant, beans, peas, cucumbers, and summer squash and zucchini. It's best for the plants to be harvested after mid-morning when the dew has dried. This helps prevent the spread of fungal diseases, and may also give the sweetest fruits. Tomatoes and melons are sweetest if you leave off irrigating for a few days prior to harvest.

Sharing the harvest

At the peak of harvest, a well-cared-for edible garden often produces more than the gardener can use, and even overwhelms our ability and time to can and freeze. Fortunately, you can share the bounty with friends and family, and it's becoming easier to also share with those in need in your community.

According to the USDA Department of Agriculture, 33 million people in our land of plenty, including 13 million children, have substandard diets or must resort to seeking help from a food bank because they cannot always afford the food they need. Groups like Plant a Row for the Hungry (PAR) and Second Harvest are raising awareness and getting people involved in their local communities to gather and distribute food to those who need it most.

The resurgence of community and school gardens is also helping to make gardening accessible to people who don't have the space, the knowledge, or the finances to grow their own food at home. Community and school gardens encourage healthier eating habits, bring neighborhoods together, and connect us to the source of our food, while encouraging environmental stewardship, self-reliance, and confidence in the safety of our food.

In our town, local businesses, the master gardeners, church groups, farmers, and social agencies have joined together to produce food for our local food pantry and create a teaching garden so others can learn to grow their own fresh, healthy food as well.

If you want to help here are some ways to get started:

- Grow more and donate it to your local food pantry or area food bank through Plant A Row for the Hungry.

- Join in an effort like "The Day of Gleaning" in Virginia or arrange to pick fruit from neighborhood trees that would otherwise go to waste.

- Volunteer at a local community or school garden to share your knowledge and experience.

- Go online to communicate with others in your area and learn about new ways to help and make a difference.

SKILL SET

···

PUTTING UP THE HARVEST FOR WINTER AND BEYOND

···

The well-maintained August garden is a wonderland of food calling out to be picked, but for the novice gardener, knowing when to harvest and how to preserve all that bounty can be challenging. One way to learn is to volunteer at a busy community garden or local farm. The Edibles A to Z section offers good information on specific crops. Here are some general suggestions for how to harvest and easy ideas for preserving the harvest.

We find that taste is the most helpful factor in determining when a new fruit variety is ready, and everyone on the farm is willing to help keep track of what color the fall gold raspberry is when it's sweetest. How floppy is the fig? What is the smell of a ripening pear? How soft is a persimmon? Our garden is a classroom and we are eager students.

Be careful not to break, nick, or bruise vegetables when harvesting. The less they are handled, the longer they will last in storage. Harvest only vegetables of high quality. Damaged goods don't last long and can spread decay to other produce.

These are some ways to keep your harvest for even longer:

- **Drying.** Dehydrators (solar and electric) are low energy and an easy way to store fruit, tomatoes, peppers, and other produce. Dehydrators for purchase and plans for building homemade solar dryers abound on the web. Many gardeners will use their oven on its lowest setting or just the fan on a convection oven for drying. Local extension offices have great handouts and demonstrations.

- **Freezing.** Proper storage in the freezer is a quick option for everything from fruit to already prepared sauces. There is a wide array of freezer plastic bags, vacuum packing, jars, individual portion sizes, and more available to help you fit your freezing efforts to the space and time you have available. Berries are my favorite to freeze; I put them on a tray, freeze overnight, and then put them in freezer bags to use as needed.

- **Canning and pickling.** For this you'll need jars, jars, and more jars; it's how my grandmother did it—and probably yours. Today the choices are many: from fermented pickles to quick refrigerator jams; water bath canning for acid foods like tomatoes; pressure canning for corn and other low-acid foods. Again, your extension service will be able to help.

- **The root cellar and alternatives.** The traditional root cellar lets gardeners keep loads of produce for winter. Now gardeners can create similar conditions in a basement, insulated closet, pantry, or garage. There are three main types of storage areas:

1 cool and dry (50–60°F and 60 percent relative humidity): best for winter squash, pumpkins

2 cold and dry (32–40°F and 65 percent relative humidity): best for onions and garlic

3 cold and moist (32–40°F and 95 percent relative humidity): best for most root crops; potatoes must stay out of the light

Get creative and make something work.

- **Long-term refrigerator storage.** This is a compromise, and never a perfect choice. Putting vegetables in perforated plastic bags in the refrigerator will provide cold and moist conditions, but only for a moderate amount of time. Fresh produce in sealed bags tends to rot.

- **Outside storage.** Traditionally, root crops are left in the ground covered with lots of mulch and a prayer that the critters don't find them.

- **Room temperature.** Don't forget our southern storage superheros, sweet potatoes and perennial onions, which can keep up to a year at cool room temperature out of the light.

·SEPTEMBER·

SECOND SPRING

Cooler nights, warm, sunny days, and gentle rains bring on a last hurrah for summer plantings of juicy tomatoes, sweet red peppers, hot peppers, eggplants, and basil, before glorious stretches of greens, frost-touched brassicas, huge heads of broccoli, and abundant root crops take us on to the pleasures of our long, lazy fall. With a little extra cover, gardeners in the Lower South can extend this time of having it all into the holiday season, but they may also have to wait for the extra rain that comes with seasonal hurricanes before finding much relief from watering duties. In most areas, cooler weather and reduced insect pressure makes it a lot easier to take care of the remaining summer crops.

TO DO THIS MONTH

PLAN, PREPARE, AND MAINTAIN

- Keep notes of plantings and harvest
- Till and prepare beds for garlic, shallots, and perennial onions
- Review fall and winter garden plans
- Inventory and evaluate row cover; order more if necessary
- Start plans for future small-fruit selection and plantings

- Take soil tests for new planting areas
- Prepare and plant new strawberry beds in early September if not done in late August
- Weed and thin earlier planted carrot and brassica beds if not already done
- Cure and store winter squash and pumpkins
- Lightly harvest rhubarb if plants look good

SOW AND PLANT

- Sow hardy lettuce every two days till 21 September, then every three days
- (In the Lower South) Sow quick-maturing varieties of summer squash and beans
- Transplant more collards and kale if necessary
- Sprout spinach in fridge for one week, then sow (if dead nettle has germinated); mid-September is last sowing date for fall harvesting in the Upper South
- Broadcast oats into spinach at planting time in September for weed control and cold-weather protection

- Sow more kale, collards, turnips, radishes, kohlrabi, daikon, and other winter radish, along with Asian greens and scallions
- Sow winter greens and salad in late September for your cold frame or covered beds
- Sow more spinach for spring harvesting
- (In the Upper South) Plant kale for spring harvest late in the month.
- Sow cover crops wherever possible in unused raised beds; use oats early in the month; and red clover, rye, or hardy Austrian winter peas in late September

FRESH HARVEST

- arugula
- Asian greens
- asparagus beans
- beans
- beets and beet greens
- broccoli
- cabbage

- cantaloupes
- carrots
- cauliflower
- celeriac
- celery
- chard
- Chinese cabbage
- corn

- cowpeas
- cucumbers
- edamame
- eggplant
- figs
- herbs
- kale
- leeks

- lettuce
- limas
- okra
- hot peppers
- sweet peppers
- radishes
- raspberries
- rhubarb

- scallions
- summer squash
- tomatoes
- turnips
- watermelons
- winter squash
- zucchini

Check potatoes, onions, and garlic in storage

This month we move along with planting the fall garden and begin filling in any gaps. Nestle in those last transplants, set up the cold frame, and lay out the row covers planned for the overwintered lettuce and greens: the race is on to take advantage of autumn's remaining light. Even the most cold-hardy plants will have a better chance of making it through until spring if they can get started when the light is still strong in early to mid-fall. The energy reserves our plants develop now, by establishing root systems and growing large and leafy, will carry them through the winter.

Planting a Winter Garden

When night temperatures are cool enough that you aren't sweating without the help of a fan or air conditioning, it is time to speed up your planting for the fall and overwintered garden. Gardeners all over the South should be figuring out how much of the cold-hardy crops they would like to eat during the winter and planning to get everything they haven't already planted in the ground soon. We are working against the shortening days and cooling temperatures of fall.

Get out a notepad and start your calculations. List the vegetables you want to harvest each week until spring. Determine how much is needed for how many times you will serve this crop each week. This will give you an estimate of how much you should be growing. The challenge now is to get all those plants in the ground as soon as possible so that they take advantage of the remaining warm days of fall. One thing that is in your favor is the ease of transplanting in fall. Use transplants liberally so you get that extra week or two of growth.

Keep these ideas in mind as you finish your fall planting:

Give fall transplants extra time. They will start off fast with the soil still warm from summer, but as the days get cooler, growth will slow and then stop. You need to get that "living refrigerator" full of well-grown plants if you want to harvest all winter.

Plant in well-drained soil. Plants die in waterlogged soil because their roots cannot breathe. The combination of heavy winter rains and chilly temperatures that slow the rate that soil moisture evaporates can be disastrous. Reduce the danger by planting winter crops in raised beds in areas with good soil drainage (on high ground if available).

Evaluate. Take a look at any waning summer plantings and replace them with crops likely to do well over the winter.

Intercrop. Use the shade of remaining summer crops to nurture your fall transplants.

Plan for cover. In the Lower South, there is still time to sow another quick planting of squash and beans. It is best to make these plantings in blocks for easy covering in case of an early frost. A good technique is to locate these new fall plantings near other crops that you'll want to cover, like late tomatoes and peppers (which often have a burst of productivity in early fall when temperatures cool enough for good pollination).

Plant and transplant. Get lots of seed for the winter greens and roots that you would like to eat in the ground now. Fall in the Southeast is a long, lazy affair. So planting plenty now allows you to have transplants ready to move when frost finally forces you to give up on those

CROPS TO OVERWINTER IN THE SOUTHEAST

HARDY, WITH NO PROTECTION EXCEPT MULCH

Brussels sprouts (very hardy)

carrots (mature roots should be harvested by midwinter)

collards (usually survive with no cover)

turnips (often survive winter)

garlic (greens only for winter harvest)

perennial onions (green onions in winter)

HARDY, BUT PERFORM BETTER WITH ROW COVER

kale (frost sweetens)

savoy cabbage (excellent for winter salads)

spinach (superb taste in winter)

leeks (great for winter soups)

scallions (slow to start in fall)

arugula (cold improves flavor)

hardy lettuce (crisp and sweet)

tatsoi (great for winter salads)

mizuna (mild in winter)

parsley (vitamin packed)

cilantro (seldom bolts in winter)

mustards (best flavor in the winter)

winter radishes (delicious kimchee)

beets (harvest mature beets before freeze)

summer plantings. In any case, the thinnings make tasty eating. Since floating row cover came on the scene, I have been able to count on periods of growth for my hardier greens up until the holidays. Fill that outdoor fridge.

Don't forget overwintered crops. Late in September and on through October in the Lower South, gardeners planning for a 12-month harvest plant spinach, kale, hardy greens, garlic, shallots, and perennial onions for harvest next year. Plants come into December with only a few leaves, but well mulched or blanketed with row cover they come through winter and take off in the warming days of February and March way ahead of spring-planted greens. Also in the Lower South, many gardeners start short-day onions from seeds in fall-planted cold frames for transplanting in January or February.

SKILL SET

SEED SAVING

It is due to the seed-saving efforts of countless unnamed farmers and gardeners over thousands of years that we have such a diversity of flavorful, unique, and productive heirloom seeds available today. Starting to save your own garden seeds is easy and connects you to this great tradition, and perhaps is the first step in creating your own family heirloom. The summer garden is winding down; fruits and seeds are ripening. Details of isolation distances for seed saving are given in the individual vegetable listings.

If you want to try your hand at seed saving, there are two steps to get you started: first, you'll need to clean (or process) your seeds, then you'll need to store them properly. There are two broad methods of seed cleaning: dry processing and wet processing.

DRY PROCESSING

Dry processing is the method to use for seeds that are held in flower heads, husks, or pods that have usually dried in place on the plant. Some examples are lettuce, beans, peas, corn, and radishes. This is the easiest method if the weather is dry. Seeds are left on the plant to dry until they are fully mature, then collected as dried flower heads, husks, or pods. The easiest method to tell if the seeds are dry enough is to look at the stem. If it is dry for ¼ inch below the seed heads, they are ready to harvest. Fall is often rainy in the Southeast, so this doesn't always work for large seeds like beans and peas. These seeds are mature as soon as the pod becomes flaccid and changes color to yellow or tan; the pods can then be harvested and spread out in one layer to finish drying inside or under cover. When the seeds are dry, the pods can be crushed and hand separated, winnowed, or screened to remove chaff before storing in a closed container—like a mason jar or freezer bag—in a cool, dry place out of the light.

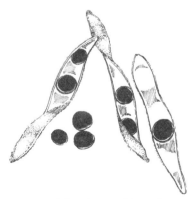

seeds bursting out of the pod

corn hanging to dry

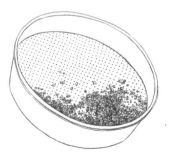

cleaning seeds with a screen

SEED SAVING CONTINUED

WET PROCESSING

Wet processing is the approach to use to separate and clean seeds that are embedded in the fleshy fruits of plants. Examples include tomatoes, cucumbers, melons, and watermelon. There are four steps:

1 **Seed extraction.** Seeds from berries or small fruits are mashed or crushed. Melon and cucumber seeds are scooped out. Take care and wear gloves when working with hot peppers (you do not want the seeds getting in your eyes!).

2 **Fermentation.** After you have extracted the seeds you will have a combination of fruit pulp, seeds, and juice. If you're unable to stir the mixture, add 15 percent water. The usual fermentation time period is three days at about 70°F. Stir twice a day.

3 **Washing seeds.** The next step is to remove all of the fruit pulp by washing the seeds. Add at least twice as much water as the volume of the seeds. Let the seeds settle to the bottom. Good seeds sink to the bottom and low-quality seeds float off with the wash (good seeds are well filled out and weigh more). Keep adding water and washing until the water is clear. Separate the seeds with a strainer.

4 **Drying seeds.** Seeds that have been extracted using fermentation or other wet-processing methods need to be dried quickly. Generally, large seeds should be dried in a single layer. Small seeds should be dried in layers no more than ⅛ inch thick. Avoid drying seeds in direct sunlight. Seeds may be dried on screens, china plates, or small Reemay bags hung in front of a box fan. When drying seeds indoors it is helpful to dry near an air conditioner, under a ceiling fan, or a safe distance away from a portable fan. When the seeds appear dry, give them at least another two to four weeks to dry before packaging. Seeds should not be packed in plastic or glass unless they are absolutely dry.

GOOD SEED STORAGE

- Make sure the seeds are dry enough (10 percent moisture is good)
- Let the seeds air dry for several weeks before storing
- Keep the temperature and humidity levels low: the sum total of both should be less than 100°F
- Pack the seeds in a sealed container, such as a mason jar
- Freeze well-dried seeds for long-term storage (always bring frozen seeds to room temperature before opening to prevent them from reabsorbing moisture)

Separate good seeds from the bad with a simple fermentation. The fleshy pulp breaks down and rinses off the good seeds at the bottom.

·OCTOBER·

SLOWING
DOWN

I love our garden in October. The summer heat is over and I can have all the garden-fresh salads I want while paying very little attention to watering, and there are almost no insect pests for months to come. We're busily harvesting and curing summer's final bounty before Jack Frost comes calling: wheelbarrows full of sweet potatoes, bushels of carrots and potatoes, baskets of herbs to dry, peanuts, dried beans, southern peas, popcorn, and more. Figs are giving their last succulent sweet fruits, fall raspberries are rushing to finish the crop, and persimmons are just beginning to mature.

All over our region, gardeners are busy. In the Lower South, we're gearing up for an extended "second spring" of fall and winter growing. In the Upper South, we're cleaning up

CONTINUED ON PAGE 121

TO DO THIS MONTH

PLAN, PREPARE, AND MAINTAIN

- Keep notes of plantings and harvest (particularly failures and successes)
- Get soil tests done if not already done in September
- Consider planning for next year as you select winter cover crops
- Finish tilling and preparing beds for garlic, shallots, and perennial onions
- Set up and refurbish cold frames
- Lay out row covers and hoops for quick response to early frosts
- Separate sweet potato seed tubers for growing next year
- Harvest sweet potatoes a few days before the first frost
- Harvest late Irish potatoes before the first frost
- Harvest peanuts immediately after the first light frost; wash, dry, cure six days, and store
- Spread lime as needed
- Weed and thin fall roots and greens, especially spinach and kale
- Set up row covers for lettuce, squash, cucumbers, spinach, celery, chard, and Chinese cabbage
- Begin frost alert: cover well or harvest beans, Chinese cabbage, peppers, tomatoes, cowpeas, limas, eggplant, melons, cucumbers, okra, winter squash, and zucchini (then breathe a sigh of relief and move on to the frost-tolerant vegetables)
- Start weeding, fertilizing with compost, and mulching the blueberries, raspberries, rhubarb, and grapes

SOW AND PLANT

- Start planting perennial onions and garlic, then mulch them
- Sow more spinach, kale, and traditional southern and Asian greens for overwintering (in the Upper South, this is your last chance)
- Sow hardy cover crops like winter wheat, rye, and Austrian winter peas as garden space becomes available
- (In the Lower South) There is still time to plant more carrots, winter radishes, beets, favas, short day onions, and peas

TO DO THIS MONTH CONTINUED

FRESH HARVEST

- arugula
- Asian greens
- asparagus beans
- beans
- beets and beet
  greens
- broccoli
- cabbage
- cantaloupes

- carrots
- cauliflower
- celeriac
- celery
- chard
- collards
- corn
- cowpeas
- cucumbers

- edamame
- eggplant
- horseradish
- hot peppers
- kohlrabi
- leeks
- lettuce
- mustards
- okra

- parsnips
- peanuts
- peppers
- potatoes
- pumpkins
- radishes
- raspberries
- rutabagas
- salsify

- scallions
- spinach
- sweet potatoes
- tomatoes
- turnips
- watermelons
- winter radishes
- winter squash
- zucchini

Check potatoes, onions, and garlic in storage

beds, mulching winter greens, and putting on protective coverings against the rapidly changing temperatures to come. Wherever you garden, bountiful harvests should remind you that the soil needs replenishing. Fall is the ideal time to work on your fertility and soil health. Composting, cover cropping, and mulching add to the bustling activity of the season.

Preparing the Garden for Winter

Fall weather makes working in the garden so easy. It's a good thing, too: there's plenty to do to prepare for winter. October is a good time to get a soil test if you haven't already done so. A recent soil test will let you know how to amend your soil, and which areas need the most attention.

Wait until spring to apply water-soluble, high-nitrogen fertilizers that break down quickly. Plants can't absorb these nutrients well at cold temperatures, so much of the value will be lost—possibly as runoff to contaminate streams or ground water. What a waste; it is better to wait and apply in spring.

Clean up crop debris. Garden hygiene is the attentive gardener's first defense against plant diseases. I don't mean washing your hands (although smokers *should* scrub their hands before handling any nightshade crops because of the chance of spreading tobacco mosaic virus); simply give your garden a thorough fall cleaning by removing any dead or diseased plant materials from the soil surface, as well as from any trellises, fences, or other structures.

Spread slow-working amendments. Apply dolomitic lime and other slow-release minerals like rock phosphate or bone meal as needed. They'll have time to break down and be incorporated into the soil so that they will be available when your plants need them in the spring.

And mulch! Apply 4–6 inches of organic mulch to any areas where you won't be planting a cover crop. I also like to layer black-and-white newspaper or cardboard underneath the mulch as an even stronger barrier against the weeds. This also helps prevent erosion and soil compaction.

Brown gold

Autumn leaves are one of the very best sources of organic matter for your garden. Leaves are packed with trace minerals that trees draw up from deep in the soil. When added to your garden, leaves feed earthworms and beneficial microbes. They lighten heavy soils and help sandy soils retain moisture. They make an attractive mulch in the herb garden. They're a fabulous source of carbon to balance the nitrogen in your compost pile. And they insulate tender plants from the cold.

First, shred up as many of them as you can. We don't have a shredder so I rake the leaves up into a pile and then drive over them a few times with the lawn mower. I have also tried putting them into a large trash barrel and using a string trimmer. Shredding leaves into smaller pieces does several good things. It increases the surface area, giving microbes many more places to work. It prevents the leaves from packing together into layers that won't let water or air penetrate. And it reduces the volume dramatically; ten bags of whole leaves become just one after shredding.

Once the leaves are shredded, I rake them up into

plastic trash bags and use them as mulch in my blueberry patch or add them to my compost pile. In time, shredded leaves left in a pile outside become leaf mold, which makes fabulous mulch. What's more, it does wonders for the soil, and looks good to boot.

Winter Cover Crops

Thick, lush stands of fall and winter cover crops are the greatest assurance of fabulous soil for next year. All cover crops, also called green manures or smother crops, add organic matter to the soil, which improves soil structure. Soil high in organic matter is better able to hold nutrients, has better aeration for plant roots, and has better drainage, while drying out less quickly. Some cover crops are organic-matter specialists, others mine the subsoil for nutrients, and still others naturally increase the available soil nitrogen.

To select a cover crop, consider which functions are your priorities, the time of year, and how long the cover crop will be in the ground. Cover crops are important tools throughout the year for filling in gaps between crops to prevent soil erosion, suppress weeds, and provide habitat for pollinators. The following are my favorites for planting in the Southeast.

Nitrogen fixers

Crimson and berseem clover. Plant six to eight weeks before the first frost date. Clovers can fix nitrogen in the soil and thus boost nitrogen for next spring's garden. Mow one or two times when about half of the crop is flowering. Allow the residue to decompose for at least two weeks before planting vegetables.

Hairy vetch. Plant six to eight weeks before the first frost date. This vine-like, vigorous, cold-tolerant, winter-hardy annual legume adds nitrogen and builds soil organic matter. Hairy vetch grows well in cereal grain mixtures and is an excellent spring weed suppressor.

Soybean and cowpeas. Plant in early to midsummer, between spring and fall crops. Mow before pods have formed or when pods are still green and have not matured. These legume family plants can fix nitrogen in the soil. They will die with the frost, leaving roots and tops to hold your soil.

Winter peas. Plant four to six weeks before the first frost. Sometimes called "black pea" and "field pea," it is a cool-season, annual legume with good, nitrogen-fixing capabilities. Usually planted with rye, oats, or barley to reduce the chance of winter kill. Cut or turn under at full bloom for maximum nitrogen.

Soil builders and subsoil looseners

Winter rye (cereal rye). Plant six weeks before the first frost date and up to two weeks after. A cold-hardy crop, rye will grow well into the spring. Rye increases soil organic matter as it decomposes. Mow one to two times when at least 12 inches tall, or when half of the crop has immature seed heads. Allow residue to decompose for at least three weeks after tilling in before planting vegetables.

Ryegrass. We sow ryegrass in late summer or early fall. This fast-growing crop tolerates flooding and does a great job "mopping up" after a crop. The plants readily absorb any leftover nitrogen in the soil, preventing it from running off. We sow ryegrass earlier than other winter cover crops, and often between vegetable crops.

The plants can become weedy, so be sure you have a very good system for killing the plants come spring.

Oats. Broadcast sow eight to ten weeks before the first frost date. Oats grow during the fall and die when cold weather rolls in. They form a surface mulch, increasing soil organic matter as they decay.

Sorghum-sudan grass hybrid. Plant in spring and summer, beginning after the soil has warmed and up until six weeks before first frost. This hybrid is unrivaled for adding organic matter to worn-out soils. These tall, fast-growing, heat-loving summer annual grasses can smother weeds, suppress some nematode species, and penetrate compacted subsoil if mowed once. It is easily killed by frost and left as a winter mulch.

Quick, warm-season cover crops

The following cover crops are excellent, fast-growing choices for filling gaps in your garden from spring through early fall. Prevent erosion, minimize runoff, and add organic matter to the soil. Mowing down these crops provides fuel for your compost pile and promotes additional root growth, so you'll add even more biomass to the soil.

The day length given in parantheses indicates the minimum number of growing days to allow for each crop. Count back from your average last frost date to make sure you have enough time before frost.

Buckwheat (35+ days) establishes quickly, suppresses weeds, and attracts pollinators. To promote extra biomass in the root systems, mow one to two times when half the crop is in flower and before hard seeds have formed. The plants are killed by frost, so don't plant too late in the fall.

Soybeans (60+ days) are very fast growing: they're the best choice for squeezing in a nitrogen-fixing legume cover crop before frost. Combine soybeans with Japanese millet for added biomass. When both are killed by your first hard frost, you can use the dead above-ground plant matter as winter mulch, ready to pull back for early spring planting. Avoid GMO soy by purchasing certified organic seed.

Cowpeas (70+ days) are another good nitrogen-fixing summer cover crop. The dense plants suppress weeds and improve the texture of poor, acid soils. For the largest nitrogen boost, work the plants into the soil to decompose when the leaves are still green. We like to undersow cowpeas between sweet corn plants when the corn seedlings are four to six weeks old: this keeps down the weeds and may help boost available nitrogen for the corn.

Japanese millet (60+ days), a fast-growing, frost-tender cover crop, can provide considerable biomass and combines well with soy. Japanese millet tolerates both drought and wet soil. Promote root growth and feed your compost pile by mowing every 40 days until the plants are killed by frost.

How to plant fall cover crops

Cover crops can be planted in any empty garden bed throughout the year or sown beneath fall cabbage, broccoli, and other plantings in the fall. Thoroughly weed the area before planting or prepare a fine seedbed in empty areas. Then scatter cover crop seed thickly. Using a rake or a hand tool, scratch seeds into the top half inch of soil and pat the soil down gently to secure them. Water the seeds in well or wait for rain in the fall. Cover crop seeds are available at many garden stores as well as online through seed companies.

Cover crops need very little maintenance during winter and only slightly more attention in the summer. Water during long dry spells and remove the odd large weed before it sets seed.

Winter cover crops in spring

In late winter or early spring, it's time to turn "green manure" into the soil. First, mow the crop and let it dry out for a week or two. Then work the crop into the soil with a garden tiller or by hand with a shovel or pitchfork. I often leave the crop as a surface mulch that will decompose over time and transplant directly into the mulch. This works well with grain-type cover crops like rye and oats or mixtures of rye and vetch.

Edible cover crops

Traditional gardeners in the Southeast always plant a big bed of winter greens (turnips, mustards, kale, and collards) to keep the garden covered and provide fresh eating until spring. Plant this beautiful cover crop in August or September to build organic matter and provide healthy meals all winter long. Try a mixture of the old southern favorites and contemporary choices like seven top turnip, lacinato kale, red Russian kale, southern giant curled mustard greens, and tatsoi.

If you are in the Upper South or in the mountains, cover your edible greens with row cover or plant in a cold frame for winter harvests. Left uncovered in cold winters, the leaves will be too damaged for good eating, but you'll have fresh new growth in early spring if winter lows aren't too bad.

GROWING GREAT GARLIC, SHALLOTS, AND PERENNIAL ONIONS

Garlic, shallots, and perennial onions are allium-family crops that are grown from bulbs or cloves, rather than from seed. These are clones of the parent plant, so there's no need to worry about isolation distance or minimum population size. Once you start growing these crops, saving seed is as easy as harvesting for the kitchen.

Plant garlic and perennial onions in the mid-fall for best yields. However, don't wait until fall to purchase seed stock: it's often worthwhile to plan ahead and order the spring before, at the same time you order seeds. The bulbs or cloves generally ship in the fall, in time for planting. At Southern Exposure, we often sell out of many varieties well in advance of fall, so we encourage pre-orders. Perennial onions are still a specialty item, and they can be impossible to find come fall.

Choose a garden site that gets plenty of sun, and provide rich soil with good drainage. It's possible to grow these crops in heavy soil, but the drainage should be improved prior to planting with the addition of organic matter or compost and making raised beds. Get your soil tested and add lime or other organic amendments as needed.

Each garlic clove you plant will produce a single bulb (which may contain up to 20 cloves). Perennial onions, which include shallots, multiplier onions, potato onions, and walking onions, produce a cluster of bulbs from each individual bulb you plant. See the garlic section of the Edibles A to Z for specific growing and harvesting instructions. We'll discuss perennial onions at length here, since the A to Z will primarily cover bulbing onions, which are grown from seed.

Perennial onions should be planted deep enough so that there is ½–1 inch of soil over the top of the bulbs. This depth is adequate for most winters, but deeper planting is recommended for mountainous areas. When planting in intensive raised beds, space your rows 12 inches apart. Large bulbs (3- to 4-inch diameter) should be planted a minimum of 6–8 inches apart, depending on bulb size. Smaller bulbs (½- to 2-inch diameter) should be planted 4–6 inches apart, depending on bulb size.

Our best planting time for garlic and perennial onions in central Virginia is mid-October to mid-November. Check with your extension service or talk to local experienced gardeners to find out the preferred time to plant in your area—they can be planted as late as mid-December further south.

Garlic and perennial onions grow well planted with other flowers and vegetables in well-maintained small or square-foot gardens. They can also be grown in large containers. Keep the plants free of weeds throughout the growing season and make sure they get an inch of water weekly until two to three weeks before harvest.

Perennial onions are ready to harvest when about half of the plants have tops that have flopped over. Bring them under cover in a cool, well-ventilated place to "cure" (that is, dry for storage). Spread them out on a tarp or hang them for two to three weeks. This is very similar to harvesting garlic, which is ready when there are only six green leaves remaining on each plant and the rest have turned brown. Cure in the same way as perennial onions. For all bulbs, you can speed dry by gently removing dirt from the surface—but don't wash them and don't damage the fragile wrappers. Wait until the tops have fully dried (about one to two weeks of curing) before very carefully wiping off the dirt with a soft cloth or old toothbrush.

Your own homegrown garlic and perennial onion bulbs are ready for kitchen use as soon as they're dry. They'll also keep in storage in a well-ventilated pantry or hung in the kitchen through summer and early fall, until it's time to replant.

·NOVEMBER·

END OF HURRICANE SEASON

Winter in the Southeast can be really fickle. In the mountains and Upper South, a summer-like day may be followed by snow the next. Temperatures are more moderate in the Lower South, but rapid temperature swings are not uncommon. Hurricane season officially ends in November, and severe weather is rare this late in the year, but storm warnings should still be heeded.

Gardeners in the Lower South are blessed with enough light to keep planting, at a slow pace, all winter: at least 10 hours of daylight for most of the winter. Late fall is the best season for growing cool-weather crops and realizing dreams of garden-fresh broccoli, frost-touched collards, crisp, tender greens, and sweet winter carrots.

TO DO THIS MONTH

PLAN, PREPARE, AND MAINTAIN

- Make notes of late plantings and harvest
- Get soil tested if not already done
- Consider plans for next year as you select winter cover crops
- Set up low tunnels and cold frames for overwintered greens
- Lay out row covers and hoops for quick response to frosts
- Check and use tomatoes and peppers brought indoors to ripen
- Finish spreading lime if soil test indicates the need
- Add needed amendments before mulching any empty beds that will not be cover cropped
- Harvest frost-sweetened kale, cabbage, spinach, and other brassica greens
- Monitor temperature in cold frames on sunny days and open as necessary
- Sheet mulch "lasagna style" to expand the garden if desired
- Cover lettuce, spinach ("burns" below 10°F), celery, zucchini, squash, and Chinese cabbage using hoops
- Mulch thickly, cover with row cover, or finish harvesting all the carrots (hardy to 12°F), beets, celeriac, kohlrabi, turnips, rutabagas (okay to 20°F), and winter radish (hardy to 20°F); wash and store
- Cut asparagus tops with weed whackers or machetes, and remove all ferns
- Cut fall raspberry canes (after leaves have dropped) to the ground with pruners
- Weed and mulch matted row style strawberries (wait to fertilize in the spring)

SOW AND PLANT

- Sow rye or wheat cover crop in empty garden beds not needed for early planting
- (In the Lower South) There's still time to sow more lettuce, kale, spinach, radish, arugula, and other hardy greens
- (In the Lower South) Plant annual row strawberries if you haven't already planted them in October
- Sow short-day onions to overwinter in cold frame
- Plant garlic, shallots, and perennial onions if not done in October
- Free trapped garlic shoots from over-thick mulch, when 50 percent have emerged.
- Weed, fertilize, and mulch grapes, rhubarb, blueberries, asparagus, and raspberries; take vine cuttings and transplant new plants if needed

FRESH HARVEST

- arugula
- Asian greens
- broccoli
- Brussels sprouts
- cabbage
- cauliflower
- carrots
- celery
- cilantro
- chard
- collards
- herbs
- kale
- leeks
- lettuce
- rutabaga
- parsnip
- peppers
- scallions
- southern peas
- summer squash
- spinach
- tomatoes
- turnips

Check garlic, onions, potatoes, sweet potatoes, and winter squash in storage

In the Upper South, we take a rest from planting while the ground is frozen or too wet to work, but we are still active in the garden, tending and harvesting the crops we planted earlier in the fall. When I look out at all the beds of winter roots, broccoli, Brussels sprouts, lettuce, leeks, and greens, it seems like more than we can eat. I have to remind myself, "What you see is what you get"—we'll resume planting when the days start to lengthen in mid-February, but until then our Virginia gardens are our outdoor pantry. Mulching is key; all of our crops and empty beds are well-mulched or covered. Careful attention to proper harvesting, maintenance, and protection is essential for bountiful harvest throughout winter.

Winter Garden Awareness

Preparation for arctic cold fronts and tropical storms begins with choosing the right site for the winter garden. You can give your plants the best chance of surviving weather's worst onslaughts by providing excellent drainage and protection from the harshest winds. Avoid local cool-air pockets prone to hard frosts.

Gardeners throughout the Southeast can enjoy winter greens, roots, salads, and brassicas. Where frosts come very late in the year, many will still be harvesting fall-planted tomatoes, peppers, and other tender crops through the holidays.

Extra Cover Needed

When the temperature drops rapidly, mulch is what counts. You should have already applied a thick layer of organic mulch last month while cleaning up the garden. This month, keep extra bags of shredded leaves, bales of hay, and row cover on hand to get through short periods of extreme weather. We sometimes cover tender plants with evergreen boughs and pile leaves up right over the plants.

Floating row cover or tarps can also cover plants or hold the fluffy mulch in place through an emergency until normal temperatures return. Row cover can rest directly on plants, but the tips of greens may be damaged during hard frosts if they touch the row cover. Put row cover on plants before frost starts—it can freeze to the ground, metal, and itself, and will tear easily and be hard to unfold without damaging it if it's already frozen. Row cover will last for two to four years if stored dry and out of sunlight when not in use. To keep row cover from blowing off, use ground staples, or heavy sticks, or just bury the edges of the row cover with garden soil.

When I lived in Canada, snow was a helpful, warming blanket that insulated my winter garden from the worst weather. Not so the wet, fleeting snow of the Southeast. It is too heavy and breaks the plants, causing more damage than the cold. So we use hoops with our row cover for tall plants like broccoli or blueberry bushes, and we try to brush the snow off these plants before it melts into a heavy, icy mess.

We like to make low tunnels using #9 wire every 4 feet or pre-cut 76-inch commercial hoops made from #10 wire for many of our winter greens. We start with spun polyester row cover and sometimes add an extra layer of slitted row plastic when the temperature is consistently cold in December (see the next chapter for details on how to make a low tunnel). On really warm days you may need to pull up one side for additional venting. I find these low tunnels really help maintain the quality of lettuce, broccoli, and Brussels sprouts in our Virginia garden, giving me bragging rights at both Thanksgiving and Christmas dinners.

Planting the winter garden in a naturally sheltered area protects plants from drying out when the wind pulls water out of the leaves and stems. Roots aren't able to take up water from frozen ground, so the winter garden is very susceptible to being dried out by wind. Ample winter rain usually keeps plants well hydrated, but if it is unseasonably dry make sure to keep your winter garden watered.

Harvesting the Winter Garden

Growth slows to a halt by mid-December, so we time our fall gardens to be mature by late November. Knowing what to harvest for indoor storage and what can be left in the "outdoor pantry" is a bit of an art. Some fast-growing vegetables like mizuna, pak choi, and turnips are best quality when harvested before hard frosts. Cold-hardy greens such as spinach, kale and arugula can be harvested throughout the winter if they have grown large enough in the fall. Later plantings of cold-hardy greens can begin the winter half grown. While not large enough for winter eating, these late plantings can survive the winter (with adequate protection) to provide the earliest spring harvests. Sauerkraut and kimchee are traditional fall ferments—not only are these stable, space-saving storage solutions for fall brassicas, fall also provides the cool weather that lets you easily make these on your countertop without much fuss.

We prefer to bring our root vegetables indoors to store, lest we have critter damage when we dig them up come spring thaw. Our winters are warm enough that we have to worry about more pest activity than gardeners in the Northeast. If you have space to store root crops inside, that's your safest choice. If you don't, mulch them well and cover them, and harvest as needed. Do bring in any overwintered root crops by March or earlier, before they begin flowering, which causes the roots to be woody and tasteless.

Carrots are our favorite winter root crop. It is extraordinary how much sweeter they are when maturing in cold weather. Apply 4–6 inches of mulch to prevent the roots from freezing and to allow harvest as needed. Break off the tops when harvesting carrots, parsnips, and other root crops so that the greens don't regrow and cause the roots to shrivel. Rinse off dirt before storing. Store roots in your refrigerator crisper for best quality. For rutabagas, radishes, and turnips, gently feel in the dirt with your fingertips to find the plants big enough to pull, and leave the little ones to continue growing. Try to harvest radishes before the first hard freeze. They're delicious with frosts, but cannot take deep soil freezes.

If you have limited garden space, greens are the most productive crop for winter growing. Harvest thinnings as the plants grow. For greens (not roots), when the plants have leaves at least 1½ inches long, thin the rows so there is a strong plant every 6 inches. Once the plants have matured and you've thinned to their final spacing, only harvest the outer leaves. The small, young inner leaves will replace them. Harvest no more than 30 percent of each plant every 10 days in mild weather; wait longer if the weather is harsh. The morning after a frost, don't harvest plants while they're still frozen—wait for the temperature to rise above freezing and for the plants to thaw out before harvesting.

Winter greens start to bolt as the weather gets warmer. Arugula is usually the first to bolt, often in February, and the other greens follow suit by April. For the best flavor, finish harvesting each crop before it begins to bolt. In reality, this means you can bring in what remains of the crop as soon as you see the first flowering stalks, or break off the first few and cross your fingers. I always try to leave some plants to flower as early spring forage for pollinators, as this is a time of year when flowers can be rare. Arugula flowers and the flowers of many other mustard greens are tasty and attractive.

SKILL SET

A LAZY, NO-DIG "LASAGNA" GARDEN BED

To expand or enrich your garden without tilling or digging, consider making a lasagna bed. This modern version of sheet mulching lets you build garden soil in place by adding layers of organic material that will cook over a few months and result in rich, fluffy soil.

One of the reasons that this method has become so popular is that it is easy. You build the bed on top of the grass or weeds just where you want the new bed. If you have crabgrass or quack grass, or other tenacious perennial weeds, you'll want to dig them out before starting, or be prepared to battle with those same weeds for years to come.

The first layer you put down, "the foundation layer," can be layered brown corrugated cardboard or layered stacks of six sheets of newspaper overlapped. My experience is that it is best to go with cardboard and use a double layer over the whole area, lest our vigorous weeds laugh at you. Next, you wet this layer thoroughly to keep it in place and get the decomposition going. The weeds and grass will break down quickly because they are smothered and deprived of light by the cardboard and other layers above it. This cardboard layer also makes a dark, moist place to attract earthworms, who will loosen the soil as they move through it.

You build the beds by adding alternate layer of green and brown material, using anything you would put in a compost pile. The possibilities are endless: one friend even used a cotton futon mattress as a layer in an herb bed and an old wool rug for another. You can use any organic materials: shredded leaves, grass clippings, vegetable scraps, even weeds. See the list of organic materials for making compost in the March chapter. Building a lasagna bed uses a lot of organic material, so it is a good idea to gather materials before starting. Fall is an easy time to start because there are so many dead leaves readily available.

STEPS

1 Start by mowing or trampling down existing vegetation (consider removing quack grass or crabgrass).

2 Layout the area of the bed. Make it narrow enough to easily reach the center (about 4 feet).

3 Cover the area completely with overlapping layers of brown cardboard (two layers is good).

4 Thoroughly wet down the base layer.

5 Add alternating layers of green and brown organic material until the bed is at least 24 inches high (generally add 3 inches of brown per 1 inch of green).

6 Use a sprinkler or seasonal rain shower to thoroughly wet down the pile.

7 Optionally cover the pile with 2–3 inches of finished compost or shredded leaves (some people cover the pile with a tarp to keep in moisture and reduce nutrient run off).

8 By spring, you should be able to directly plant into your new bed.

REST AND REFLECTION

In December, we're at the peak of the "Persephone Days," when light levels are so low that plant growth almost stops. Both garden and gardener can take a much-needed rest. For the next few months, most of our fresh harvests will be the result of careful planning and planting in July through September. On clear, sunny days, I go outside to catch a little warmth and vitamin D while giving our perennials some much-needed pruning and mulching. This is my favorite time to reflect on the season past, read great garden books, and dream of that most beautiful garden of all, the one that grows in my mind!

TO DO THIS MONTH

PLAN, PREPARE, AND MAINTAIN

- Make notes about problems and successes as you finish preparing the garden for winter
- Finish garden cleanup—clean and oil shovels, rakes, hoes, trowels, and other metal tools
- Service your rototiller now rather than during the spring rush
- Make sure your row cover is secure on overwintered crops
- Weed and mulch the strawberries, raspberries, and blackberries
- Prune grapevines now if they are dormant (when they lose their leaves); use the prunings for holiday wreaths
- Transplant new blueberries if needed—leaves are one of the best mulches for blueberry bushes; you can shred them by running over them with a mower
- Parsnips, turnips, beets, and carrots can be dug and stored in the fridge
- Check greenhouses and cold frames daily—they heat up quickly on sunny days

SOW AND PLANT

- This is the last chance to plant potato onions in most areas
- (In the Lower South) Sow short-day bulbing onions if you haven't already
- Plant more carrots, beets, and hardy greens.
- Look out for pests such as aphids, caterpillars, snails, and slugs in the garden

FRESH HARVEST

- arugula
- beets
- cabbage
- carrots
- celeriac
- celery
- Chinese cabbage
- cilantro
- collards
- kale
- kohlrabi
- leeks
- lettuce
- mustard greens
- onions
- parsley
- parsley
- parsnips
- radishes
- rosemary
- rutabaga
- salsify
- spinach
- thyme
- turnips

Check garlic, onions, potatoes, sweet potatoes, kohlrabi, and winter squash in storage

Herbs, Preserves, and Gifts from the Garden

The holidays are a time for giving, but who needs another garden stone? Sharing your time, gardening knowledge, and the bounty of your gardens are great ways to give gardeners on your list something special.

- Gift the gardeners or the gardeners-to-be in your life with gift certificates to your favorite local nursery or mail-order garden seed company. Include a catalog with your gift to help with inspiration.

- Herbal jams and jellies make wonderful, tasty, and unusual gifts. Use the frozen fruits and cubes of fresh herbs from last summer (see the August chapter for freezing instructions). You can also use your stored winter squash to make delicious pumpkin-butter gifts. A book or a copy of your recipe is a nice touch.

- The seeds that you saved in September and October make lovely homegrown seed packets. Include growing instructions and a recipe. This is a great holiday project to do with kids—both saving the seeds and making the packets.

- You can make handmade wreaths from the branches and stems that you gather as you prune and clean up your garden for winter. Decorate them with unusual "flowers," such as garlic bulbs, perennial onions, sprigs of rosemary or sage, lavender leaves, dried okra pods, or whatever takes your fancy.

- Offer a gift certificate of your time. You can help a new gardener get started or an aging gardener to finish a difficult task. I treasure the time I can spend in the garden with friends.

- Artfully arrange a basket of fresh winter greens, lettuces, stored squash, sweet potatoes, and dried flowers to make a unique hostess gift (much healthier than the Christmas cookies I used to bring my friends).

- Jars of homemade pickles, gussied up with recipes and pretty cloth swatches, make lovely gifts.

- Gorgeous glass bottles of herbal vinegars make tasty gifts. There's still time to infuse vinegar with thyme, rosemary, or other herbs. Using fresh herbs, I loosely fill the jar about halfway with the herbs, then pour the vinegar over, and let it sit for up to a week. Then strain the vinegar into a fancy-looking small-mouth bottle and add a few sprigs of fresh herbs for decoration. Label it nicely and tie a ribbon around the top.

- If I've grown enough dried beans, I'll make soup mixes in glass jars, with colorful layers of dried beans, dehydrated garlic or onions, and herbs, along with a recipe for a simple one pot meal. I actually have a collection of old-fashioned glass-topped mason jars just for this purpose, but a modern mason jar will do just fine.

- Share your love of garlic with friends and family by arranging a garlic sampler basket, using a pretty assortment of different, labeled bulbs. Even if your friends don't have space to plant them all, they can enjoy the culinary adventure of comparing the different varieties. Include a book on growing garlic for new gardeners.

- Make baskets from willow or grapevine cuttings.

GARDEN DREAMS: INSPIRING GARDENING BOOKS

December is when I indulge in books I didn't have time for earlier. The kind of read that inspires me not only to garden, but to work for a more environmentally sustainable and just world, starting in my own back-yard. Attending winter agricultural conferences and gardening workshops is another fun way to learn new gardening skills and maybe even get your new garden book autographed by the author. Some of my favorites for the southern gardener are:

The Seed Underground
Janisse Ray

I am an avid seed saver, but this book inspires me to do even more. Ray is a Georgia naturalist and environmen-talist best known for *Ecology of a Cracker Childhood*. She's sometimes called the Rachel Carson of the South. In *The Seed Underground*, Ray shares the profound stories of ordinary gardeners saving time-honored, open-pollinated plant varieties like old time Tennessee muskmelon and Long County Longhorn okra—varieties that will be lost if people don't grow, save, and swap the seeds.

A Southern Garden
Elizabeth Lawrence

Elizabeth Lawrence takes you through a year in the middle south and leaves you wanting to be out there in your garden, enjoying it in every season. Her table of bloom dates for over 800 flowering plants helps you welcome pollinators all year. Her writing feels just like a most knowledgeable friend sharing everything she knows. Her gardens in Charlotte are a National Historic site.

The Southern Living Garden Book
edited by Steve Bender

Although not focused on food growing, this book will save you money and the heartache, by helping you choose the flowers, trees, and insectary plants that enjoy our sultry summers.

Animal, Vegetable, Miracle: A Year of Food Life
Barbara Kingsolver, Steven Hopp, and Camille Kingsolver

I recommend this book to all of our farm interns. The story of one family and a year in which they made every attempt to eat food produced locally is a family adventure shedding light on our food system, our beliefs, life in Appalachian Virginia, and the trials and successes of living locally. Read it and heed the call to action.

A Rich Spot of Earth: Thomas Jefferson's Revolutionary Garden at Monticello
Peter Hatch

I never fail to find inspiration for my own gardens in the work of Thomas Jefferson at Monticello. Peter Hatch, who led the restoration of the gardens at Monticello, takes us on a tour of the gardens' history, from the first artichokes and asparagus planted in 1770 through the horticultural experi-ments of Jefferson's retirement years.

Vermicomposting

Worm composting or "vermicomposting" lets you make compost quickly and efficiently indoors. Making compost is one of the best things you can do for your garden, but during the cool winter months your outdoor pile slows to a halt. Starting a worm bin indoors is a great way to make excellent compost during winter and a chance to introduce any young gardeners in your household to the role of earthworms in the garden.

There is a wide range of worm bins on the market. They work great, but can be pricey. Making your own lowers your cost and can be a fun project. Use a dark-colored plastic storage container or tote, or a wooden box. Use an awl or drill to make small holes in the upper half of the sides to let air in. To keep the worms' living conditions moist but well drained, put in a divider or "floor" that sits a couple of inches off the bottom. A loose cover keeps flies and light out and worms and moisture in.

To start your little worm farm, fill the bin with moistened, shredded newspaper, cardboard (cheap and easy to find), or coir (coconut fiber, available from garden supply stores, catalogs, or online). Mix in a handful or two of garden soil and some crushed eggshells to help the worms break down their food. Make sure the mix is as damp as a wrung-out sponge, rather than wet.

Introduce a pound or so of composting worms or red wigglers (*Eisenia fetida*) from a garden center, bait shop, or online. Or get them free from a friend with a healthy worm bin. Most commercially available worms are species that live only in manure or very rich soil and will not survive in average garden soil.

Feed your worms well-chopped vegetable matter mixed with a bit of water. Bury your scraps at least 6 inches deep to avoid fruit flies and unpleasant orders. Soft foods in small amounts are best for the first few days. When the worms have multiplied, you can increase the amount of food. For faster composting, run the food through a blender, since worms don't have teeth to tear off large chunks. Think of worms as vegetarians and stay away from meat, dairy, and oily wastes. If there's a bad smell, your bin may be too wet, or may not be getting enough air, or you may be adding too much food. It will take a few weeks for your worms to adjust and start to work efficiently. Be patient and pay some attention. After about 60 days, your bin should be full of rich compost.

Harvest your compost when most of the bedding looks like coffee grounds and smells like good soil. To harvest, first push the compost to one side of the bin. Add new bedding to the empty side. For the next few days, place all new food scraps in the side with new bedding. The worms will migrate to the side with the new bedding and food scraps. Now you can remove the finished compost and add new bedding in its place. Your rich worm castings are ready for using in the garden or adding to potting mix as needed.

READING GARDEN CATALOGS

Garden catalogs seem to start coming in earlier each year. By Christmas, the pile is getting high and the urge to order seeds is getting stronger. Have you noticed that most seed catalogs come from companies in the Northeast and California? Read on for hints on how to make the best choices for your southeastern garden.

Know where the seed company is located—check their address and find out where their trial gardens are located. Some companies have several trial gardens, but they're usually in the same place as the company's offices. When a catalog from up north says "full sun," be careful to check my recommendations in the Edibles A to Z section of this book and ask local gardeners. Many plants prefer afternoon shade in the Southeast, especially in the heat of summer. Crops often take longer to mature up north, so don't trust the "days to maturity" dates in northern catalogs.

Even though it's best to buy from regional companies, don't be afraid to check out what they're selling up north. I find that for our mild winters, many of the cool-season varieties developed in the Pacific Northwest do really well. California and the Southwest have much drier climates, but from there we can find great heat-tolerance and also some really interesting Asian vegetables. Our friends to the Northeast are doing great breeding work for disease resistance. Even though they're not specifically being adapted to the Southeast, we often give things a try.

Select varieties with excellent pest and disease resistances. Sometimes these are listed as codes in seed catalogs. Be sure to look at the catalog key to understand these codes, because they vary by company, but some of them are universal. VFN indicates resistance to Verticillium wilt, Fusarium wilt, and nematodes. VF, also common, indicates resistance to just the first two. Look for varieties that come out of land grant university breeding programs in southeastern universities. Some of our favorite tomatoes have come out of the University of Florida (Tropic and Neptune) and the University of Arkansas (Ozark Pink). The nematode-resistant bell peppers (Carolina Wonder and Charleston Bell) developed in South Carolina at the USDA experimental station are godsends for many southern gardeners.

For warm-season crops look for words like "heat tolerant," "drought resistant," and "good pollination in heat." For cool-season vegetables, look for "bolt resistant," "long holding," and, especially for spring plantings, "early." A short number of days to maturity is just one measure of earliness; being able to grow well in cool, low-light conditions is just as important for having an early harvest.

Those in the Lower South who plant warm-season crops in spring and fall, taking a garden break during the dog days of summer, should look for quick-maturing and early varieties. You might not be able grow the really large long-season tomatoes, but you can grow two reliable crops of lovely, medium-sized slicers on either side of the hot rest period.

EDIBLES
A TO Z

UPPER SOUTH
PLANTING AND HARVESTING CHART

■ Planting
■ Harvesting

These charts show the planting and harvesting periods for annual plants grown in an open garden without additional protection. Exact planting dates will vary depending on the year and your microclimate.

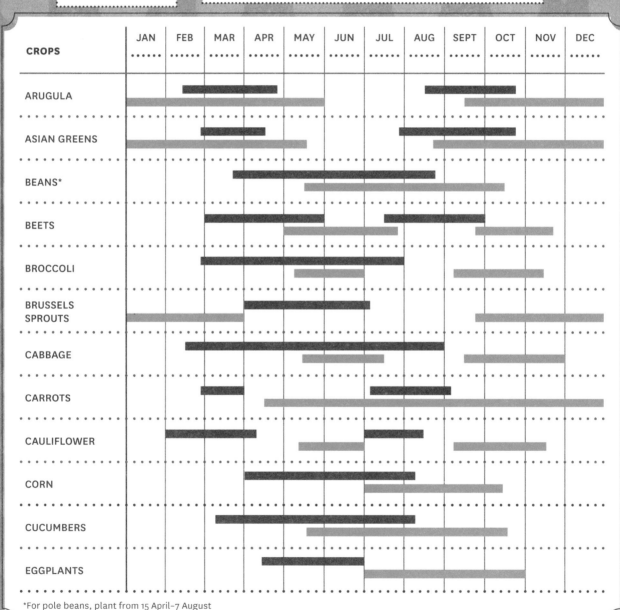

CROPS	JAN	FEB	MAR	APR	MAY	JUN	JUL	AUG	SEPT	OCT	NOV	DEC
ARUGULA												
ASIAN GREENS												
BEANS*												
BEETS												
BROCCOLI												
BRUSSELS SPROUTS												
CABBAGE												
CARROTS												
CAULIFLOWER												
CORN												
CUCUMBERS												
EGGPLANTS												

*For pole beans, plant from 15 April–7 August

CROPS	JAN	FEB	MAR	APR	MAY	JUN	JUL	AUG	SEPT	OCT	NOV	DEC
FAVA BEANS**		▓	▓			░						
GARLIC					░					▓	▓	
KOHLRABI			▓	▓	░	░	▓	▓	▓	░		
LETTUCE	░	░	▓	▓	░	░	░	▓	▓	░	░	░
LIMA BEANS				▓	▓	▓	▓░	░	░	░	░	
MELONS				▓	▓	▓░	░	░	░	░		
MUSTARDS	░	░	▓	▓	░	░		▓	▓	░	░	░
OKRA				▓	▓	▓	▓░	░	░	░		
ONIONS		▓	▓			░	░	░	▓	░	░	░
PARSNIPS	░	░	▓	▓							░	░
PEAS		▓	▓	▓	░		▓	▓	░			
PEPPERS				▓	▓	▓	▓░	░	░	░		
POTATOES			▓	▓	▓	▓	▓░					
RADISHES			▓	▓	░			▓	▓	▓░	░	
RUNNER BEANS			▓		░	░	▓	▓	░	░		

**One harvest only

Planting
Harvesting

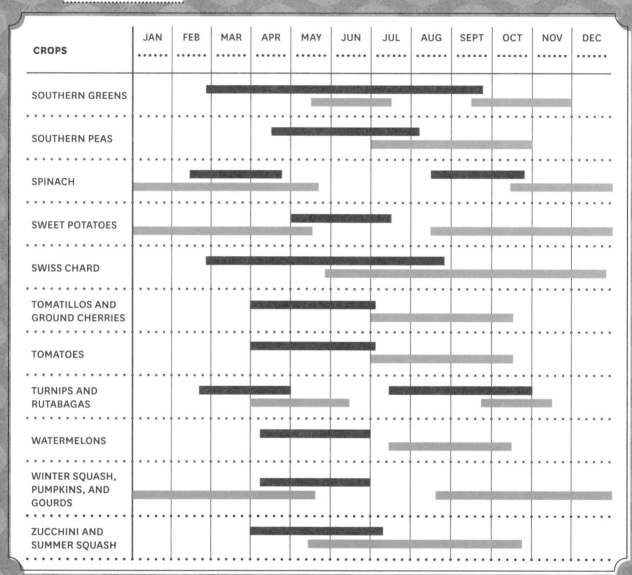

CROPS	JAN	FEB	MAR	APR	MAY	JUN	JUL	AUG	SEPT	OCT	NOV	DEC
SOUTHERN GREENS												
SOUTHERN PEAS												
SPINACH												
SWEET POTATOES												
SWISS CHARD												
TOMATILLOS AND GROUND CHERRIES												
TOMATOES												
TURNIPS AND RUTABAGAS												
WATERMELONS												
WINTER SQUASH, PUMPKINS, AND GOURDS												
ZUCCHINI AND SUMMER SQUASH												

In coastal regions, milder weather generally allows planting two to four weeks earlier in spring and later in fall. Mountain gardeners will need to delay spring plantings by up to four weeks, but can extend cool-weather crops well into summer. Additionally, where winters are severe the fall garden should be planted toward the early end of these ranges to ensure adequate growth for surviving the cold.

LOWER SOUTH
PLANTING AND HARVESTING CHART

Planting
Harvesting

These charts show the planting and harvesting periods for annual plants grown in an open garden without additional protection. Exact planting dates will vary depending on the year and your microclimate.

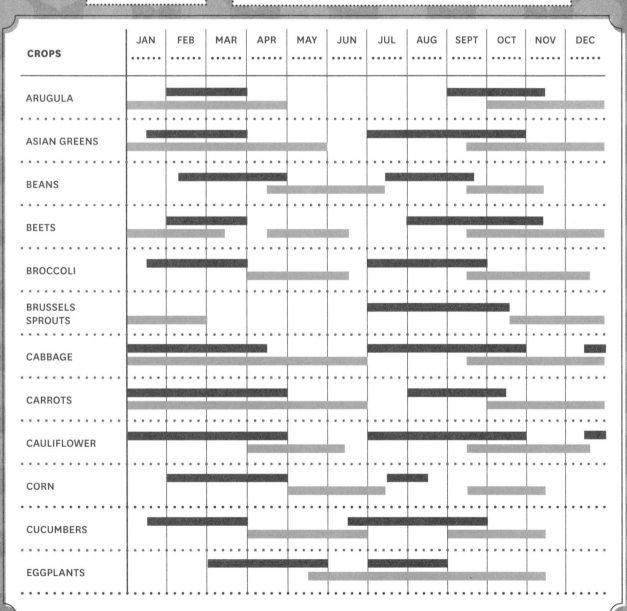

CROPS	JAN	FEB	MAR	APR	MAY	JUN	JUL	AUG	SEPT	OCT	NOV	DEC
ARUGULA												
ASIAN GREENS												
BEANS												
BEETS												
BROCCOLI												
BRUSSELS SPROUTS												
CABBAGE												
CARROTS												
CAULIFLOWER												
CORN												
CUCUMBERS												
EGGPLANTS												

- ■ Planting
- ▬ Harvesting

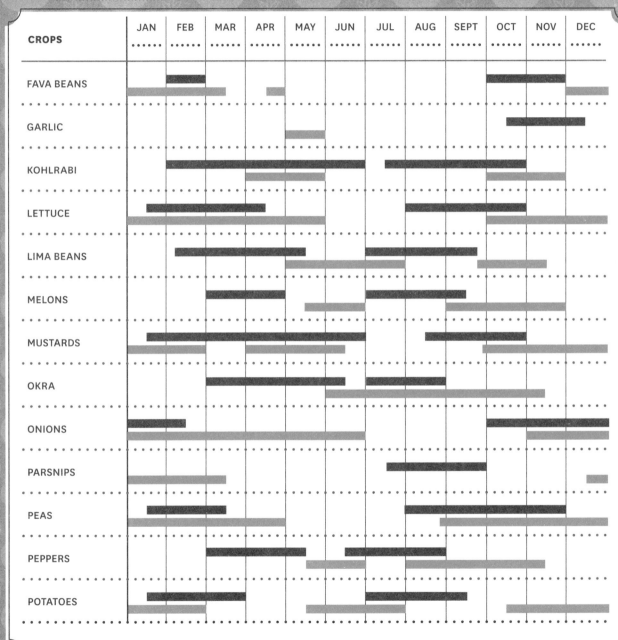

CROPS	JAN	FEB	MAR	APR	MAY	JUN	JUL	AUG	SEPT	OCT	NOV	DEC
FAVA BEANS	H	P	H	H						P	P	H
GARLIC					H					P	P	
KOHLRABI			P	P	P	P	P	P	P	P		
LETTUCE	H	P	P	P	H	H	H	P	P	PH	H	H
LIMA BEANS			P	P	P/H	H	P/H	P/H		H	H	
MELONS			P	P		H	P	P	H	H		
MUSTARDS	H	P	P	P	H			P	P	PH	H	H
OKRA			P	P	P	H	P/H	P/H	H	H		
ONIONS	P/H	P/H	H	H	H	H	H	H	H	PH	PH	PH
PARSNIPS	H	H	H				P	P				H
PEAS		P	P					P	P/H	H	H	
PEPPERS			P	P	H	P/H	P/H	P/H	H	H		
POTATOES		P	P		H	H	P	P	H	H	H	

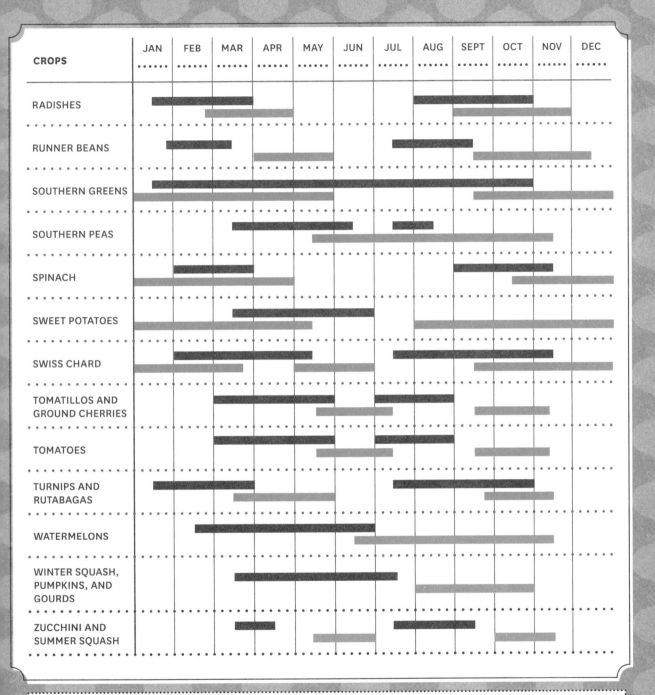

In coastal regions, milder weather generally allows planting two to four weeks earlier in spring and later in fall. Mountain gardeners will need to delay spring plantings by up to four weeks, but can extend cool-weather crops well into summer. Additionally, where winters are severe the fall garden should be planted toward the early end of these ranges to ensure adequate growth for surviving the cold.

Artichokes

Artichokes are one of the most unusual and delicious vegetables. As artichokes don't handle extreme heat and cold, it's best to treat them as annuals in most of the Southeast. Thomas Jefferson grew artichokes at Monticello and modern-day farmers in Texas are successfully growing them for market. If you have enough space for the large, attractive plants, you can have you own garden-fresh "baby chokes."

GROWING Plant in full sun to partial shade. Artichokes thrive in fertile, well-drained soil. Start seedlings in the fall to overwinter in a cold frame, or indoors in spring at least two months before the last frost. Excellent drainage is essential for success with fall sowing or overwintering artichoke plants. Sow seeds ¼ inch deep and ½ inch apart. Keep warm until the seeds sprout, then move to a cooler area. The plants need eight to ten days at 50°F or less to initiate buds. Transplant to 3- to 4-inch pots. Two weeks before the last frost, plant outside 2–4 feet apart in rows 3–4 feet apart. Use spun polyester row cover to protect from frost. Use mulch to keep the roots cool and retain even soil moisture. One frustrated gardener in north Florida determined to have homegrown artichokes trimmed back his plants, dug up the roots, and stored them in an extra refrigerator over the summer; he then replanted the roots in fall and reported to me that he was getting lots of artichokes the following spring.

HARVESTING Cut the stems 1½ inches below the bud when they reach full size, but before the bracts open.

Homegrown artichokes are often small and tender, perfect for eating whole. Harvest is generally early to midsummer.

VARIETIES **Tavor** (95 days) and other **Imperial Star** (85 to 95 days) varieties are bred to produce in one season and are excellent choices for the Southeast. Many gardeners in the Lower South have success with the old standard **Green Globe** (90 days) and purple-tinted **Violetta** (95 days), as well as the Imperial Star types planted in fall in a cold frame or other sheltered place and transplanted in early spring. Look for new annual varieties selected for the Southeast by breeders developing crops for the growing local-foods specialty market.

SEED SAVING Cut flower heads when they are completely open and beginning to show their white seed plumes. Separate seeds from fuzz. Place seeds in a dry location, away from direct sunlight, until dry and brittle. Store in a glass jar in a cool dry place.

Arugula

Zesty arugula, with its sharp, peppery leaves, has taken the Southeast by storm, moving from upscale restaurants in Atlanta and DC to gardens all over the region. This cool-season native of the Mediterranean is a perfect addition to the winter garden. Greens past their prime can be steamed or blended fresh with garlic and olive oil for a deliciously different take on pesto.

GROWING Arugula thrives in cooler weather, so it can be harvested all winter. Light mulch or row cover may be needed at higher elevations and in the Upper South. Loose, rich, moist soil keeps plants growing quickly from seed to plate in four weeks. Sow seeds ¼ inch deep, 1 inch apart, in rows 12–16 inches apart starting in early spring. Plant successions every two to three weeks until the weather starts to get hot. In the late spring and early summer, choose a partially shaded location. Resume succession plantings in early fall for delicious greens all winter. Row cover is not necessary for growing arugula but it can be used to maintain higher leaf quality during the winter.

HARVESTING Harvest leaves regularly while they are still young and tender, at 2–3 inches. Leave the center growing points intact for future harvest. Arugula flowers are tasty additions to salads early in the spring. Leave a few plants to feed the beneficial insects and self sow for surprise arugula plants come fall.

VARIETIES There are two main types of open-pollinated arugula. The smooth-leaved Italian types tend to be milder than the finely toothed "wild" varieties. Try each to see which you like best.

SEED SAVING About 40 days after seeding, the plants send up stalks of little white flowers with dark veins that quickly form seed pods. Support the stalks if they fall over. Harvest the pods when they turn brown, and bring them inside to finish drying.

Asian Greens

There are more different kinds of Asian greens available every year, which is a boon to winter gardening in the Southeast. These nutritious, cool-weather, brassica-family crops add spice and variety to the greens we can harvest all winter. Harvest the tender greens fall through spring for mixed salads, oriental dishes, and flavorful cooked greens.

GROWING Direct sow ¼ inch deep in rows 12 inches apart or broadcast for baby greens. Sow two or three plantings starting in early spring for harvests until summer, take a break for the heat, then make one or two large sowings in late summer and early fall for fall and winter greens. Thin the rapidly growing plants to 6 inches for leafy greens like mizuna and 12 inches for heading types. Cover with spun polyester row cover for protection from flea beetles and for extended winter harvest.

HARVESTING In cold weather, wait for the plants to thaw before harvesting. Frost sweetens the flavor of these greens. Thinnings and small leaves can be added to mixed salads. The plants can be harvested whole or a few leaves at a time for steaming and stir-fries. Mature fall-planted Chinese cabbages are perfect for mixing with winter radishes to make kimchee.

VARIETIES For those who don't like intense spiciness, **Early Mizuna** (37 days) has superior mild flavor and quick growth. **Wong Bok** Chinese cabbage (75 days) is a short-barrel type perfect for kimchee. Sweet and spicy extra winter hardy greens, like **Tender Tat Tatsoi** (43 days) and **New Star Mustard** (45 days), are bred to withstand temperatures as low as 6°F without protection. **Tatsoi** (43 days), with its rich, dark green leaves, is my personal favorite winter green. The ground-hugging plants continue growing during the winter with any hint of warmth. **Tokyo Bekana** (44 days) is mild and sweet, especially planted in fall.

SEED SAVING While many varieties flower in hot temperatures, for best-quality seed Asian greens should be grown as biennials in the Southeast. Direct sow in the fall and harvest the seed pods the following spring when they turn tan. Complete the drying process under cover. Check the species and isolate by 600 feet for home use.

Asparagus

Asparagus is one of spring's luxuries. Plan where you'll place this perennial crop carefully: the tall, luxuriant ferns will shade the area to their north for most of the growing season for years to come.

GROWING Like many Mediterranean natives, asparagus requires good drainage, rich soil, and full sun. Amend the soil with lime and up to 5 inches of compost if needed. Asparagus can be started from crowns or seed. Sow ¾ inch deep in 3-inch pots 12 weeks before the last frost. Plant seedlings or crowns 8–14 inches apart in 6-inch furrows at least 3 feet apart in early spring. In the Lower South and coastal areas, you can plant in November and December. Apply a thick layer of mulch to keep the plants evenly moist and free of weeds. Each fall, cut and remove the ferns when they die back (removing the ferns helps keep down pests), then add compost and 2–4 inches of mulch. In warmer areas where asparagus ferns don't die back in the fall, give the plants a rest period by not irrigating during the summer, letting them grow through the winter, and limiting the harvest period next season.

HARVESTING Wait until the second year of growth to harvest spears grown from crowns and the third year for seed. Snap off the spears at ground level when they reach 7 inches. Avoid cutting, as it can damage emerging roots and spread disease. Harvest for two weeks the first year, then increase the harvest period two weeks each year up to eight weeks total. Store spears in the refrigerator with the bottom 1–2 inches submerged in water.

VARIETIES No asparagus variety is particularly well suited to real heat, but a number will do well enough if having asparagus is a priority and you have reasonable expectations regarding yields. For seed, we prefer old standards like **Martha Washington** or **Purple Passion**. For crowns, one of the all-male varieties in the **Jersey** series or the more heat-tolerant **UC137** are good choices.

SEED SAVING Protect the red berries that form in fall from birds until they begin to shrivel. Mash the berries, use a screen to separate the seeds from the pulp, and rinse and thoroughly dry the seeds. Modern all-male varieties like Jersey Knight don't produce seed.

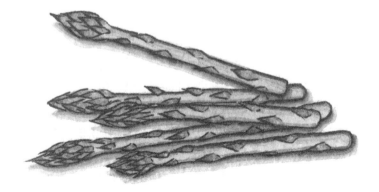

Beans

Beans are easy to grow, nutritious, delicious, and truly Southern fare. Country pintos, "green beans and new potatoes," and leather britches are all traditional dishes. Most beans are descendants of those grown by native peoples in traditional Three Sisters Gardens. Beans are grown for whole-pod snap beans (green, purple, or yellow), fresh shelling beans, and dry soup beans.

GROWING Beans are nitrogen-fixing legumes that can add fertility to your soil. Overly rich soils may actually reduce yields, so don't add nitrogen-rich amendments before planting. Soil should be well drained with pH above 6.0. After the last frost-free date, plant seeds 1 inch deep and 2 inches apart in rows 12–18 inches apart, thinning to 4 inches apart. Succession plant bush-type beans every three weeks, since they only produce one or two heavy harvests per planting (that's good for canning and freezing). Pole beans require trellising but produce all season if kept well picked and growing conditions are good. Mexican bean beetles can be a real problem with pole beans so we order pedio wasp when we spot the first bean beetle eggs as a biological control.

HARVESTING For fresh snap beans, pick when pods are small, before the seeds develop, and keep the plants well picked for an extended harvest. For shell beans, choose shelling varieties and pick the pods when they're plump, but before the beans start to dry and become starchy.

Many heirloom beans, such as greasy bean varieties, remain tender even as the pod fills and make a tasty, nutritious snack seldom seen outside of Appalachia. Dry beans should be harvested once the pods turn yellow and flaccid. Bring inside to complete drying under cover to avoid moldy beans.

VARIETIES **Contender** (42 days) is my choice for early and late bush bean plantings. **Royalty Purple Pod** (52 day) is good for planting early in cool soil. **Kebarika** (72 days) excels as a dry bush bean. **Kentucky Wonder** (62 days) remains our most popular pole bean. **Grady Bailey Greasy** (80 days) is a tasty snap bean that stays tender for "shelly" beans (snaps with beans formed in pod).

SEED SAVING Isolate varieties 25 feet for home use. Harvest like dry beans. After pods have turned leathery and begun to turn brown, pick off the pods and allow them to dry in a single layer out of direct sunlight until a week after the seeds rattle in the pods.

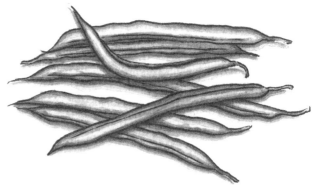

Beets

Formerly called "blood turnips," beets were originally grown for greens, but were replaced by spinach and the closely related chard. We southerners love these roots pickled. Beets come in yellow or red-striped versions besides the traditional dark blood red. The colorful, tender leaves are good for steaming and add color to salads.

GROWING Beets are traditionally planted early in the spring, but in the Southeast I think the best-quality beets grow in the cool days of fall. Sow seeds ½ to ¾ inch deep, in rows 12 inches apart, directly in the garden from February through early June and again in early September. Thin to six plants per foot for fresh beets, three plants per foot for beets for winter storage. Beets need neutral pH, light soil, and even moisture. For good yields of tender roots, irrigate and add ashes or lime as needed.

HARVESTING Harvest beets when they reach your desired size. Use the early thinnings for young greens and baby beets. Most varieties have the best flavor and quality when harvested small, at less than 2 inches diameter, but some storage varieties stay tender at much larger sizes. Hot weather can cause the roots to toughen, so harvest small if you expect heat. Greens are best from tiny thinnings up to 6 inches tall. Leave at least 1 inch of stems on the roots to prevent bleeding during cooking. The plants survive mild frosts, but bring the roots into storage before the ground freezes solid.

VARIETIES **Chioggia** (52 days) is an early, beautiful, red-and-white-striped heirloom. **Bull's Blood** (35 days for leaves; 60 days for roots) is grown for the dark reddish-purple color the greens add to baby salad mixes. The color is strongest in cool weather. **Cylindra** (55 days) is an elongated Danish heirloom that's easy to peel and slice for pickling. **Detroit Dark Red** (60 days) is my favorite dark red beet. It's a famous old variety that keeps its rich red color when pickled. **Lutz Winter Keeper** (76 days) is a longer-season variety that remains tender even when very large and retains sweetness and texture in storage.

SEED SAVING Beets are biennial, so for seed it's best to sow them in the fall, overwinter the roots, and harvest the seeds the following spring. Harvest the pods when dry and papery, and bring under cover to finish drying. Beets cross with chard. Isolate crops by ¼ mile for home use.

Blueberries

Blueberries are the natural choice of small fruit to grow in the Southeast. Native rabbiteye blueberries are nearly disease free, easy to grow, and will live about twenty years. One mature rabbiteye blueberry bush yields 15 pounds of berries in a season. In the Upper South, you can also grow highbush blueberries, which are earlier, sweeter, and larger, but require more care. Newer southern highbush varieties let gardeners grow blueberries as far south as Florida. The attractive upright blueberry plants of either type make a great choice for edible landscapes, with stunning fall colors, interesting flowers in spring, and loads of beautiful delicious berries in summer. In addition to taste and appearance, blueberries are ripe with medical advantages. They help lower cholesterol and studies suggest that blueberries also reduce the risk of some cancers.

GROWING Blueberries require acidic soil with pH levels of 4.0 to 4.5 and plenty of organic material. They need moisture-retentive, well-drained, humus-rich soil with good aeration. Blueberries are shallow rooted and poor competitors against large rooted trees, shrubs, and weeds that compete for water and nutrients. All types of blueberries grow best in full sun. Get a soil test and amend the soil a year before planting.

First dig a 3- to 4-foot-diameter hole for each plant. Then take 40 percent of the soil from the hole and mix with 40 percent pre-moistened sphagnum peat moss and 20 percent organic compost to ensure continued low pH. Mix in any amendments and fill in the hole around the bush after planting, making sure the soil is in good contact with the shallow roots.

Plant in the spring after all danger of frost has passed, or in the fall once the plants are dormant. Choose at least two varieties and space them 4–6 feet apart for cross-pollination and better fruit set. Cover the area with 3–6 inches of acidic organic mulch like pine needle, shredded bark, or leaf mold. Renew the mulch yearly and make sure the plants get 1 inch of water per week during the growing season.

HARVESTING Five plants provide enough blueberries for fresh eating, drying, and preserving for a family of four. A rich blue color indicates ripeness, but don't be too eager; berries do not continue to ripen after picking. Use shallow bowls or trays for harvesting. Do not wash berries until you are ready to eat them. Store your berries in open containers in the refrigerator.

To easily freeze blueberries, spread the berries on a cookie sheet or tray and freeze overnight. The next morning, transfer to a sealable container or plastic tub, label and return to the freezer until needed.

VARIETIES Rabbiteye (zones 6 to 9): **Climax** has early ripening large berries, **PowderBlue** is known for its sweet, dark blue fruit, and **Tifblue** has outstanding flavor. Northern highbush (zones 4 to 7): Good cultivars are **Bluecrop**, with richly flavored berries on vigorous bushes, and **Reka**, with great early season flavor. Southern highbush (zones 7 to 10): **Jubilee** does well in heavier soil and summer heat and **Sharpblue** blooms throughout the year in warmer areas.

SEED SAVING Blueberries do not come true from seeds. Propagate from stem cutting in spring and early summer.

Broccoli

Broccoli is tasty, nutritious, and full of antioxidants. Broccoli was served by Thomas Jefferson at Monticello, but it wasn't until 1922 that the D'Angelo brothers made it popular in the US. Harvest while the weather is cool for large, flavorful heads: in the Southeast, we plant broccoli in the early spring and fall. Choose the right varieties and pay attention to timing and you'll find that broccoli is easy to grow throughout the region. With harvests possible right up until heavy frost, broccoli is an important part of the year-round edible garden.

GROWING For spring plantings, transplant outside before 15 February in the Lower South and coastal regions, and as late as 1 April in the mountains and Upper South. Start your transplants four to six weeks before setting out. Sow seeds ¼–½ inch deep, two per inch, in rows 6 inches apart. Transplant at 12–16 inches apart in raised beds or 3- to 4-foot rows. Keep your plants growing steadily with even moisture and fertile, well-drained soil. A deep layer of mulch will help cool the plants in warm weather. For fall broccoli, sow seeds directly in a garden seedling bed under row cover or in flats kept in a shady place 10 to 12 weeks before the first hard freeze. Keep the seed bed moist, but don't delay waiting for wetter, cooler weather. If you don't have water for keeping seedlings moist outside, start transplants indoors instead. Use row cover to protect from flea beetles and cabbage worms, especially on young plants. Remove when plants are full size. Broccoli is an ideal fall crop to follow tomatoes or melons in areas with mild winters.

HARVESTING Harvest broccoli while the cluster of flower buds is still tight. Open yellow flowers indicate over-maturity.

VARIETIES Since timing is everything with spring plantings, try quick-maturing hybrids like **Premium Crop** (58 to 62 days; makes large heads) and **Arcadia** (63 days; stands up well to both cold and heat). For fall crops, try productive, open-pollinated varieties like **Nutribud** (55 to 70 days), **De Cicco** (49 to 78 days), **Purple Peacock** (70 days; a broccoli/kale cross), and **Waltham 29** (74 to 90 days; drought and cold tolerant). These types may have smaller main heads, but continue to make tasty side shoots until very hard freezes hit.

SEED SAVING Broccoli will cross with Brussels sprouts, cabbage, cauliflower, kale, and kohlrabi. Isolate by ⅛ mile for home use.

Brussels Sprouts

A prized holiday dish, roasted Brussels sprouts with butter and crumbled bacon confer bragging rights to both gardener and chef. Fresh-picked and sweetened by frost, they're delicious lightly steamed or as a pickled salad. The attractive plants can provide months of delicious sprouts where winters are mild. French settlers brought Brussels sprouts to Louisiana in the 1800s and they were grown at Monticello in 1812. Sprouts are grown successfully as a commercial winter crop in the Deep South.

GROWING Cool weather is obligatory to form firm, crunchy heads, so don't rush planting. If possible, time your harvest so the Brussels sprouts will be sweetened by frost. Gardeners in the Upper South sow in early to mid-June, while those in the Lower South wait until mid-July or early August. Sow the seeds ¼–½ inch deep in flats or pots. Four to six weeks later, when the plants have three or four true leaves, transplant outside with 18–24 inches between plants, in irrigated, fertile soil. Water before plants are stressed by drying out. Pests and diseases are similar to cabbage. Control flea beetles and cabbage worms with floating row cover.

HARVESTING You can either harvest continuously as they get large (about ¾ inch across), or harvest the whole stalks at once. For continuous harvests, twist off individual sprouts, and break off the leaf below each sprout to keep the plant from forming new sprouts. The plants are cold-hardy to 0°F.

If you're growing just a few plants and want all the Brussels sprouts to be ready at the same time, "top" the plants by pinching off the growing tips (the top ½ inch) when the stalk is about ¾ inch thick. You can cook and eat the sprout tops.

VARIETIES My favorite variety for continuous harvests all winter is **Catskill (Long Island Improved)** (85 to 110 days). If you're growing just a couple plants and want a concentrated harvest, try **Mezzo Nano** (100 to 110 days). These traditional Italian plants are shorter and a little earlier than some open-pollinated varieties, and the sprouts mature all at once.

SEED SAVING Brussels sprouts will cross with broccoli, cabbage, cauliflower, kale, and kohlrabi. Isolate by ⅛ mile for home use.

Cabbage

A staple garden crop, cabbage is eaten fresh, boiled, stir-fried, or fermented, from microgreens to coleslaw to sauerkraut. It has a place on the table of every good southern cook and a place in most good southern gardens. Cabbage is widely cultivated as both a spring and fall garden standard throughout the Southeast. It can also be grown during the summer in the mountainous areas. Plus it stores well under the right conditions.

GROWING Cabbage grows best in rich, moist, well-drained loam with high fertility. Choose varieties appropriate for the time of year. Early varieties require more fertility than mid- or late-season varieties. The plants are shallow-rooted, so irrigation may be necessary. Cabbage needs a steady supply of water and full sun throughout the growing season. The heads may split if a heavy rain follows a long dry spell without irrigation. A thick mulch layer will hold moisture, control weeds, and extend the harvest.

In spring, start your transplants four to six weeks before moving them out to the garden. Sow ¼ inch deep, two to three seeds per container. Germinate at room temperature, and then reduce the temperature for growing. After the seedlings emerge, choose the most vigorous one and cut the others at the soil line. Harden off before transplanting in mid-February to late-March. Space 12–18 inches apart in rows 3–4 feet apart. Fall cabbage is transplanted, or direct seeded, six to twelve seeds per foot at a depth of ¼–½ inch. Maintain adequate soil moisture during germination.

Control diseases by using clean germination soil mix, inspecting your seedlings regularly, rotating all cabbage-family crops, and maintaining good garden sanitation. To control pests, use floating row cover immediately after transplanting. For an early season treat, succession plant microgreens in flats. Grow at 60°F or cooler. Maintain even moisture by misting.

HARVESTING When the head of the cabbage is fully formed, it is ready to harvest. After harvest, select the strongest side sprout and allow it to develop into a second, smaller head. Harvest microgreens with scissors or a sharp knife at 10 to 15 days (½–2 inches). Use like fresh sprouts.

VARIETIES Since 1840, **Early Jersey Wakefield** (64 days), with its distinctive 3-pound cone-shaped heads, has been an early season favorite in the Southeast. **Red Acre** (76 days) and **Late Flat Dutch** (100 days) are good choices for sauerkraut and winter storage. Red cabbage has colorful appeal for microgreens.

SEED SAVING Cabbage will cross with Brussels sprouts, broccoli, cauliflower, kale, and kohlrabi. Isolate by ⅛ mile for home use.

Carrots

Many gardeners believe carrots are hard to grow, but with just a little attention to timing you can easily grow these classic root vegetables in the Southeast in both spring and fall.

GROWING Carrots need well-drained soil, free of rocks, loosened to 8–10 inches deep (12 inches for long, tapering types.) Sandy soils are best, but don't despair if you have clay: just add lots of organic matter and pay extra attention to loosening the soil. Sow directly in the ground ¼ inch deep, three seeds per inch, in 12-inch rows. Cover with very fine soil. Carrots germinate slowly, so mix in a few radish seeds (which sprout quickly) to mark the row and keep the soil from crusting. When the plants emerge, thin to 1–2 inches apart. Thinning is crucial: the roots won't bulk up if they're crowded. Don't bother trying to transplant, as the plants never resume growth.

Provide even soil moisture to prevent root cracking. Control weeds with shallow cultivation and organic mulches. (Carrots are poor competitors so prioritize weeding this crop!).

Plant your earliest crop of spring carrots four weeks before the last spring frost, and continue every two weeks until May. Fall plantings can start in August and continue until four weeks before the first fall frost.

HARVESTING Carrots are ready to harvest 65 to 75 days after sowing, earlier if you like younger roots. Best-quality roots are no larger than an inch across for most varieties. Use a garden fork to loosen the soil, being careful not to damage the roots (push straight down before lifting). Harvest spring crops promptly before they become bitter and fibrous. Carrots get sweeter with cool temperatures. Fall carrots can be left in well-mulched raised beds as needed until spring (unless you start finding animal damage). If your ground freezes hard, however, harvest fall carrots and store somewhere cool, moist, and well ventilated. A root cellar is ideal, but perforated plastic bags in the refrigerator may last several months.

VARIETIES Beyond the classic tapered orange roots, carrots come in a delightful variety of colors and sizes, from red-cored, blocky French classics like **Chantenay Red Core** (65 days), to purple skinned beauties like **Cosmic Purple** (70 days), to heirloom whites and whimsical rounds. "Blocky" carrots such as **Danvers 126** (75 days) and **Scarlet Nantes** (70 days) are the best choice for heavy soils.

SEED SAVING Saving carrot seeds is not a project for beginners in the Southeast. The plants readily cross with any Queen Anne's Lace within a half mile, so extra care must be taken to prevent hybrids. Isolate from other carrot varieties and Queen Anne's Lace by at least 330 feet for seeds for home use, and save seeds from at least 50 plants (200 is the commercial recommendation).

Carrots are biennial, so they flower and produce seed in the spring of the second year after planting. To save seed, sow in the fall and apply heavy mulch before hard freezes. Alternatively, pull up the carrots before frost kills the tops, store the roots in sawdust in a cool dark place, and replant the following spring as soon as the ground can be worked. Monitor for wild Queen Anne's Lace in the area and cut back any flowering stalks until after the carrots form seeds. Label blossoms that open before Queen Anne's Lace and only harvest seeds from those seed heads. If you can, grow your carrot seed crop in a cold frame or greenhouse. This will help prevent contamination, and also promote early flowering before Queen Anne's Lace.

Cauliflower

Cauliflower isn't the easiest member of the cabbage family to grow in the Southeast, but it's worth the effort for adding a crisp fresh taste as well as a lot of class to your veggie trays and mixed pickles.

GROWING Cauliflower is similar to broccoli and cabbage, but a little more temperature sensitive. Plant in fertile soil rich in organic matter, and in full sun. Spring crops are usually started indoors or in a greenhouse or cold frame. Germinates best at 70–75°F but then seedlings prefer 60°F. Fall/winter crops can be started in a seedling bed from July to September, depending on your location. Cover transplants and outdoor seedlings with floating row cover or other protection, or the bugs will almost certainly devastate your babies. At all times keep soil evenly moist. Cauliflower doesn't like heat, so start spring plants early (it might feel like winter still to you). But you must also harden them off and protect them from too much cold (10 or more days below 50°F causes bolting). Cauliflower prefers a mostly neutral soil. During the growing season, avoid dry weather stress. Don't hesitate to irrigate, especially at the beginning of the season, and as the heads are maturing. Keep well mulched. Cauliflower is a heavy feeder, so supplement with compost or other nitrogen-rich amendments. Nice white heads require blanching (tying the inner leaves around the head), unless you plant the newer self-blanching varieties. Control diseases by using clean potting mix, watching your seedlings for disease, rotating all cabbage family beds, and keeping your garden cleaned up.

HARVESTING Harvest when the head is full but the "curds" haven't started to separate or turn yellowish. Cut the stem, leaving a whorl of leaves attached to the head so it won't dry out.

VARIETIES If you have the room and the enthusiasm for cauliflower, you can prolong the season by planting different varieties. **Early Snowball** (50 days) and **Snowball Y** (50 to 60 days) are popular, somewhat-heat-tolerant, and early maturing varieties, but both still perform better in fall. My favorite for fall is **Snowball Self Blanching** (68 days), because the leaves self wrap in cool weather, but not when it's hot.

SEED SAVING Cauliflower will cross with broccoli, Brussels sprouts, cabbage, kale, and kohlrabi. Isolate by ⅛ mile for home use. Allow overwintered plants to bolt in spring and harvest the siliques (long, slender seed pods) when they and the seeds inside them are brown. Allow them to dry in a layer no more then ¼ inch thick for two weeks before storing.

Celery and Celeriac

Celery is a standby for snacks and flavoring soups, but it can be a challenge to gardeners. Celeriac, or root-celery, the flavorful root vegetable, and cutting celery, which grows like parsley, are easier to grow than celery and equally delicious in soups. All these crops thrive in cool weather. They are easy to start inside and transplant to the garden in the early spring, but the challenge is providing shade and adequate moisture through the summer.

GROWING Celery and celeriac require rich, continuously moist soil, high in organic matter. They need at least six to eight hours of sun a day but also appreciate some shade in the hot summer. Beginners may want to buy local starts but producing your own gives you many more variety choices. Pre-soak seeds overnight to speed up their slow germination. Start seeds in sterile potting mix eight to ten weeks before your last frost date. Sow the tiny seed very shallowly and barely cover with soil. Keep moist and thin as needed. Move to larger pots or flats as they grow. Harden off and remove a few outside leaves before setting out. Space plants 8 inches apart in 2- to 3-foot rows. In the mid and Upper South, set out celery after the last spring frost and mulch well. Cut back your celery plants by late summer and they will produce tasty side bunches for fall harvest. In the Deep South, sow celery and celeriac in a seedling bed in midsummer, move celery starts to their permanent location in the garden by October. Moisture control is essential. Celery and celeriac will not tolerate drying out. Drip irrigation is your friend for low-fuss, frequent watering.

HARVESTING If you want to blanch your celery, use boards leaned up against each side of the row, or surround each plant with open-ended milk cartons. Leave in place 7 to 14 days. You can harvest the whole celery plant by cutting it off just below the soil line. Or harvest individual outer stalks as needed. If you want your summer crop to regrow for another fall harvest, cut the plants a little above the soil line, making sure to leave intact the central growing tip and any visible side shoots. Harvest celeriac before the first deep frost by carefully digging up the roots with a fork. You can harvest small amounts of celeriac leaves during the season to add that wonderful celery flavor to soups and stews.

VARIETIES Bright green **Ventura** celery (85 days) is a favorite producing great fall re-growth. **Tall Utah** celery (110 days) has lots of crisp, tender, tasty stalks. **Large Smooth Prague** celeriac (110 days) is an excellent keeper for winter use. **Affina Cutting** celery (80 days) is so easy.

SEED SAVING These are biennial plants, so they typically have to be left in the ground through the winter before they will flower and form seeds. The plants will get quite large, so transplant your best plants, or thin out the plants around them, to give them lots of space. Isolate by ¼ mile from other celery varieties. Harvest seeds when the seed heads are brown and allow them to dry in a single layer for two weeks.

Corn

Fresh-picked sweet corn is one of the joys of summer. Nothing beats the taste of sweet corn harvested, cooked, and served immediately. If you have the space, consider growing dent, flint, popcorn, or flour corns ("field corn") for fresh grits, polenta, and cornbread. It's not by chance that the Southeast is famous for corn.

GROWING Don't rush planting sweet corn; wait until after your average last spring frost to sow outdoors. Separate sweet corn from field corn by at least 100 feet to ensure sweet flavor and tenderness. Corn is a "heavy feeder"—enrich your soil with organic material and plenty of compost for enough phosphorous and nitrogen.

Sow an inch deep in well-drained soil in full sun, in rows 2–3 feet apart. It's best to sow extra seed, but rather than sow "one for the mouse, one for the crow, one to rot and one to grow," as the traditional saying goes, I sow twice what we need and thin to 8–12 inches apart when the plants have two true leaves. Corn is wind pollinated, so for full, plump ears you'll need to plant in blocks at least four rows wide, unless you want to learn how to hand pollinate.

For a steady supply, try planting both an early and a late variety with each planting, and succession plant every three to four weeks. Maintain even moisture (at least an inch of rain or irrigation per week), especially during pollination and while the ears are plumping up. Keep well weeded but cultivate shallowly. Six to eight inches of mulch helps conserve moisture and keeps out the weeds.

HARVESTING Harvest sweet corn when all the silks are brown and the ears are full down to the tip. Pick just before cooking for the best taste. To store sweet corn, cool it as soon as you can. To harvest popcorn, dent, flour, and flint corns, wait until the husks and ears are dry to the touch, then finish drying indoors.

VARIETIES I like the old-fashioned taste of open-pollinated sweet corns like **Texas Honey June** (97 days) and **Country Gentleman** (90 to 92 days). The tight husks on these varieties help keep out corn earworms. Many gardeners prefer sugary enhanced hybrids like **Silver Queen** (90 days) or **Early Sunglow** (67 days). **Pennsylvania Butter Flavor Popcorn** (102 days) and **Cherokee Long Ear Short Popcorn** (100 days) are both outstanding heirloom popcorns. For delicious polenta and cornbread, **Floriani Red Flint** (100 days) is both tasty and colorful.

SEED SAVING Separate varieties by 600 feet for home use. Save seeds from at least 50 plants to maintain vigor and diversity (200 is the commercial recommendation).

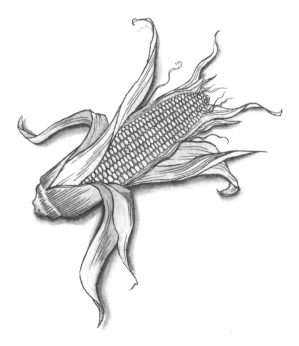

Cucumbers

Southerners have been growing (and pickling!) cucumbers since colonial times. All summer long we may struggle to keep up with the production, but we also enjoy cucumber salads, cucumber sandwiches, and white gazpacho. Most slicing types also make good pickles when picked small, and it's a great way to preserve the harvest.

GROWING Cucumbers prefer full sun and rich, well-drained soil with plenty of organic matter and even moisture. For this warm-weather crop, wait until after all danger of frost has past, then either direct sow ½ inch deep or transplant out two- to three-week-old seedlings grown in pots. Seeds will not germinate in cold soil. Harden off the transplants and handle them very gently. Space 12 inches apart in rows 3–5 feet apart. Floating row cover protects from pests and adds warmth early in the season, which improves your production. Use trellises or cages to take advantage of vertical space. Long cucumbers will grow straighter this way and the improved air circulation helps prevent disease. To control disease, choose resistant varieties, keep your plants vigorous, and remove old plants.

HARVESTING Pick cucumbers while still crisp, tender, and green. (Over-mature fruits get very hard or very soft, depending on conditions.) Harvest young fruits frequently (as in, daily) to get the most cucumbers. Remove large fruit you might have missed. You can pickle small, young slicing varieties, but some pickling types make poor slicers because they get soft and yellow at slicing size.

VARIETIES **Marketmore 80** (58 to 65 days), **Poinsett 76** (67 days), **Straight Eight** (57 days), and **Ashley** (66 days) are excellent stand-by green, American slicing cucumbers with great flavor and multiple disease resistances. For pickling, **Little Leaf H-19** (55 days) has multiple disease resistances, easy-to-find fruit, and naturally parthenocarpic flowers that don't require pollination. **Suyo Long** (61 days) is a sweet-flavored, heat-resistant, "burpless" cucumber from China. Heirlooms like round, yellow **Lemon** (67 days) cucumber and ivory-colored **White Wonder** (58 days) are crisp, refreshing, and productive in our hot, humid summers.

SEED SAVING Isolate from other cucumber varieties by ⅛ mile for home use. Harvest large fruits that have turned yellow or brown and cure in dry, room-temperature conditions for two to three weeks. Cut open each fruit and scoop out the seeds into a container. Add water just to cover and let sit at room temperature for one or two days, stirring every twelve hours. Add additional water and pour off the bad seeds that float on top. Add water again, rinse, strain, and spread the seeds into a thin layer and allow to dry for three weeks.

Eggplant

Eggplant loves hot weather and grows well in all parts of the Southeast. As the rest of your spring/summer garden succumbs to the sweltering heat and relentless sun of late summer in the Lower South, eggplants can be counted on to keep producing until cool weather arrives in early fall.

GROWING Grow eggplant similarly to peppers, with full sun and a long season. Choose well-drained soil or use raised beds. If you buy your starts, choose sturdy, dark green plants that are not in bloom. Inspect the top and undersides of leaves for apparent insect problems and to make sure diseases are not present as well. Start seeds ¼ inch deep eight to ten weeks before setting out. Because eggplant seeds are prone to rot, I recommend sowing into a soil-less seed-starting mixture (available at most garden stores, or make your own with perlite, peat, and compost). Harden off and plant in warm soil, preferably before flower buds appear. Don't rush the season; cold-shock can stunt these heat-loving plants. Space 24 inches apart in a block, or 20 inches apart in rows 36 inches apart. Use row cover to control flea beetles on young plants. Eggplants are heavy feeders and may need extra fertilizer to produce a good crop but don't give too much nitrogen or you'll get big plants and not many fruit. Maintain even moisture, especially during fruit set and development. Mulch once the soil is good and warm to reduce weeding and watering. Keep plants well picked to encourage more production. Remove over-mature fruits. Plant resistant varieties and rotate all nightshade family plants (tomatoes, peppers, eggplants, potatoes) to control disease.

HARVESTING Fruit are best quality before the seeds form. They are ripe when the skin appears glossy and is resilient to thumb pressure. If the seeds are brown, it's too late. Cut the tough stem with clippers or a sharp knife.

VARIETIES The old standard **Black Beauty** (74 days) produces egg-shaped, glossy, purple-black fruit 6–9 inches long perfect for Italian dishes. My favorites are **Ping Tung Long** (62 days), a slender Japanese eggplant with a thin skin and more delicate flavor, and **Rosita** (70 to 80 days), a lavender heirloom from Puerto Rico with few seeds, tender skin, and melt-in-your-mouth taste when grilled.

SEED SAVING Isolate varieties by a minimum of 150 feet for home use. Harvest after the fruits turn dull yellow. Cut into 1–2 inch cubes and cover with water for 24 hours at room temperature (stirring once midway). Use your hands to squish seeds out of the fruit. Let sit for 12 hours more if seed is still difficult to remove. Rinse and spread in a thin layer to dry for three weeks.

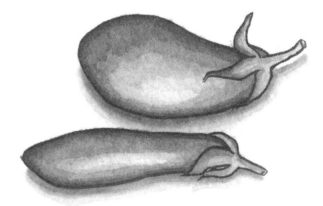

Fava Beans

* *

Fava beans, also known as "broad beans," are large lima-shaped, cool-weather legumes that grow similarly to peas in the Upper South, or as a fall-planted bean in the Lower South. They're versatile. Eat the immature pods as you would a snap bean. Eat the next stage as a green shelled bean. Or eat the fully mature dry bean.

GROWING Direct sow favas like peas in the early spring in the Upper South. We sow ours by March here in central Virginia. The spring window for good germination is short. In the Lower South, it's best to sow in September or October. Sow seeds 4–6 inches apart and thin to 8–10 inches. The 3- to 4½-foot-tall plants prefer full sun, well-drained soil, and a pH level of 6.0–6.8. Provide sturdy trellising. Keep the vines well picked to keep them producing. Practice good plant hygiene—try not to handle the plants when they're wet to prevent the spread of fungal disease. To assure high yields, apply a nitrogen-fixing inoculant when sowing.

HARVESTING Favas are ready for harvest when the pods are full and 5–7 inches, but still green. Shell them, and blanch the seed/beans (unless they are very small and tender). Next, remove the outer casing, I just give each one a "squeeze" and out comes the tender bean inside. Then they are ready to prepare in your recipe. They won't need much cooking in that tender stage.

VARIETIES **Broad Windsor** (95 days) is the most widely available heirloom fava. We like to use this this fava instead of chickpeas in hummus, for a delicate, nutty flavor. **Sweet Lorane** (95 days) is an especially cold-hardy fava bred to survive through winter in mild areas. The vines may survive lows to −10°F.

SEED SAVING For home use, isolate fava varieties by a minimum of 75–150 feet. Process the seeds like other beans.

Figs

Growing figs has a long history in the Southeast. In 1692, John Smith wrote of a fig "prospering exceedingly" at Jamestown, Virginia. Large trees still provide shade to courtyards in New Orleans and summer visitors to Monticello leave lusting after the ripe, luscious fruit on trees planted against a south-facing terrace wall. From patio planter to small shade trees with an edible bonus, there is a fig to fit the needs of every southern gardener.

GROWING In all areas of our region figs are easy-care plants once established. They tolerate a wide range of soils as long there is good drainage. Avoid drain fields and sewer pipes or the thirsty, fibrous roots will clog them. In the Upper South, choose a location that will protect fig trees from the cold winter lows. Plant in front of a sunny south-facing wall, in a sheltered area, or beside a blacktop driveway. It's best to plant figs when dormant in fall or spring.

Dig a hole 3 inches deeper than the pot the tree was set in at the nursery and twice as wide. Gently place the root ball in the hole, being sure to spread out the roots so they're generally directly downward and outward, and definitely not circling the trunk. Mix compost into the reserved soil, and fill in around the root ball, applying gentle pressure to set the tree. Cut the top back by half on bare root plants. Water thoroughly and keep well watered through at least the first summer.

In my Piedmont, Virginia, garden I mulch my fig trees heavily with straw, effectively covering the trees, after the leaves drop in the fall. Gardeners at higher elevations mound soil around the base of the plant for even more protection.

HARVESTING Figs are ripe when they change color, their necks wilt and the fruit droops. If they are still exuding a white milky sap they are not fully ripe. Pick early when the figs are a little under-ripe for making preserves or to avoid bird and insect damage.

VARIETIES **Brown Turkey** (10°F) is the most popular fig in the Southeast and will ripen fruit even when frozen to the ground. **Hardy Chicago** is an even more cold-hardy selection of Brown Turkey. **Celeste** (0°F) has excellent eating quality and a short ripening season.

SEED SAVING Figs do not come true from seed; propagate from cuttings or suckers.

Garlic

Savory garlic is essential for the cook's garden and a star of winter plantings. Never before have there been so many varieties available to gardeners from so many reputable online sources. Many farmers markets allow you to buy stock acclimated to your local area.

GROWING Each garlic head grows from a single clove. You can actually replant any garlic clove, as long as it has been stored well for use as seed garlic, although you'll have the best results if you use a variety you know is adapted to your climate. Choose a location in full sun and provide fertile, well-drained soil with lots of organic matter. Raised beds are excellent for garlic (and other root crops) if you have heavy soil. Test your soil; pH should be neutral. Tradition says, "plant garlic the shortest day of the year and harvest the longest day of the year," but I find it's better to plant in October or November and harvest in May or June. The ultimate bulb size is determined by how much leafy growth the plants put on early in life, so you'll have much larger bulbs if your plants get started a bit earlier in the

fall. When choosing which cloves to plant, think big: large cloves from large bulbs. (Cook with your smaller ones.) Plant 1 inch deep, 4 inches apart, in rows 12–16 inches apart. Gently place the cloves right side up (pointy end up, scarred end down), and cover well with soil, keeping them pointed the right way as best you can. Mulch immediately, but remember to "liberate" young plants having trouble getting out of the mulch. Liberation is best done when you first start seeing the green shoots, about a month after planting. In late spring, you'll need to remove the scapes (the flowering stalks for bulblets) from hardneck garlic varieties. Scapes are delicious pickled, or you can use them like green onions for fresh garlic flavor. Garlic doesn't compete well, so keep it well weeded. Maintain even moisture throughout the season.

HARVESTING Timing is important. Harvest when the bottom third of the leaves are brown and the top four to eight leaves are still green. The green leaves form the papery wrapper layers needed for good storage. (If you harvest too early, the cloves will be very small; harvest too late and the bulb will have split.) Handle the bulbs gently, as they bruise easily before they're cured. To cure garlic, simply hang or lay out the bulbs in a shaded, airy space protected from rain for at least a month, leaving adequate room for good ventilation between bulbs. (For softneck varieties, garlic braids are a convenient way to cure and later store garlic.) Once the bulbs are dry, trim the tops and roots. Garlic stores best in the dark with good ventilation, at either 32–40°F or 55–70°F. The cloves will sprout prematurely if kept at 40–50°F (the temperature of most refrigerators).

VARIETIES Most gardeners in the Southeast grow soft-neck (braiding) varieties for their large bulbs with many cloves and good storage quality. **Asian Tempest** is one of the earliest to mature. **Inchelium Red** won a taste test among 20 varieties at the Rodale Institute and continues to be a favorite variety. **Nootka Rose** is my favorite long-storing silverskin. **Red Toch** and **Lorz Italian** boast robust flavor and medium storage quality. For gardeners in the Upper South, hardneck (rocamble) varieties like **Music**

and **Kilarney Red** offer robust flavor and large, easy-to-peel cloves. Hardneck varieties do not store well. Some gardeners will grow some of each type and cook with their hardneck garlic first while the cloves are still good quality.

SEED SAVING Garlic does not form true seeds in the Southeast. Select large cloves from disease-free bulbs to save for planting.

Grapes, Muscadines

Muscadines, also called scuppernongs, are the grape of choice for organic gardeners in the South. Known for their unique sweet flavor, they are very different from the California seedless grapes at local stores. Muscadines have a stronger flavor, seeds, and a thick, tough skin. There is a technique to eating these that those of us from the South have perfected. Just squeeze the pulp and juice into your mouth through the stem end, enjoy the essence of the fruit, and spit out the seeds. The fruit is very popular with southerners for wine, juice, pies (from the cooked skins) and jellies. The large vines are prolific producers of sweet, delicious fruit and need little care once established.

GROWING Muscadines grow best in fertile, sandy loam, but can tolerate a wide variety of soils with good drainage. Success of newly planted and young vines depends on consistent irrigation and weed control. Bare root vines should be planted December through February. Container-grown vines can be planted throughout the year.

Muscadines need sturdy trellising to climb: they can be planted on an arbor for home fruit production, or in a traditional post-and-wire configuration. The vines are relatively drought tolerant once they've had time to grow their roots. They will have a long life given a good location.

What really makes these native grapes shine, and why you should grow them rather than a traditional grape, is that they are so resistant to pests and plant diseases in our climate. The hardy, vigorous plants are almost always grown entirely without chemicals. Some of the newer bunch grapes and concords are being grown organically in the Upper South but none so easily as these native varieties. For the novice gardener, I advise sticking with muscadine varieties.

Grapes, Muscadines, continued

HARVESTING Most cultivars have an extended ripening period, often four to six weeks, ideal for enjoying table grapes. Harvest by picking individual grapes or bunches of grapes by hand. If you're going to be processing muscadines for juice or jelly, you'll want a faster harvest method: simply shake the berries loose into tarps below the vines. The fruits may have some bruising, but it won't matter since you'll be crushing them soon anyway.

VARIETIES Many popular varieties only have female flowers, so you'll need to plant a self-fruitful (perfect flowers with male and female parts) alongside, or only grow self-fertile varieties. **Fry** needs a pollinator and is one of the most popular muscadines for fresh eating. It ripens very large, bronze grapes for six weeks. **Pollyanna** is self-fertile; the grapes are medium-large and dark purple. **Noble** is another self-fruitful, popular red muscadine for wine or juice production.

SEED SAVING Muscadines do not come true from seed; propagate cultivars by cuttings or peggings. To peg, wound a low-growing shoot by making light cuts in the bark and then cover the cuts with moist soil. Leave the shoot tip exposed. After about a month, roots should have formed, and the shoot may be separated from the mother vine.

Jerusalem Artichokes, Sunchokes

A very easy-to-grow perennial, these nutty little tubers are a traditional Native American food source that can be grown throughout most of the Southeast. Also called "sunchokes," Jerusalem artichokes are sunflower relatives. The lovely yellow blossoms on stalks growing to 12 feet or more make a sunny addition to the fall garden, and they produce an almost unending supply of food. The roots taste similarly to water chestnuts. Cook them just like potatoes. They're especially nice in stir-fries and salads. Unlike most starchy vegetables, the principal storage carbohydrate is inulin rather than starch. Inulin is converted in the human digestive tract to fructose rather than glucose, which is better tolerated by diabetics.

GROWING Choose a sunny location to plant whole tubers or pieces of tubers that are no less than 2 ounces and have two or three prominent buds. After the weather cools in the fall (or in the very early spring), plant the tubers 3–4 inches deep and 12–16 inches apart in rows 3 feet apart. Do not allow the cut tuber pieces to dry before planting. Jerusalem artichokes tolerate a wide range of soils but for larger tubers plant in loose, fertile soil.

If the plants become crowded, the roots will become smaller and smaller. Since Jerusalem artichokes are perennial and aggressive growers, they are best planted in a permanent location.

HARVESTING The tubers will be large and ready for harvest by the first fall after planting, starting when the plants are in blossom. They are best left in the garden and dug as needed. Tubers will keep all winter in the ground until they start to grow again in the spring. The skin is very thin, so harvest gently to avoid cuts and bruises. The skin is also susceptible to rapid moisture loss. Small amounts can be stored in the refrigerator or root cellar provided that they are not allowed to dry out.

VARIETIES Named varieties of Jerusalem artichokes are hard to find but include: **Mammoth French White**, **French White Improved**, **Stampede**, **Fuseau**, and **Red Fuseau**. All of these varieties are recommended for high inulin content. Frankly, most people get started with Jerusalem artichokes by getting tubers from a gardening friend, health food store, or by mail order as an unnamed variety.

SEED SAVING Don't bother saving seeds with these plants, simply allow some tubers to remain in the soil to begin growing again the following spring. It's best to dig them up in the fall or spring and spread out your seed tubers to give the plants plenty of room to grow new tubers.

Kohlrabi

Kohlrabi is grown for its bulbous stem and its leaves. The mild and crisp-tasting flesh can be cooked or used grated for salads. Kohlrabi stores very well when refrigerated. Young kohlrabi leaves can be harvested for salad. Purple-leaved varieties are pretty in salad mixes.

GROWING Kohlrabi needs full sun and prefers well-drained, fertile soil high in organic matter. It's a heavy feeder that loves compost and also needs plentiful, consistent moisture. It likes cool weather; a little frost can improve flavor.

Start indoors or direct sow four weeks before your last frost date. For an early crop, set out hardened seedlings at four weeks. For fall/winter crops, direct sow eight weeks before your first frost date. Soil must be kept moist but not wet for good germination and early growth. Sow $\frac{1}{4}$–$\frac{1}{2}$ inch deep and 1 inch apart in rows 12 inches apart. Thin to a 4–6 inch spacing depending on the variety and desired size. Mulch to maintain moisture, reduce weeding, and add organic matter. Row cover helps control flea beetles on all fall brassicas and is almost essential for young plants in late summer and fall.

HARVESTING Most kohlrabi are best when the globe is 2–3 inches across (some storage varieties grow larger). Plants left too long will get tough and fibrous stems. Cut between globe and root. Kohlrabi stores well in a cold, humid place.

VARIETIES **Early Purple Vienna** (55 days) is an early variety that is less subject to cracking and damage from

Kohlrabi, continued

variable spring weather than the extra-early **Kolibri** (45 days). The Czechoslovakian heirloom **Giant Winter** (130 days) typically remains tender at 8–10 inches, making it perfect for winter storage. It can also remain in the garden all winter for harvest as needed in the warmer areas of the Lower South.

SEED SAVING Kohlrabi will cross with Brussels sprouts, cabbage, cauliflower, and kale. Isolate by ⅛ mile for home use. Allow overwintered plants to bolt in spring and harvest the siliques (long, slender seed pods) when they and the seeds inside them are brown. Allow them to dry in a layer no more then ¼ inch thick for two weeks.

Lettuce

Lettuce comes in an astounding variety of textures, colors, and patterns. Explore the full variety and discover your favorites, from succulent romaines to tight, crisp butterheads, from elegant, nutrition-dense looseleafs to classic, tiny crispheads. Fast-growing lettuce is perfect for frequent, small plantings that make use of those handy, unused corners of the garden (even in partial shade).

GROWING I want the same crisp, sweet, flavorful, juicy lettuce for salads year round, but the way we grow this crop changes with every season. Some things remain the same: the tiny seeds need light to germinate, so you should gently press the seeds into the soil surface or cover very lightly with fine compost. The first week after sowing is crucial: keep the soil evenly moist (don't let it crust over), but not soggy. The seeds won't germinate over 80°F, so take whatever measures necessary to keep the soil cool (more about this below). Lettuce doesn't compete well with weeds, so you should cultivate early and often.

We recommend spacing lettuce at 10–16 inches apart in rows 12–24 apart, giving more space for larger varieties. For direct sowing, sow four seeds per foot and use the thinnings as baby lettuce, or broadcast seeds in an area for cut-and-come-again baby leaves. You can also sow a thick lettuce "hedge" (two plants per foot) and mow the top 6 inches every few days once the plants mature. This method only works well in cool weather; the plants will become bitter if the weather is the least bit warm. I have given more details about year-round lettuce production in the June chapter, so you'll seldom be without sweet, crisp lettuce.

HARVESTING For best quality and maximum sweetness, harvest early in the day while it's still cool. If you have to harvest during the heat of the day, revive the heads by chilling in cold water for up to half an hour.

VARIETIES **Buttercrunch** (55 days green, semi-heading), **Sierra** (54 days), summer crisp (even in high summer on our farm) green with red tips, **Jericho** (60 days, Israeli), the most heat-tolerant green romaine for Caesar salad all year round, **Rouge d'Hiver** (62 days), cold-tolerant deep red French crisp heirloom, romaine-type, **Tom Thumb** (48 days), miniature heirloom butterhead beloved by Thomas Jefferson.

SEED SAVING Isolate varieties by a minimum of 12 feet for home use. Harvest after the plants have begun to "feather"

like dandelions by knocking the seeds off into a bucket by vibrating the plants. Remove the fluff and store in a cool dry place.

Lima Beans

Lima beans love the heat and are as much a part of southern cuisine as cornbread. Large limas, served boiled and salted, have a creamy texture that for me conjures memories of Sunday dinners on hot summer days at my grandma's house. Limas are also delicious pureed with cilantro, lime, and cumin for a distinctly Latin American flavor that I learned to love during the summer I spent in Texas. These heat-loving beans come in a variety of sizes and colors; there is a perfect fit for every southeastern vegetable garden.

GROWING Lima beans thrive in a sunny, well-drained site with plenty of organic material and a neutral pH. Limas need warmer soil than other beans, so wait until two weeks after your average last frost date to sow the seeds 2–3 inches apart. Thin to 4–6 inches apart. Provide a sturdy trellis for pole types. For a continuous harvest throughout the growing season, sow succession plantings of bush lima beans every two weeks or follow an early crop of bush plants with a planting of pole lima beans. Pole limas have an extended harvest period that will see you through the remainder of the season. Lima beans will not set pods in temperatures above 80°F or in cold or wet weather. Time your plantings to avoid hot weather. In the Lower South, lima beans can be sown again in late summer for autumn harvest. Make sure your plants get 1 inch of water per week.

Side dress plants with compost or other low-nitrogen fertilizer when they begin to bloom for increased yields.

HARVESTING When the pods are filled out but still firm and bright green they are ready for shelling out for fresh beans. Continue to pick pods as soon as they become plump to extend flowering and the production of new pods. Unshelled fresh lima beans will keep in the refrigerator for one week. Shelled fresh lima beans can be blanched and frozen. For dried lima beans, wait until the pods are dry before harvesting and finish drying indoors before threshing out the beans.

VARIETIES **Fordhook 242** (72 days) is an excellent bush lima for the Upper South with dense foliage and good production of nutlike seeds. **Thorogreen** (65 days), the 1943 AAS winner, has a concentrated set of beans with good flavor for fresh eating, canning, or freezing. **Christmas** (84 days) has large quarter-size limas on 5- to 6-foot vines and is a productive and heat-resistant variety.

SEED SAVING Isolate from other varieties of lima beans by at least 125 feet. Pick the pods when the seeds rattle inside and allow them to dry in a layer no more than ½ inch thick for two weeks.

Melons

....

Melons are a frost-tender, warm-season crop well suited to the Southeast. Muskmelons include the green- and orange-fleshed melons often mistakenly called cantaloupes in the United States. Melons use a lot of garden space but you can grow smaller varieties on trellises, supporting the growing fruit with a sling of old pantyhose or other porous material. Muskmelons are good for both beginning gardeners and new seed savers because they slip or easily separate from the vine when fully ripe.

GROWING Melons require a loose, warm, sandy loam with a pH of 6–7. Improve soil tilth and fertility with compost, cover crops, and mulch. Start indoors two to four weeks before last frost in pots, not flats. Sow two to three seeds per 3-inch pot, ½ inch deep. Best germination temp is 85–90°F. When seedlings emerge, thin to one plant per pot by snipping at the base. Maintain seedling soil temperature at 75°F or above. Keep the soil moist but not soggy. Harden young plants before transplanting in warm garden soil. Handle gently and water well. Space plants 12–18 inches apart in rows 5–6 feet apart, or two or three plants per hill.

For direct seeding, once soil temperature averages 70°F, sow seeds ½–¾ inch deep. For early plantings, black plastic mulch and row covers warm the soil, conserve moisture, suppress weeds and pests, reduce fruit rot, and hasten maturity. Plastic mulch works best with drip irrigation, which saves water and work for you, and reduces foliage disease. Remove row cover when female flowers appear. Maintain adequate moisture in early growing stages and fruit setting. Later on, water only when soil is quite dry and leaves show signs of wilting in mid-day. Fungal diseases can be a problem.

HARVESTING When ripe, most varieties of melon slip from the vine in response to thumb pressure at the base of the stem. Ripe melons also develop a sweet aroma. Honeydews mature a little later than muskmelons and are overripe by the time the stem can be tugged from the fruit. These must be cut from the vine.

VARIETIES **Eden Gem** (also called **Rocky Ford**) (89 days) is a popular, green-fleshed, 2–3 pound muskmelon with sweet-flavored flesh. **Kansas** (90 days) is a productive variety with sweet taste, great texture, and disease resistance. My recommended honeydew variety is **Earlidew** (90 days).

SEED SAVING Muskmelon will not cross with watermelon, cucumber, pumpkin, or squash, but varieties within the species intercross freely. Isolate melons by a minimum of ⅛ mile for home use, or ½–1 mile for pure seed.

Mustards

A common sight in the South, mustard greens are at their peak from November thru April. Fresh-harvested small, tender, bright green leaves with just a hint of spiciness cook quickly with just the water left from washing them, or can be chopped up and added to a salad. Bright yellow mustard flowers are a tasty, peppery addition to salads. The dry seeds are good for homemade mustard or dressing if you catch them before they shatter onto the ground.

GROWING Plant early in the spring (three weeks before the frost-free date) and again three weeks later. Resume planting from midsummer on for fall harvest. Sow seeds ⅓–½ inch deep and thin seedlings to 3–5 inches apart. Thinnings can be eaten. Protect summer plantings from flea beetles with row cover or insect netting. Fall plantings are usually of higher quality because they mature under cooler conditions in most locations. This cool-weather nutritious crop shares cultural requirements with members of the cabbage family.

HARVESTING Harvest the leaves when they are young and tender. Do not use wilted or yellowed leaves. You can cut the entire plant or pick individual leaves as they grow. The smaller the leaves the more tender they are. The leaf texture becomes tough and the flavor strong in summer. You can either clip off the leaves with a scissors or a knife and allow them to grow back to be harvested again, or you can cut the entire plant. Fall mustard leaves should continue to grow until you start getting regular frosts. Wrap unwashed mustard greens tightly and store in the refrigerator's crisper drawer for up to one week. Mustard greens tend to hold sand and dirt, so wash thoroughly before cooking.

VARIETIES **Florida Broadleaf** (45 days) has very large leaves and is slow to bolt in hot weather. The very heavily curled, dark green leaves of **Green Wave** (45 days) also stay tasty despite the heat. Also very slow to bolt is **Southern Giant Curled** (50 days), with bright green, curly, well-crinkled leaves.

SEED SAVING If you want a variety to be stable from year to year, you'll need to isolate it from other mustard plants (and Chinese cabbage) of the same species by a minimum of 600 feet for home use. For pure seed, isolate varieties by ¼–½ mile. Allow overwintered plants to bolt in spring and harvest the siliques (long, slender seed pods) when they and the seeds inside them are brown. Allow them to dry in a layer no more then ¼ inch thick for two weeks.

Okra

Breaded and fried, pickled with hot peppers, or thickening Creole gumbo, okra is a favorite throughout the Southeast. Okra was probably brought to the region early in the 1700s by enslaved people from West Africa. The tall plants are beautiful in edible landscapes, and the mature pods can be used in dried flower arrangements and decorations.

GROWING Plant okra in full sun and warm, well-drained soil. For faster germination, I recommend soaking the seeds overnight before sowing. Sow straight into the ground outside, three to four weeks after your average last frost, ¾ inch deep in rows 3–6 feet apart. Thin to 9–18 inches apart (taller varieties need more space). For small plantings, sow two or three seeds at each spot where you want a mature plant, and pick the strongest seedling to keep. (You can extend your season by starting transplants indoors four weeks beforehand, but handle the fragile roots carefully.) Four or five plants are enough for most families. Use plentiful organic mulch to control weeds, especially when the plants are young. Crop rotation and wide spacing (good air circulation) help prevent diseases like root knot nematodes and mildew.

HARVESTING Harvest when the pods are still young and tender, generally 2–3 inches long, but some varieties stay tender when much larger. Cut the pods off the branches, leaving about ¼ inch of stem; don't pull them off. If the thorny plants bother your skin, you'll want to wear gloves and long sleeves. For high yields, harvest okra daily or every other day. Any hard, fibrous older pods should be removed and composted, as leaving them on the plants stops production. Okra stores best at 45–50°F and high humidity.

VARIETIES **Clemson Spineless** (56 days), 1993 AAS winner, is the most widely grown okra in the US. Choose dwarf varieties for small gardens. The heirloom **Cajun Jewel** (53 days) is my favorite dwarf plant (2½–4 feet) for abundant, early delicious pods. **Hill County Heirloom Red** (64 days) is my pick for an edible and ornamental hedge planting.

SEED SAVING Isolate varieties by ⅛ mile for home use. Allow the okra pods to get large and dry off naturally on the stalk before harvesting. Dry the pods thoroughly for several more days under cover. Then remove the seeds and store in a cool, dry place in tightly closed jars.

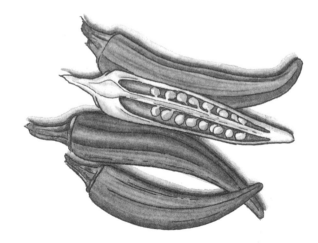

Onions

Onions have a reputation for being a challenging crop, but these culinary essentials are actually a cinch when you choose the right types and use the right timing for our region. For a year-round kitchen staple, choose storage types, like pungent yellow bulbing onions and lesser-known—but extremely easy to grow in our region—perennial multiplier onions. Crisp green onions give your cooking a professional touch, and they're very easy to grow. For a growing guide for perennial multiplier onions (i.e., potato onions and shallots) see the October chapter; if you plan to grow perennial onions, be sure to order bulbs well in advance of fall planting.

GROWING Bulbing onions have only a short window of time to grow before spring heat or lengthening days trigger the bulbs to stop growing and start drying down. To ensure they have enough time to grow before this happens, Southeast gardeners sow onion seeds in the fall through very early spring, and choose the right varieties for our latitude. Short Day (SD) types bulb with 10–12 hours of daylight; grow these south of 35°N. Northern gardeners grow Long Day (LD) types, which bulb with 14–16 hours of daylight; these are best grown north of 38°N. If you're in between these latitudes, like many of us in the Upper South, choose LD varieties that mature on the early side (look at the day length), or choose SD varieties. You'll have the best results if you sow in fall and keep the seedlings growing over winter in the greenhouse, cold frame, or under row cover.

In the Upper South, sow bulbing onion seeds in a cold frame or greenhouse. In the Lower South, gardeners can direct sow bulbing onion seeds in the garden. Sow the seeds ½ inch apart if you plan to transplant later, or 2 inches apart if you direct sow. Thin to about 3 inches apart. Cover with fine soil or compost, ¼–½ inch deep. Be sure to transplant when the seedlings are still a little narrower than a pencil, and by early spring (February). Onions don't tolerate weeds, so prioritize weeding this crop. Provide ample moisture. Organic mulch helps keep down the weeds and keeps in water and nutrients. Practice crop rotation of at least three years to control pests and diseases.

Traditional green onions (often sold as bunching onions) only do really well in our region in the fall through spring (under cover where winters are cold). Sow them just like bulbing onions, but at about ½ inch apart and thin or transplant to at least 1 inch apart. (Turn to perennial bunching chives for green onion style in the hottest months.) Sow just once in the fall, or for lots sow once in the fall and again in the early spring. A single sowing can be harvested over an extended period.

HARVESTING For bulbing onions, pull up the whole crop in one harvest for the easiest curing and storage. When half of the tops have fallen over, pull up the bulbs and cure them by hanging or spreading under cover with good ventilation, for two to three weeks. They're done curing when the necks have thoroughly dried. Clip off the tops to within

1 inch of the bulb and store in mesh bags in a well-ventilated place. For green onions, whenever the tops are big enough, you can start harvesting. Pull them up whole.

VARIETIES Short Day (SD) varieties: **Texas Early Grano** (100 days) is often called the mother of all sweet onions, and **Granex hybrid** (80 days) is one of the famous sweet Vidalia types. Long Day (LD) varieties: **Yellow of Parma** (110 days) was the best storage onion in our 2011 trials, and

Red Wethersfield (100 days) was grown by Jefferson at Monticello.

For green onions, **Deep Purple** (60 days) brings extra color, just on the bottoms. **Evergreen Hardy White** (65 days) reliably overwinters even in The North.

SEED SAVING Isolate varieties by a minimum of 150 feet. For pure seed, cage plants or isolate by ¼–½ mile.

Parsnips

Sweet, nutty parsnips are hardy, easy-to-grow root vegetables, closely related to carrots. Parsnips are slow growing, so be patient! They're worth the wait. Heavy frosts sweeten the roots, and they'll happily wait in the ground until you're ready to harvest. For gardeners looking to eat locally year round, parsnips are an old staple worth rediscovering.

GROWING Sow parsnip seeds ½ inch deep, one to two seeds per inch, in rows 18 inches apart, as soon as the soil can be worked in the spring, and by July at the latest. Very far-south and coastal areas may have better results sowing in September for spring harvest. Soak the seeds for 24 hours before sowing to help germination. When your plants emerge, thin to 4-inch spacing. Your soil should be well drained and not too rich. The top 10 inches or deeper should be loose and clod free. Don't let the soil dry out while the seeds are germinating, which can take up to three weeks. Sow radishes every 3–4 inches to prevent soil crusting and mark the rows. Liberal mulch will help give even moisture to the plants.

HARVESTING Use a garden fork to loosen the soil around the roots before pulling them. For the best-tasting parsnips, harvest after a few frosts. You can leave the plants in the ground all winter, but cover them with a thick layer of organic mulch and harvest before new top growth starts in the spring. Parsnips grown in frost-free areas may not develop the same "frost-touched" sweetness. Cut off the leaves ¼ inch above the top of the root and store as you would carrots.

VARIETIES Heirloom varieties **Hollow Crown** and **Turga** both have stout roots good for clay soils. Both are ready in about 100 days, perfect for either spring or fall sowings.

SEED SAVING Isolate varieties of this biennial by ¼ mile for home use. Overwinter and allow to flower. Harvest seeds when they are brown and allow them to dry in a single layer for two weeks.

Peanuts

Originally from Brazil, peanuts were introduced into the southeastern United States during the 1700s. The first commercial peanuts were grown near Wilmington, NC, in about 1800. Most nuts and high-protein crops take a long time and a lot of space before they produce, but this is not the case with peanuts. They are easy to grow, and easy to harvest, and can produce heavy crops. If you have a couple of rows to spare in your garden, give them a try. You can't beat homegrown, home-roasted peanuts (or homemade peanut butter!).

GROWING Shell out the nuts and sow 2 inches deep and 10–12 inches apart in rows 30–36 inches apart. If planting in hills, plant three nuts per hill, 10–12 inches apart, in hills 2–3 feet apart. To get a head start on the season you can start peanuts indoors for four to five weeks before transplanting. Loose, well-drained soil is important for good germination, and a slightly acidic soil pH of 5.8–6.2 will give the best results. Plant after last frost. Peanuts require 100 to 140 days of hot weather and ample rainfall to yield a good crop. When the plants are 12 inches tall, hill them up with loose soil as you would with potatoes, and mulch between the rows to keep the soil loose for easy pegging (when the runners dip into the ground to form peanuts). Keep the soil moist until the plants begin to flower, then water less, allowing the soil to dry between watering. Too much water during flowering can lead to poor germination and empty pods.

HARVESTING Harvest in mid- to late October or after a light frost. Peanuts are ready for harvest when the leaves turn yellow and begin to wither, usually 120 to 150 days after planting. Lift pods with a garden fork, pulling up the whole plant. Shake away loose soil and hang the whole plant to dry for about two weeks in a warm, dry place. Seeds can be removed when the hulls are completely dry.

VARIETIES **Tennessee Red Valencia** (110 days) is a quick variety for the Upper South. **Shronce's Deep Black** (110 days) is gorgeous pan fried with oil. **Carwile's Virginia** (120 days) is a delicious heirloom variety of the classic Virginia peanut.

SEED SAVING Raw peanuts may be left in the shell and saved for replanting the following spring. Once dried, place the peanuts in mesh bags and store them in a cool, well-ventilated place.

Peas

Fresh peas are a joy of the spring garden. Thomas Jefferson delighted his neighbors at Monticello by growing the earliest spring peas. Before the 1940s, all peas were shelling peas or snow peas, but edible-podded sugar snap peas have fast become a garden standard. In cool weather, peas are a trouble-free crop and a delightful snack straight off the vine.

GROWING Pea vines are more resistant to freezing than the pods, so spring-sown peas can get a running start. Sow peas as soon as the soil can be worked in the spring and sow successions every two to three weeks. Where winters are mild, gardeners can make fall and even overwintered plantings. Sow the seeds 1 inch deep and 1–2 inches apart in double rows with an appropriate trellis. Tamp down the soil. You won't need to thin peas.

Peas work with bacteria to "fix" nitrogen from the atmosphere. In new gardens, "pepper" the moistened seeds with nitrogen-fixing soil inoculant just before planting. Peas need well-drained soil, rich in phosphorus and potassium. Too much nitrogen promotes leafy growth and a poor harvest. Pre-sprouting peas is worth the effort. Soak the seeds overnight and then keep them moist in a sprouting jar or damp paper towel in a plastic bag for a few days before planting. Get them in the ground as soon as the tiny roots emerge and then use the edges of the beds for spinach or other greens. Choose resistant varieties, avoid touching the plants when they're damp, and use a three- to four-year rotation for disease control.

HARVESTING Peas should be harvested frequently, preferably every other day or even daily. Harvest in the morning for best flavor, but wait for the dew to dry off first. Touching damp plants can spread fungal disease. Chill promptly. The sooner you eat or freeze peas, the sweeter they will be. Snap peas and shelling peas are ready for harvest as soon as the pods are filled out. Snow peas are best picked when the pods are still thin, dark green, and tender. Harvest shelling peas when the pods are full but still green.

VARIETIES **Wando** (68 days) is heat tolerant and has been a popular shelling pea in the South since its introduction in 1943. **Sugar Snap** (73 days) has crisp, thick pods that remain sweet and tender when mature. **Sugar Ann** (56 days) is an extra early, crisp, sweet snap pea that does not require staking. **Mammoth Melting Sugar** (70 days) has sweet flavorful pods that hold their quality even if harvested a little late.

SEED SAVING Isolate varieties by a minimum of 50 feet for home use.

Peppers

Peppers are flavorful, nutritious, and ornamental. We southerners are lucky to have the long warm season that peppers need. Everyone knows the familiar sweet bell peppers, but many gardeners are just discovering the joys of growing early-maturing pimentos; the many flavors, colors, and heat-levels of hot peppers; savory Italian frying peppers; and novel ornamental peppers.

GROWING Peppers prefer moderately fertile, well-drained soil, with lots of organic matter. Start your seeds indoors six to eight weeks before the last frost date and transplant to 3-inch pots when several leaves have developed. Harden off your peppers before transplanting out at 18-inch spacing. The plants need warm soil and air temperatures, so don't hurry to move transplants outside (old timers wait until the dogwood blossoms have fallen). Cultivate when the weeds are still small to avoid damaging the shallow roots. Mulch and afternoon shade are very beneficial in late summer. Short stakes may be necessary to prevent large-fruited varieties from falling over when the peppers start maturing.

HARVESTING Keep your plants productive by picking the peppers as soon as they ripen (usually indicated by color—most peppers can be picked at several different color stages). To harvest, use shears or scissors to cut the stem an inch above the fruit. Don't try to twist them off by hand, or you'll risk breaking off whole branches. Peppers will keep for about a week in cool, moist conditions, like the crisper of your refrigerator. Before your first killing frost,

uproot the plants, place the roots in a bucket of water, and store in a cool place. The peppers will continue ripening on the plants for up to a month.

VARIETIES For sweet bell peppers, try **Keystone Giant** (79 days) or nematode-resistant **Charleston Belle** (67 days). **Kevin's Early Orange Bell** (70 to 80 days) is my preferred orange bell. Hot peppers are more disease resistant and there are so many kinds: from classic **Jalapenos** (72 days) and **Hungarian Yellow Wax** (60 days) to the milder **Aji Dulce** (111 days) or classic **Hungarian Paprika** (70 days). Small-fruited sweet varieties like **Doe Hill Golden Bell** (60 days), **Lipstick** (55 days), and **Feherozn** (55 days) are all early, tasty, and productive.

SEED SAVING For home seed savers, isolate varieties by at least 50 feet. After the fruits are completely ripe (in their last color phase), cut them open, scrape the seeds onto a paper plate in a single layer, and allow them to dry for two weeks.

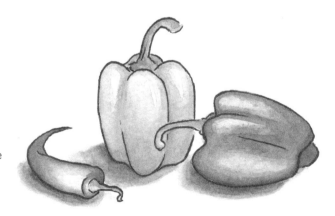

Potatoes

Potato diversity is incredible: the home gardener can choose from an array of colors, textures, flavors, shapes, and sizes. There are 5000 different potato varieties grown worldwide, 3000 in their native Andes. Freshly dug potatoes are tender, flavorful, and cook quickly. Too many to eat right away? Cure your potatoes for a nutritious staple all winter. Best of all, potatoes are easy to grow and a great use of space.

GROWING In the Southeast, we grow two potato crops each year, one in spring and one in fall. Make your early spring planting up to two weeks before average last frost. For fall crops, use early varieties and plant at least 90 days before the average first frost.

You'll need to "chit" your seed potatoes for one to three weeks before planting by spreading them in a single layer in a warm room with bright, indirect light. The skin will green up and grow compact sprouts, or "eyes." Sprouts less than 1 inch long are ideal.

The day before planting, cut any large seed potatoes into pieces no smaller than an egg, with at least two eyes. Potatoes need loose soil well amended with compost. Gently place the seed potatoes at a 12-inch spacing in 4- to 6-inch-deep furrows, 3–4 feet apart. Use a rake to fully cover the potatoes, pushing down with gentle pressure.

After two to three weeks, when the green plants are 6 inches high, apply compost to the soil around the plants and "hill" by mounding soil against the plants to two-thirds of their height. Hill again when the plants have grown another 6 inches. The more stem covered with soil, the more potatoes you'll get. You may want to hill a third time, especially for high-setting potatoes like fingerlings. Any potatoes that get exposed to sunlight will turn green and become toxic, so hilling is very important. The plants benefit from an inch of water weekly, but stop watering two weeks before harvest.

HARVESTING When the plants have turned brown, it's time to dig. Use a heavy garden fork, pushing straight down at least 8 inches from the plant center before angling inward. Spread the harvest on the ground to dry for a few hours before bringing indoors. Any potatoes badly scratched during harvest should be eaten right away. Curing will heal minor scratches and thicken the skin for storage: place the potatoes in a warm, dark place in shallow bins for a week. After curing, you can store potatoes in deeper bins in a dark place at 40–45°F for six months or more.

VARIETIES For early potatoes, **Red Gold** (less than 90 days) is a winner, with attractive golden flesh and red skin. My favorite warm-season potato is yellow-fleshed, tan-skinned **Carola** (90 days). For company, serve **Rose Finn Apple Fingerling**.

SEED SAVING Save only the healthiest, small (1–4 ounce) potatoes for planting. Where winters are mild, viruses build up making seed saving difficult. Southeast gardeners should use certified seed potatoes for disease free stock.

Radishes

Spring radishes come in a rainbow of colors that perk up salads and delight children. Storage radishes are larger and were winter staples in colonial Virginia. Nowadays, they are used for cooking, kimchee, and other pickles as well as a crisp addition to sandwiches and salads. Both are easy-to-grow additions to your garden and your diet.

GROWING For spring radishes, plant as soon as the soil can be worked. Sow ½ inch deep, ¾–1 inch apart in rows or bands. Thin as needed. Even moisture is important for rapid growth and best quality (tender and mild, of course). Start harvesting as soon as the roots are big enough. Succession plant until warm weather makes radishes hot and woody. Plant again in the fall once it's cool out.

For storage radishes, grow these large root veggies in deeply dug soil or raised beds. Start sowing 10 weeks before your first frost date. Make succession plantings to insure against bad weather conditions. Sow seeds ½ inch deep, 2 inches apart, in rows 12–18 inches apart. Thin plants to 4–6 inches apart. In warm weather, mulch radishes to maintain moisture and control weeds. Use row cover to control flea beetles on late summer plantings and extend the fall harvest.

HARVESTING Harvest spring radishes frequently, when they're still small, tender, and mild. Harvest winter radishes through the fall and winter as needed. Use a garden fork to lift roots carefully. Winter radishes store well refrigerated in perforated plastic bags to maintain humidity.

VARIETIES Children love to grow and eat the many colors of round radishes in the "Easter Egg" mix (24 days). Heirloom **White Icicle** (29 days) is elongated, crisp, and sweet. For fall planting, **Daikon** (65 days) is preferred for traditional kimchee. **Misato Rose** (60 days), the lovely "watermelon radish," has a mild flavor and stays crisp and sweet all winter.

SEED SAVING Isolate a minimum of ⅛ mile for home use. Allow overwintered plants (which make the best seed) to bolt in spring and harvest the siliques (long, slender seed pods) when they and the seeds inside them are brown. Allow them to dry in a layer no more then ¼ inch thick for two weeks.

Runner Beans

Runner beans are perennials from Central America that twist the opposite way from other beans—which is interesting, but isn't the best part. The flowers are gorgeous and edible (both the plump buds and the open flowers). The showy, decorative plants quickly climb way up high (so use a trellis). Hummingbirds love them. The young pods are tasty eaten like snap beans, or you can let them fill out and dry for a very pretty soup bean.

GROWING Direct sow runner beans 1 inch deep outside when the soil is 60°F or warmer in the spring, start indoors two weeks before last frost date, or plant in late summer for a fall harvest. Runner beans are frost tender and slower than pole beans to start producing, so don't delay sowing. Keep the pods picked to promote more flowers, even if you don't eat them. For best eating, pick them young and tender. For all peas and beans, avoid handling wet plants. Rotate crops to help control disease. Apply a nitrogen-fixing inoculant to increase yields of these and other legumes.

Provide a tall trellis, as these vines can "run" quite long. In the fall when frosts threaten to kill the vines, dig up the storage root and store it indoors to replant the following spring. The vines will come back more vigorously than from seed, giving you a jump on the season.

HARVESTING Runner beans are harvested and eaten like a green bean when they are young and tender. Pinch off the flowers and buds at any time for a pretty snack. For dry beans, let the pods dry out on the vines before harvesting the beans to finish drying indoors.

VARIETIES **Scarlet Runner** bean (68 days) has beautiful flowers and makes a terrific green bean, especially in the mountains.

SEED SAVING For home use, isolate runner bean varieties by a minimum of 75–150 feet. Process the seeds like other beans.

Southern Greens: Collards and Kale

Classic southern greens are a highly nutritious staple of most any garden in the Southeast. Heat-tolerant collards and frost-loving kale are enjoying a resurgence of popularity. Winter kale can be tender enough for fresh salads, and young collards need only be lightly steamed. Plant lots of kale and collards in the fall with a little cold protection, and you'll be able to harvest these greens all year round. Highly decorative curly kales and variegated collards are striking along a path or in a cool-weather flowerbed. These plants are also excellent choices for container gardening, as they are cut-and-come-again—you can harvest from the same plant for many months.

GROWING Collards and kale are both non-heading cabbage family relatives. Collards are more heat tolerant. Both can be overwintered in much of the South and have improved flavor after being frosted. Kale is best as a cooked green during summer, when it tends to be less tender and stronger flavored, but during the winter it's delicious and tender raw in salad. Use collards lightly steamed when young and tender, or slow cook the larger leaves southern style. Direct sow ¼–½ inch deep, 2 inches apart, in rows 36 inches apart, in fertile, well-drained soil. Thin to about 12–18 inches apart when the plants have two to three true (non-seedling) leaves. These plants transplant very well: space transplants 12–18 inches apart. Keep direct-sown fall plantings moist for best germination (you'll probably need to sow while the weather is still hot in order to get much growth before cool weather). Mulching helps maintain even moisture and keep the leaves clean. Row cover provides excellent protection against flea beetles for fall plantings, helps plants survive and thrive during winter lows, and gets you a head start on spring growth.

HARVESTING Snip off or twist off the large outer leaves before they reach 12 inches long; leave the inner leaves to continue growing. Harvest regularly, but never take more than 40 percent of the leaves at one time, and give the plants a few days to recover. One technique is to establish a harvest rotation, where you cycle through three or four beds on each successive day. Older leaves become tough and stringy, and should be discarded. You can also harvest whole plants, but you'll need to plant in successions for continuous harvests of young plants. Most varieties produce tender young greens in about 40 days.

VARIETIES The dark green leaves of Italian heirloom **Lacinato** kale (60 days), also known as dinosaur kale, are a good substitute for cooked spinach. Curly leaved **Vates** kale (55 days) is flavorful and easily grows through winter in our region. **Georgia Green** (75 days) was my grandmother's favorite collard in our sandy Florida garden. I still enjoy its sweet, tender fall leaves here in our red Virginia clay. **Variegated** (80 days) collards are an interesting addition to an insectary planting, as the variegation appears with flowering. Another interesting collard is **Green Glaze** (79 days), with smooth, bright green leaves, rich flavor, and excellent resistance to cabbage worms.

SEED SAVING Collards and kale (*Brassica oleracea*) will cross with each other and with broccoli, Brussels sprouts, cabbage, cauliflower, and kohlrabi. Isolate by ⅛ mile for home use. Red Russian–type kale (*Brassica napus*) crosses with rutabaga and some rapeseed (canola).

Southern Peas: Crowder Peas, Black-Eyed Peas; Asparagus Beans

Southern peas are delicious, pest-resistant, drought-tolerant stars of the summer garden in the Southeast. These African legumes were brought to the United States by slaves and served as a tasty treat during hard times. They have low fertility requirements because, like other legumes, they fix nitrogen in root nodules formed by symbiotic bacteria. Asparagus or yard-long beans are a close relative from Asia that many Americans only know from stir-fry dishes at Asian buffets.

GROWING Southern peas and asparagus beans thrive in hot weather with full sun and well-drained soil. They are drought tolerant and grow well throughout the South without irrigation. Wait until the soil has really warmed up before planting. Sow seed 1 inch deep, 3–6 inches apart, in rows 18–42 inches apart. Most varieties of asparagus beans are vining and need a sturdy 6-foot trellis. Most cowpeas are also easier to harvest with a short trellis. Cowpeas actually prefer a less nitrogen-rich soil—too much fertilizer will give you lots of green and no beans.

HARVESTING Asparagus beans are best harvested long and thin at 12–15 inches long before peas begin to fill out the pods. Pick cowpeas either as green shelling peas or for dry cooking peas. The yield is similar to green beans. For fresh eating, wait until the pods begin to thin for easier shelling. The pods will become more flexible and the pod color will change. When you think they are ready, shell out a few to see. For dry soup beans, wait until the pods are brittle, papery husks, and finish drying indoors.

VARIETIES The three main types are mild-flavored black-eyed peas, stronger-flavored crowder peas, and mildest-flavored cream peas. Among the mostly bush black-eyed peas, I really like **Queen Anne Blackeye Pea** (68 days) and **Pink Eye Purple Hull** (65 days), a short bush type with pods held high for easy picking. My favorite crowder peas are **Colossus** (75 days), **Mississippi Silver** (64 days), and **Whippoorwill** (75 days), all larger vining plants that require staking. **Lady** (66 days) and **Zipper Cream** (65 to 70 days) are small bush types. **Chinese Red Noodle** asparagus beans (95 days) are tasty and make a striking ornamental edible growing on a strong trellis.

SEED SAVING Isolate from other southern peas and asparagus beans by a minimum of 50 feet for home use. Harvest like dry beans.

Spinach

Popeye's favorite food has come a long way, from the prickly spinach grown by Jefferson, to acres of winter spinach near Norfolk in the 1930s, to the commercial fields in the Texas Garden belt today. It's easy for home gardeners to grow spinach in cooler weather from fall through spring, and it's a standby for winter harvests. Spinach makes great fresh salads, wonderful soups, quiches, and soufflés.

GROWING Spinach likes cool weather, short days, high soil fertility, and ample water. Neutral soil (pH 6.5–7.5) is important, so get a soil test. For acid soil, incorporate limestone three months before planting. If you miss your chance, add some in the row as you plant. In heavy soil, raised beds improve drainage and lessen damping-off. Sow ¼–½ inch deep as soon as the ground can be worked. Thin seedlings to 4–6 inches apart. Use the thinnings in salads. Make new succession plantings every 10 to 14 days in the spring and fall for a steady supply of tender leaves. First spring plantings should be in full sun. Later plantings may need partial shade. Mulch keeps roots cool to reduce bolting, lessen weeding, and conserve moisture. Fall plantings starting six weeks before the first frost give a more sustained harvest than spring plantings. Extend fall harvest through until spring with floating row cover.

HARVESTING Pick the outer leaves as needed. Smaller leaves are more tender. Discard the stem if it's tough. Rinse well. Harvest baby spinach in three to five weeks. Fresh spinach keeps for 10 to 14 days in cool temperatures and high humidity. Spinach freezes well but with a good fall/winter garden, you can have fresh spinach for eight months of the year.

VARIETIES **Bloomsdale Long Standing** (42 days) is the best-known heirloom spinach and my personal favorite for its attractive, savoyed dark green leaves, good flavor, and slow bolting. **America** (45 days) won a 1955 All-America selection for its multiple disease resistances. For a summer substitute, try **Malabar** spinach (70 days), a highly ornamental vine that can be trellised for easy harvesting, or **New Zealand** spinach (62 days)—neither is a true spinach.

SEED SAVING Plant only one variety or isolate by ¼ mile for home use. Allow the plants to bolt. They will declare themselves male or female plants. Harvest the seed from the female plants when they are brown and allow them to dry in a single layer for two weeks.

Strawberries

Strawberries are delicious and highly nutritious. One cup of juicy red berries supplies an adult's daily requirement for vitamin C. Strawberries are one of the easiest-to-grow and most popular fruits for the home garden. A range of different varieties is available from local independent nurseries and reliable online merchants, so it is easy to get started growing a variety well suited to your location.

GROWING Select a site with full sun (at least eight hours a day) and rich, well-drained soil, or plant in raised beds or rows well amended with compost and any organic amendments indicated by a soil test. Strawberries prefer a slightly acidic soil so follow any recommendations for altering pH as well. In any case, work in a 3-inch layer of compost to add organic matter. There are two systems of strawberry culture in common use in the Southeast: matted rows and annual rows. The matted row system involves planting the mother plants 2 feet apart the first spring, then letting runners fill the bed the first summer. The flowers are removed the first year, so no fruit is produced until the second year. In the Upper South, beds using the matted row system and bare root plants are usually started in early spring. In the Lower South, because of disease pressure, the fall-planted annual row system (where plants are discarded after harvest) is the norm using plug plants. Fall-planted plugs are spaced 12 inches apart. Plants of appropriate varieties are available seasonally at local nurseries and through reputable online merchants. Proper placement of plants so the crown is at ground level and not buried is important.

Mulching or regular cultivation is essential and regular watering is also essential for good yields.

HARVESTING Strawberries will be ready for harvesting four to six weeks after blossoming. Harvest continues for about three weeks. Look for fully red berries. Harvest by the stem every three days. Store unwashed berries in fridge for three to five days or freeze whole berries for longer storage.

VARIETIES **Chandler** is the variety of choice for annual row planting with high yields, good fruit color, and excellent flavor. **Sparkle** produces berries with excellent flavor late in the season. For an everbearer, **Ozark Beauty** has excellent flavor and production. Most everbearing strawberries take a summer snooze if the temperatures get really high; we find everbearing plants only produce in spring and fall in our region.

SEED SAVING Strawberries are propagated from runners. Save healthy young plants instead of the original mother plants. Start new beds in a distant location to avoid buildup of nematodes and viruses in the soil.

Sweet Potatoes

....

Sweet potatoes are delicious, nutritious, and easy to grow in the Southeast. Typically yielding well over one pound per plant, this easy-to-grow summer crop does not need refrigeration for long-term storage.

GROWING Sweet potatoes need at least four months of frost-free growing. Most gardeners start with slips (young plants) purchased from a local garden center or reputable mail order source. Your new slips may not have roots, but don't worry, they'll grow roots once they're in the ground. Transplant your slips into the ground outdoors 2–3 inches deep, with the leaves above the ground, 10–18 inches apart, in rows at least 3 feet apart (to make room for the sprawling vines). Transplant in the evening and water immediately. Continue to water every few days until the plants are established.

Sweet potatoes like loose, well-drained soil. If you have clay soil or drainage problems, work in lots of compost and make raised beds or planting ridges 8–12 inches high. Keep the young plants well weeded, until the vigorous vines shade out new weeds. In most areas, sweet potatoes can produce a decent crop without additional watering after the plants are established, but irrigation will assure a larger harvest and prevent splitting and cracks.

HARVESTING You can harvest sweet potato leaves and young shoots for greens at any time. The tubers are ready to harvest as soon as they reach your preferred size. To harvest, begin by pulling up the vines and setting them aside so you can see where you are digging. Use a garden fork to carefully loosen the soil around the sweet potatoes (avoid damaging them with your fork). Dig sweet potatoes before the soil temperature drops below 55°F or the storage quality will be reduced. Freshly dug sweet potatoes are easily bruised by rough handling. Cure the potatoes by holding them at high humidity and 85°F for a week before storing.

VARIETIES Most gardeners prefer quick-maturing varieties like **Beauregard** (100 days) and **Georgia Jet** (100 days). The white-fleshed **O'Henry** (100 days) is good mashed and in savory dishes. **Bush Porto Rico** (also sold as **Puerto Rico**) (110 days) is a good choice for small gardens and large containers.

SEED SAVING Select well-formed, small- to medium-sized roots from your best-producing plants to save for seed and grow your own slips the following spring.

Swiss Chard

The multi-colored Rainbow varieties of chard have made a splash with both gardeners and cooks. A few plants can produce tasty and nutritious greens in spring, summer, and fall. In the Southeast, the mild green leaves provide an excellent substitute for cooked spinach in warmer months.

GROWING Swiss chard prefers full sun or light shade and fertile, well-drained soil with neutral pH. It tolerates some frost. Start indoors or in a cold frame a month before setting out. Or direct sow at the frost-free date and again in late summer for fall. Soak seeds overnight for quicker germination and plant ½ inch deep. For full-size plants, thin to 12 inches apart in rows 15 inches apart. Snip and eat your thinnings. Mulch to maintain moisture, reduce weeding, cool the soil, and keep the leaves clean. Remove older leaves to keep your plants growing vigorously. Extend the season in winter with floating row cover.

HARVESTING Pick outer leaves as needed when they are over 6 inches long. Leave the center of the plant intact. Soak leaves immediately in cold water, drain, and refrigerate. Clip tender young plants as needed for salads. Like spinach, chard is easy to blanch and freeze.

VARIETIES Multi-colored varieties like **Bright Lights** (60 days) and **Rainbow** (**Five Colored Silverbeet**) are the queens of edible ornamentals. **Leaf Beet** (50 days) varieties, which are often called perpetual spinach, have thinner stems and smaller leaves, excellent for creamed soups and quiche. White-stemmed varieties like **Lucullus** (50 days) are more productive and bolt resistant with more tender stems (petioles). The broad, white stems can be cut out, parboiled in salt water, lightly misted with olive oil, or spread with butter and sprinkled with Parmesan cheese. They are delicious bubbly right from the oven.

SEED SAVING Chard is a biennial that crosses readily with beets. Isolate varieties by at least ¼ mile for home use. Choose the best plants in March. Chard is usually simply overwintered in place. Harvest the seeds in late spring when they are brown and allow them to dry in a single layer for two weeks. The tall heavy seed stalks may require staking or they will fall over.

Tomatillos and Ground Cherries

Bring a taste of Mexico into your garden with tomatillos, an essential ingredient of salsa verde. They have a tangy sweetness some describe as "citrus-y." Ground cherries are smaller, sweeter, and grow closer to the ground, perfect for pies and jam. These drought-tolerant treats in a papery husk love the heat, so they're naturals for the Southeast garden. The fruit varies from cherry size to 4 inches across.

GROWING Grow tomatillos and ground cherries like an indeterminate tomato, in full sun and well-drained soil. Start indoors four to six weeks before last frost date. The seeds germinate best at 75–85°F soil temperature. Harden off and set plants out when soil is warm. Space at least 3 feet apart in rows 3–5 feet apart. The bushy, sprawling plants bear fruit until frost. Trellis or cage upright varieties to save space and maintain good air circulation. Once established, the plants are somewhat drought tolerant but will produce better with an inch of water each week. Keep weeded with shallow cultivation. A 4-inch layer of mulch really helps conserve moisture, control weeds, and keep your fruit clean and looking good.

HARVESTING The fruits are edible at all stages but are sweeter for pies when they start to change color and burst out of their papery husk. Pick the fruits off the ground or directly from the plant when they are still green or yellow-green. For maximum sweetness, let them finish ripening inside until golden hued (some varieties will remain greenish). For distinctive tangy salsa flavor, use tomatillos while they're still a bit green and tart. The fruits will keep for weeks if stored in the husk at about 50°F.

VARIETIES **Cossack Pineapple** (60 days), with its sweet, fruity taste, is my preferred ground cherry for jam, sauces, and pies. Tart-yet-sweet **Tomate Verde** (75 days) is a classic for salsa verde. **Cisineros Grande** (85 days) produces lots of very large fruit for easy harvest.

SEED SAVING Be careful because husk tomatoes self-sow easily and can become weedy. Isolate varieties by 150 feet for pure seed. Allow the tomatillos to ripen for a week or longer after picking, then remove the husks, and select the ripest for seed. Add water to a blender, leaving room for a quarter of the volume of halved fruits to be processed. Blend briefly at lowest speed. The good seeds are heavier than water, and will sink to the bottom. Add more water to float off the pulp and bad seeds on top. Pour the remaining water and seed through a fine strainer. Spread the seeds on a screen or a plate to dry. Fully dry your seeds and store in an airtight container.

Tomatoes

Garden-fresh, vine-ripened tomatoes taste so much better than store bought! Tomatoes thrive in our long, hot summers. This "high-value" crop is a priority for almost every gardener. Even in a small garden, a few plants bring a lot of pleasure. Many busy gardeners buy "starts" from the local greenhouse or farmers market, but starting your own plants from seed lets you choose more exciting and unusual varieties.

GROWING Tomatoes will grow in any fertile, well-drained soil. They need full sun and high organic matter. Start your transplants five to six weeks before the last frost date. Sow seeds ¼ inch deep in 2 inches of potting mix. For high germination, keep the soil warm and moist but not soggy. Provide plenty of light: keep your seedlings in a sunny, south-facing window, under grow lights, or in a greenhouse. Move the seedlings to 3-inch pots when they have two to three true leaves. Harden off when they are 6–10 inches tall by moving them outside during the day. Transplant outside when soil is warm, starting around your average last frost date, into rows 5 feet apart. In-row spacing should be 24 inches for trellises and 3–4 feet for cages. Set each plant in the ground in a shallow, diagonal trench, so that only two or three sets of true leaves are above ground level. Protect your plants when frost threatens by covering them overnight. Trellis or cage plants to keep the fruit off the ground, increase air circulation, and make harvesting easier.

Prevention is the best strategy for pests and diseases. Most tomato diseases can be prevented by keeping your plants growing well with good fertility and soil moisture, keeping the plants dry (by planting in full sun), and maintaining good air circulation (by planning for adequate space between plants). Even soil moisture will prevent fruit cracking. Apply mulch once the ground is warm to help keep the soil moist. Consider using drip irrigation or soaker hoses. Be sure to buy your seeds and starts from a reputable source. Rotate nightshade crops to prevent disease.

HARVESTING Start harvesting any time after the fruit are fully colored. Tomatoes are best stored in a cool (but not cold) place, above 50°F.

VARIETIES There are hundreds of tomato varieties to choose from and each one is someone's favorite. Determinate varieties are often earlier and shorter, but indeterminate varieties will keep producing tomatoes right up until frost. As a seed saver, I prefer open-pollinated (OP) and heirloom varieties, but I look for disease resistance, flavor, and productivity as well. In our test gardens at Southern Exposure Seed Exchange and at the large public tomato tasting we sponsor at the Heritage Harvest Festival at Monticello, these varieties have been consistent winners.

Cherry tomatoes are easy to grow and a great choice for new gardeners. **Matt's Wild Cherry** (60 days) produces loads of intensely flavored, small, deep red cherry tomatoes until frost. **Amy's Apricot** (70 days) is a flavor contender for an OP alternative to the ever-popular hybrid **Sungold** (58 days).

Red slicers are red-orange globes perfect for salads and sandwiches. **Old Virginia** (80 days) is a productive, heirloom, 5–7 ounce red slicer with a real old-timey sweet, tart flavor. **Tropic VFN** (80 days) is a vigorous,

Tomatoes, continued

disease-resistant, large, orange red 12-ounce tomato that came out of the traditional breeding program at the University of Florida in Pensacola.

Paste tomatoes are a must for salsa and marinara sauce. **Roma Virginia Select** (75 days) is a farmer-selected paste tomato that delivers large quantities of paste tomatoes even under disease pressure. **Amish Paste** (80 to 90 days) is the largest paste tomato I have grown.

For unusual colors, **Garden Peach** (73 days) resembles a peach in both color and in its fuzzy, textured skin. The very large, flavorful **Cherokee Purple** (85 days) ripens to a unique dark, dusty pink-purple. Pink tomatoes aren't really pink: **Eva Purple Ball** (78 days) is one of my all-time favorites, and the color could be described as a deep rose. It's classified as a pink, while purple tomatoes tend to be red-brown.

Large, flavorful heirlooms are the reason some people want homegrown tomatoes: they're perfect for sandwiches. Here are a few of our favorite big slicers: **Granny Cantrell's** (69 to 80 days) is a large, German, red-pink tomato with a flavor like the famous **Brandywine** (82 days); **Mortgage Lifter VFN** (83 days) is a delicious, large red tomato with an unforgettable story from West Virginia.

SEED SAVING Isolate varieties by a minimum of 35 feet for home use or bag fruit clusters to maintain purity. Harvest fruit when fully ripe and scoop the center of the fruit with the pulp and seeds into a container with a loose lid. Let it sit at room temperature until bubbles stop forming (about three days) stirring every 12 hours. Add water and float or pull off the pulp and floating seeds. Rinse and then spread the heavier seed from the bottom of the container in a thin layer on a screen or plate and allow to dry for three weeks before storing.

Turnips and Rutabagas

With the public's new interest in local foods, both turnips and rutabagas are experiencing a renaissance in interest from gardeners and gourmet chefs looking for local winter fare. Turnips are an early spring or fall crop that produce smaller, paler roots (often actually white). They are quick growing and frequently are eaten while quite small. These qualities make them good for greenhouse and hoop-house growing. Some turnip varieties keep pretty well, others don't. Some are grown mainly for their greens. Rutabagas are also called Swedish turnips or Swedes, and are usually planted as a fall/winter crop producing larger, yellower roots. They are more productive than turnips and store very well. In milder areas, they can overwinter in the ground.

GROWING Both turnips and rutabagas prefer full sun and loose soil. Maintain even moisture (don't let them dry out) and don't crowd the roots. They don't need a lot of nitrogen. Plant turnips in early spring and then again in the late summer, allowing 70 days to mature. Sow ½ inch deep and keep moist. Keep them well weeded. Thin to 1 inch apart first, then 3 inches apart; eventually thin larger varieties to 5 inches apart. Young thinnings make good eating. Plant rutabagas so they will grow 90 to 100 days before hard frost. Thin to 4 inches when they're 1 inch tall and 10 inches apart when 3 inches tall. Flea beetles can savage young plants so use row cover or the newer insect netting to protect summer plantings. Keep your crop weeded and watered for vigorous growth. The best disease control is good sanitation (removing residue) and rotating all cabbage family plants.

HARVESTING Most turnips are best harvested young and tender at 2–3 inches. Harvest rutabagas at 3–6 inches. Trim roots and tops right away (unless you're selling bunched young turnips). To overwinter rutabagas, mulch heavily once the temperature gets down to around 20°F. Harvest greens when they're still young and tender and chill them immediately for best quality.

VARIETIES **Hakurei** (38 days) is the best-known gourmet salad turnip. **Scarlett Ohno Revival** (55 days) is a lovely, tender, red-skinned Japanese variety. **Seven Top** (45 days) is the variety of choice for traditional southern salad greens.

SEED SAVING Isolate a minimum of 600 feet for home use. Allow overwintered plants to bolt in spring and harvest the siliques (long, slender seed pods) when they and the seeds inside them are brown. Allow them to dry in a layer no more then ¼ inch thick for two weeks.

Watermelon

Few things satisfy like an ice-cold slice of sweet, juicy watermelon. From petite icebox melons to large county-fair-size rattlesnake types, watermelons are symbolic of summer in the South. It is an easy crop to grow if you have a long season and enough space. Ingenious gardeners have even gotten around the space issue by growing small melons on a chain-link fence using a sling to hold the developing melons. Now if only there was a quick way to learn how to tell when your watermelon is ready to harvest.

GROWING Watermelons are similar to muskmelons in that they prefer a location with full sun and excellent drainage. Direct seed in late spring after the chance of frost has past. Sow seeds 12–18 inches apart in rows or hills 6–8 feet apart. Vines require anywhere from 36–100 square feet of vine space per hill, depending on variety. Be careful not to disturb watermelon vines while cultivating around them. When planted in good soil under good environmental conditions, melons will do well, but are not as consistent producers as some other crops.

HARVESTING Determining when a watermelon is ripe is an acquired skill that is important because watermelons don't continue ripening after harvest. The first clues are visual. Gently roll or lift the melon and look at the underside. Ripe melons turn a creamy, light yellow color that is hard to mistake once you have some practice. Next ,look to see if the tendril closest to the melon has dried up. The real test is sound. A ripe melon sounds hollow. Once you hear it, it will become a welcome harmony and you'll seldom harvest a less-than-ripe melon afterwards.

VARIETIES Sugar Baby (77 days) is my most reliable small, red-fleshed sweet watermelon. **Orangeglo** (85 days) is one of the best orange-fleshed watermelons. **Crimson Sweet** (85 days) has it all: red-fleshed, exceptionally sweet, disease resistant, and a consistent producer of medium-size melons. It has been a favorite with gardeners for over fifty years.

SEED SAVING Isolate varieties by at least ⅛ mile for home use, or ½–1 mile for pure seed. When fruits are fully ripe, scoop the flesh out into a bucket and leave at room temperature for two to three days, stirring every 12 hours. Rinse seeds through a strainer and spread in a thin layer to dry for three weeks.

Winter Squash, Pumpkins, and Gourds

Winter squash and pumpkins have been grown in the Southeast for thousands of years. They come in a variety of different sizes, shapes, and colors. Some of the best-tasting pumpkin pies are actually made from squash, but who can resist an autumn field strewn with bright orange jack-o-lanterns and baby boos? In addition to having fine flesh for roasting, baking, boiling, mashing, and pies, all have tasty, nutritious edible seeds.

GROWING Winter squash, pumpkins, and gourds have similar growing requirements. All do best in rich, well-drained soil. Where drainage is a problem, plant in elevated " hills." Otherwise, I use enriched stations on the flat.

For a fresh supply as soon as possible, make two sowings: one in the spring around your average last frost, and another in midsummer, timed so the fruits will mature just before first frost. The second sowing is for winter storage, so it should be larger than the first. The plants started in the spring will generally have fewer insect and disease problems, but the fruits won't keep as well in storage. Gardeners in the deep South should time the two crops to avoid the worst summer heat; choose faster-maturing varieties, like acorn and butternut.

You can buy starts at a local nursery to have a lot of different types, but direct sowing will result in stronger taproots and better drought tolerance. Starting this crop from seed is easy; just sow a few extra seeds, ½–1 inch deep, at each final location, and thin. Bush varieties should be spaced 18–30 inches apart in rows 4 feet apart, or 6–8 seeds per hill, in hills 4 feet apart. Plant vining varieties at the same plant spacing, but leave more space (6–8 feet) between rows or hills. Treat gourds like vining squash.

Maintain even soil moisture by mulching heavily once the soil is warm and providing deep irrigation as needed. It's critical to supply adequate water while the fruits are forming. Use floating row cover to conserve warmth early in the season and provide protection from insect pests, but ensure good pollination by uncovering as soon as the flowers begin to open. Weeding becomes difficult once the vines spread, so keep on top of those weeds early. In small gardens, save space by growing small-fruited varieties on a sturdy trellis. Support the fruits once they get heavy.

Squash and pumpkins can be seriously challenged by insects and disease, but you can fight back! First, choose resistant varieties, like butternuts or any other varieties from the species Cucurbita moschata. Second, fertile soil and good conditions go a long way toward helping your squash and pumpkins survive. Use green manures, cover crops, mulch, and compost to improve soil fertility and tilth. Use a three-year rotation for squash plantings. Maintain even moisture. Floating row cover can sometimes mean the difference between a good crop and no crop at all.

HARVESTING Winter squash and pumpkins are mature when the rind can no longer be easily dented by a fingernail. Harvest before first frost. Use pruning shears to cut the stems, leaving an inch or more on the fruit. Take care not to bruise or cut the fruit. Make sure and save the seeds for toasting and serving as a salted treat. The early male squash blooms can be harvested just like from summer squash for stuffing.

Winter Squash, Pumpkins, and Gourds, continued

Cure pumpkins and winter squash in the field to dry and toughen the skin if weather is warm, sunny, and dry, or indoors at temperatures from 80–85°F with 75–80 percent relative humidity for seven to ten days. Store in a cool, dry place. Move gourds to a dry, well-ventilated place for extended drying until they feel light and you can hear the seeds rattling inside.

VARIETIES Some of my favorites for winter squash are **Waltham Butternut** (95 days), which was the 1970 AAS winner, and is the standard for flavor in the South; **Cornell's Bush Butternut** (90 days) is a butternut on compact, bush plants, perfect for small gardens and containers; and **Table Queen Acorn** (85 days) is a classic heirloom with enduring appeal. An heirloom purportedly of Seminole origin, **Seminole Pumpkin** (95 days) can keep in storage for over a year. The vines are very sprawling.

For pie types, **Small Sugar** (100 days) is just right for a small jack-o-lantern and the sweet flesh is excellent for baking. **Winter Luxury Pie** (100 days) is an attractive pumpkin that also makes delicious pies.

Big Max (115 days) is an extra-large, classic Halloween pumpkin, perfect for entering in the County Fair.

SEED SAVING There are four species of cultivated squash and pumpkins: *Cucurbit pepo*, *C. moschata*, *C. maxima*, and *C. mixta*. Crossing occurs easily within each species, and rarely between species. For home use, isolate varieties of the same species by a minimum of ⅛ mile. Let the fruits remain on the plants until the vines fully wither away and the fruits become very large and hard. Bring them in somewhere protected from the rain, at around room temperature, to cure for one month. Cut the fruit, scoop out the seeds, and rinse them, removing all the fleshy matter. Spread them into a thin layer to dry for three weeks.

Zucchini and Summer Squash

Deciding what to do with all those zucchini is one of our favorite summer rituals. Some gardeners host zucchini parties, with prizes for the most inventive dish and creative carving. Zucchini and summer squash come in a range of shapes and colors, but all are versatile. Grill with salt and olive oil, bake in dessert breads, slice raw for salads or in thin strips for low-carb "pasta." The large, yellow blossoms are edible; use them in salads or roast them with cheese and nut filling. Most varieties are young fruits of the species Cucurbita pepo. *Southeast gardeners sometimes have trouble with this species, with vine borers and plant diseases: if that's the case, you have options! Read on for varieties and alternatives especially suited to hot climates.*

GROWING We usually direct sow (½–1 inch deep) and set out two- to three-week old transplants at the same time, right around our average last frost date. One or the other set usually performs better, depending on conditions. Start transplants in 2- or 3-inch pots and be sure to move them to their final location while they're still small. Give bush varieties at least 4 square feet, vining varieties at least 9 square feet. Mulch well once the soil is warm.

Where pests and diseases cut harvests short, start a new crop every four weeks until late summer (generally we'll make three plantings, if you're in the deep South take a rest in high summer). Choose resistant varieties, maintain even moisture and soil fertility (including calcium), use a three-year crop rotation for all squash, and clean up last season's crop debris. Later sowings tend to have more insect problems; use floating row cover to protect the young plants, but remove it as soon as the blossoms open to allow for pollination.

HARVESTING Pick the fruits small for the best flavor and texture, generally at 5–8 inches. Pick "Patty Pan" types at 3–4 inches. Pick the fruits often to find them before they become giants. If you discover a very large fruit lurking in the undergrowth, hollow it out, fill with your stuffing of choice, and roast or grill.

VARIETIES **Benning's Green Tint Scallop** (52 days), a delicious pale green southern heirloom Patty Pan, and **Yellow Crookneck** (55 days) are traditional southern favorites. **Black Zucchini** (48 days) is the best-known zucchini, but **Tender Grey** (42 days) has remarkable flavor even when large. **Butter Blossom** (50 days) has large, firm male blossoms perfect for stuffing.

For hot climates, the Italian variety **Tromboncino** (*Cucurbita moschata*) (80 days) is a boon to gardeners plagued by vine borers, but you'll need a sturdy trellis or plenty of space for the vigorous vines. The fruits stay tender and sweet to 10 inches; let them mature for winter squash similar to butternut. Young **Luffa** gourds and young **Butternut** winter squash perform well where pests are an issue.

SEED SAVING Isolate varieties of the same species by a minimum of ⅛ mile for home use.

Resources

Appalachian Seeds
Burnsville, NC
www.appalachianseeds.com
(828) 400-7014
Heirloom tomato seeds, certified
organic tomato, herb, perennial
flower, and gourmet vegetable plants.

Baker Creek Heirloom Seeds
Mansfield, MO
www.rareseeds.com
(417) 924-8917
One of the largest selections of
heirloom, open-pollinated, NON-GMO
seeds.

Berlin Seeds
Millersburg, OH
(877) 464-0892
Amish garden seed and supply
company offering good growing tips
and old-style equipment. Write for
catalog.

Big Horse Creek Nursery
Lansing, NC
www.bighorsecreekfarm.com
(336) 384-1134
Specializing in antique and heirloom
apple trees and custom grafting
services.

Bountiful Gardens
Willits, CA
www.bountifulgardens.org
(707) 459-6410
Open-pollinated vegetables, herbs,
flowers, grains, green manures, bio-
intensive products.

Eden Brothers
Dahlonega, GA
www.edenbrothers.com
(877) 333-6276
Large selection of vegetable seeds,
bulbs, and wildflower mixes shipped
from both coasts.

Edible Landscaping
Afton, VA
www.ediblelandscaping.com
(804) 361-9134
Large selection of container grown
fruits, berries, vines, nuts, and herbs
for edible landscaping.

Fedco Seeds
Clinton, ME
www.fedcoseeds.com
(207) 426-9900
Coop offering great selection and low
prices for short-season vegetable,
herb, and flower seeds.

Finch Blueberry Nursery
Bailey, NC
www.danfinch.com
(800) 245-4662
A big selection of rabbiteye
blueberries, with some unique
varieties, including rare creepers.

Gourmet Garlic Gardens
Bangs, TX
www.gourmetgarlicgardens.com
(325) 348-3049
Offering excellent information about
growing garlic in the South and many
unusual varieties of garlic.

Gourmet Seed International LLC
Tatum, NM
www.gourmetseed.com
(575) 398-6111
Generous packets of vegetable, herb,
and flower seeds from around the
world. Organic gardeners should note
that some seed is treated.

Hidden Springs Nursery
Cookeville, TN
www.hiddenspringsnursery.com
(931) 268-2592
Hector Black's unusual fruits,
including medlar and autumn olive.

Ison's Nursery & Vineyards

Brooks, GA

www.isons.com

(800) 733-0324

Large selection of fruit and nut trees for the South: muscadines, scuppernongs (over 40 varieties), blueberries, brambleberries, grapes, and more.

Johnny's Selected Seeds

Winslow, ME

www.johnnyseeds.com

(877) 564-6697

Excellent selection of quality heirloom, organic, and hybrid seeds with a slightly northern bias. Cool tools.

Johnson Nursery

Ellijay, GA

www.johnsonnursery.com

(888) 276-3187

Hardy fruit trees and small fruits for the home orchard, including antique and disease-resistant varieties, and orchard supplies.

JW Jung Seed Co.

Randolph, WI

www.jungseed.com

(800) 297-3123

Supplier of quality seeds, fruits, and horticultural products. Not to be confused with Monsanto-owned Jung Seed Genetics.

New Hope Seed Company

Bon Aqua, TN

www.newhopeseed.com

info@newhopeseed.com

Open-pollinated vegetable seeds including many family heirlooms.

Niche Gardens

Chapel Hill, NC

www.nichegardens.com

(919) 967-0078

A Southeast nursery with native perennials, underused trees, and shrubs.

Park Seed

Greenwood, SC

parkseed.com

(800) 845-3369

One of the oldest seed companies in the South offering flower, herb, and vegetable seeds plus a huge trial garden.

Peaceful Valley Farm Supply

Grass Valley, CA

www.groworganic.com

(888) 784-1722

California company offering organic gardeners the seeds, plants, supplies, and information they need since 1976.

The Pepper Gal

Fort Lauderdale, FL

www.peppergal.com

(954) 537-5540

One-woman show with a great selection of pepper seeds.

Pepper Joe's, Inc.

Timonium, MD

www.pepperjoe.com

(843) 742-5116

Offering seeds for some of the hottest peppers in the world.

Pinetree Garden Seeds

New Gloucester, ME

www.superseeds.com

(207) 926-3400

Good selection of very small packets for the home gardener.

Sandy Mush Herb Nursery

Leicester, NC

www.sandymushherbs.com

(704) 683-2014

Extensive listing of herb plants and unusual perennials.

Seed Savers Exchange

Decorah, IA

www.seedsavers.org

(563) 382-5990

A nonprofit membership organization, offers wonderful heirloom seed, a beautiful catalog, and a great mission to preserve our vegetable seed heritage.

Seeds for the South

Graniteville, SC

www.seedsforthesouth.com

orders@vegetableseedwarehouse.com

Untreated heirloom and hybrid vegetable seeds for the South.

Southern Exposure Seed Exchange
Mineral, VA
www.southernexposure.com
(540) 894-9480
Over 700 heirloom, organic, NON-GMO, open-pollinated varieties selected for flavor and regional adaptability. Heirloom garlic, multiplier onion, okra, southern peas, and other regional specialties.

Sow True Seeds
Asheville, NC
www.sowtrueseed.com
(828) 254-0708
Open-pollinated, non-GMO seeds, including many heirloom, organic, and traditional varieties for western North Carolina.

Sustainable Mountain Agricultural Center
Berea, KY
www.heirlooms.org
(859) 986-3204
Nonprofit preserving southern Appalachian heirloom beans, tomatoes, and knowledge about seed saving.

Territorial Seed Co.
Cottage Grove, OR
www.territorialseed.com
(800) 626-0866
Quality vegetable, herb, and flower seed selected for the Pacific Northwest and beyond.

Tomato Growers Supply
Fort Myers, FL
www.tomatogrowers.com
(888) 478-7333
Huge selection of heirloom and hybrid tomato, pepper, and eggplant seeds.

Vintage Virginia Apples
North Garden, VA
www.vintagevirginiaapples.com
(434) 297-2326
Offers workshops, roots, grafting supplies, and trees for historic and contemporary apples of distinction.

White Harvest Seed Company
Hartville, MO
whiteharvestseed.com
(866) 424-3185
Christian family business offering heirloom seeds and survival kits.

COMMUNITY RESOURCES

ATTRA
www.attra.ncat.org
ATTRA is The National Sustainable Agriculture Information Service. It is developed and managed by the National Center for Appropriate Technology (NCAT). It has excellent publications, mostly free for digital copies.

Carolina Farm Stewardship Association
www.carolinafarmstewards.org
Supports local and organic agriculture in the Carolinas.

Georgia Organics
www.georgiaorganics.org
Advocates for tasty food, healthy communities, and thriving farmers, working to provide good food for all.

Growing Small Farms
www.growingsmallfarms.org
Debbie Roos has a wealth of searchable information and amazing insect pictures on her site.

Grow It, Eat It
https://extension.umd.edu/growit
Vegetable gardening information and resources for gardeners in Maryland.

Grow Veg

www.GrowVeg.com

An online garden planner for whatever the size or shape of your garden or plot.

Mother Earth News

www.motherearthnews.com/
Organic-Gardening.aspx

Thirty years of articles on "using natural organic gardening methods to grow the freshest food."

Plant a Row for the Hungry

www.gardenwriters.org/gwa.
php?p=par/index.html

A very worthwhile program to encourage gardeners to grow for the needy in their communities.

Southern Sustainable Agriculture Working Group (SSAWG)

www.ssawg.org

A nonprofit organization that promotes sustainable agriculture in the southern United States.

State Extension Services

www.csrees.usda.gov/Extension/

Use this page on the USDA website to find your state Cooperative Extension Service.

Symbiont Biological Pest Management Company

drmcbug.com

Home website for "Dr. McBug," specializing in utilizing naturally occurring, beneficial insects to control pest insects and weeds in a variety of situations, from farm to home.

Virginia Association for Biological Farming (VABF)

www.vabf.org

Detailed information about a variety of topics in sustainable agriculture.

WEATHER AND CLIMATE

American Horticulture Society: Heat Zone Map

www.ahs.org/publications/heat_
zone_map.htm

National Weather Service Southeast Regional Forecast

graphical.weather.gov/sectors/
southeast.php

USDA Plant Hardiness Map

www.usna.usda.gov/Hardzone/
ushzmap.html

TOOLS AND SUPPLIES

Berry Hill Drip Irrigation

Buffalo Junction, VA

www.berryhilldrip.com

(434) 374-5555

Farmer D Organics Garden Center

Atlanta, GA

www.farmerd.com

(404) 325-0128

Purple Mountain Tools

Tacoma Park, MD

www.purpletools.net

(877) 538-9901

Seven Springs Farm

Check, VA

www.7springsfarm.com

(800) 540-9181

Wood Creek Farm and Supply

Cana, VA

www.woodcreekfarm.com

(276) 755-4902

SOIL TESTING

AU Soil Testing Lab

Auburn University, AL

www.aces.edu/anr/soillab

(334) 844-3958

Micro-Macro International, Inc.

Athens, GA

www.mmilabs.com

(706) 548-4557

Soil & Plant Testing Laboratory

Amherst, MA

www.umass.edu/soiltest

(413) 545-2311

Texas Plant & Soil Lab

Edinburg, TX

texasplantandsoillab.com

(956) 383-0739

MORE GOOD BOOKS

There are many good books about gardening, food, and gardens. I enjoy reading inspiring stories about gardeners and food, as well as good books about how to get things done in the garden. Reading about others' experiences and gaining new knowledge reminds me why I want to grow good food and live sustainably. Here are a few of my favorite garden books.

Ashworth, Suzanne. 2002. *Seed to Seed: Seed Saving and Growing Techniques for Vegetable Gardeners*. Decorah, IA: Seed Savers Exchange.

Dawling, Pam. 2013. *Sustainable Market Farming: Intensive Vegetable Production on a Few Acres*. Gabriola Island, BC, Canada: New Society Publishers.

Deppe, Carol. 2010. *The Resilient Gardener: Food Production and Self-Reliance in Uncertain Times*. White River Junction, VT: Chelsea Green.

Greene, Wesley. 2012. *Vegetable Gardening the Colonial Williamsburg Way: 18th-Century Methods for Today's Organic Gardeners*. Emmaus, PA: Rodale Press.

Lowenfels, Jeff, and Wayne Lewis. 2010. *Teaming with Microbes: The Organic Gardener's Guide to the Soil Food Web*, Revised Edition. Portland, OR: Timber Press.

Pleasant, Barbara, and Deborah L. Martin. 2008. *The Complete Compost Gardening Guide*. North Adams, MA: Storey Publishing.

Tallamy, Douglas. 2009. *Bringing Nature Home: How You Can Sustain Wildlife with Native Plants*, Updated and Expanded. Portland, OR: Timber Press.

Glossary of Basic Garden and Seed Saving Terms

Annual. A plant that completes its life cycle and makes seed in one year. Includes most vegetable crops. Examples are corn, beans, and tomatoes.

Biennial. Plants that grow one year and need a period of winter cold (vernalization) before making seed the second year. Examples are carrots, beets, celery and parsley.

Cold frame. A structure built to protect plants from wind, cold, and other adverse weather conditions. All cold frames have a transparent or translucent top to let in light. The sides can be a permanent wooden structure or a temporary structure made from a variety of materials like straw bales or wire hoops. Gardeners in the Southeast often add a shade-cloth covering to use it for starting seedlings in summer for the fall garden as well as the spring and winter uses discussed in the Gardening 101 chapter.

Compost. The dark, rich, earthy smelling product of naturally decomposed organic material. In the hot southeast we are constantly losing organic material—making compost is one way to recycle organic waste and replenish our soil. Information on how to make compost is covered in the March chapter.

Cover crop. Plants grown to revitalize the soil, help soil texture, and add organic matter. Cover crops are planted in vacant space during the gardening season or over winter and worked into the soil after they grow instead of being eaten.

Direct sowing. Planting seeds in the garden right where they are to grow. Some seeds like beans and corn do better direct sown. As with all plantings, making sure that you have favorable soil temperature is important to success. When seeds have sprouted, thin to recommended spacing.

Double digging. A deep method of intensive soil conditioning favored by biodynamic and bio-intensive gardeners. It involves removing the top shovel full of soil, loosening the next layer, and replacing the topsoil. This method creates a deep bed, although modern research questions the process as it dramatically disturbs the soil life.

Germination. The process of a seed's initial growth, from taking up water until you see the little sprouts. It can be helped and sped up by providing the right conditions for each plant. Read your seed package or see the Edibles A to Z section for specific details.

Hardening off. The process of gradually preparing seedlings for the transition to outdoor conditions by "toughening them up" through exposure to increased direct sunlight, wind, variable outdoor temperatures, and slightly restricted watering.

Hardy. Annual seeds can tolerate being frozen, and plants can stand a slight freeze—but not sustained freezing without appropriate cover. Good choices for fall and winter in the Southeast. Half-hardy plants can be sown when the soil is cool, but temperatures are above freezing. Tender annuals like tomatoes need to wait for warm soil and weather.

Heirloom. An open-pollinated variety passed down through generations of a family or a commercial variety more than 50 years old (mostly developed before World War II). Seed breeds true with proper isolation distance.

Hybrid. Varieties created by crossing two different parent lines that may have superior qualities in the first (F1) generation, but will be variable in following generations. This means that you cannot reliably save seed.

Intercropping. Growing more than one crop side by side mixed in the same bed. This is a helpful technique in the small garden.

Isolation distance. How far apart from each other two varieties of a crop need to be for pure seed.

Mulch. Covering for garden soil to control weeds and retain moisture. Plastic mulches can be used, but organic mulches offer the added benefits of nurturing earthworms and other soil life as well as building the soil as it decomposes.

Open pollinated. Varieties that breed true seed when randomly mated in a planting with only minor variations.

Organic matter. Decaying plant material that can help plant roots improve their uptake of water and nutrients. It also helps make a good environment for all beneficial soil microbes and organisms. Organic matter can improve the texture of all types of soils, from gritty sand to heavy clay.

Plant family. Closely related grouping of plants with similar growth requirements and some potential for cross pollination when seed saving. In terms of botanical scientific nomenclature, family is the principle classification, falling just above genus. Potatoes, tomatoes, peppers, and eggplants are all in the nightshade family (Solanaceae).

pH. A pH test measures the acidity or alkalinity of your soil on a scale of 1.0 to 14.0 with 7.0 being neutral. Most vegetables prefer a neutral to very slightly acid soil at 6.3 to 7.0. When pH is below 6.0 or above 7.5 many of the nutrients in your soil are not available to plants, so crops suffer. Adjusting pH is cheap and easy but takes a little time, so get your soil tested early.

Relay planting. A variation on intercropping where the next is seeded or transplanted into a standing crop part way through its growth cycle. The first crop is harvested when ready, leaving the second crop to finish maturing in the bed. For example, snap peas planted down the middle of a bed of overwintered spinach.

Row cover. Also called horticultural fleece, row cover is available in many spun or woven polyester fabrics. It will extend your growing season, protect your plants from insects, and provide isolation for seed saving.

Shade covering. Window screens, burlap, sheer curtains, or anything else used to provide temporary shade for plants and seeds being established during the heat of summer.

Spacing. Gardeners refer to both the distance between individual plants in rows and the distance between rows or hills as spacing. The Edibles A to Z section and your seed packets have details on spacing.

Thinning. Seeds are usually sown thicker than what is optimal for mature plant spacing. Removing or transplanting the excess plants is known as thinning. Leafy greens may be used for salads or braised greens.

Variety. Particular strains, population, or hybrid of a vegetable that is uniform for certain characteristics like color, size, disease resistance, hardiness, or taste. Only open-pollinated varieties breed true.

Index

About the Author

TRAV WILLIAMS

Ira Wallace serves on the board of the Organic Seed Alliance and is a worker/owner of the cooperatively managed Southern Exposure Seed Exchange, which offers over 700 varieties of open-pollinated heirloom and organic seeds selected for flavor and regional adaptability. Ira is a Central Virginia Master Gardener and also an organizer of the Heritage Harvest Festival at Monticello, a fun, family-friendly event featuring an old-time seed swap, local food, hands-on workshops, demos, and more. She currently writes about heirloom vegetable varieties for magazines and blogs including *Mother Earth News*, *Fine Gardening*, and *Southern Exposure*.